THE

RELIGION OF THE PRESENT

AND OF THE FUTURE.

THE

RELIGION OF THE PRESENT

THE FUTURE.

SERMONS PREACHED CHIEFLY AT YALE COLLEGE,

THEODORE D. WOOLSEY.

NEW YORK:
CHARLES SCRIBNER AND COMPANY.
1871.

JAS. B. RODGERS CO.
ELECTROTYPERS,
52 & 54 North Sixth Street, Philad'a.

TO THOSE

WHO HAVE NOW AND THEN HEARD MY VOICE

IN THE PULPIT OF YALE COLLEGE,

AND ESPECIALLY

TO THE GRADUATES WHO HAVE GONE FORTH FROM THESE HALLS,

LEAVING ME HERE UNTIL NOW,

WHEN MY TIME OF GRADUATION IS NEARLY COME,

I AFFECTIONATELY

INSCRIBE THESE DISCOURSES,

AS AN ACKNOWLEDGMENT OF THE RESPECT AND LOVE

WHICH THEY HAVE SHOWN ME.

PREFACE.

SOON after making known, in December, 1870, my intention to resign the Presidency of Yale College, it was suggested to me by the eminent publishing house, whose name is on the title-page, that I should put into their hands for publication a selection of Sermons preached by me in the College Chapel. A request to the same effect came some time before from members of one of the classes just before their graduation, and I have been encouraged to do this by persons on whose judgment I rely.

It is proper to say, for the information of some who may meet with this book, that my ministrations were confined to special occasions and to intervals when there was no regular preacher.

I may be permitted to add that two of the Discourses, the nineteenth and twentieth, were delivered elsewhere, and not in the College pulpit.

In regard to the Sermons selected I desire to say, that some of them are devoted to subjects of especial importance at the present time; others consider aspects of religious life which need, as it seems to me, to be brought before the public in this country, and above all, before students; while others still are taken up with the prospects of Christianity in the future. Hence the title—The Religion of the Present and the Future—appeared to be not altogether inappropriate.

YALE COLLEGE, *May*, 1871.

CONTENTS.

SERMON I.

THE EARLY YEARS OF CHRIST.

LUKE ii. 51, 52. And he went down with them, and came to Nazareth, and was subject unto them; but His mother kept all these sayings in her heart. And Jesus increased in wisdom and stature, (ἡλικίᾳ, age) and in favor with God and Man.

FROM the time when Jesus at the age of twelve visited Jerusalem with His parents, there is an interval of eighteen years until the date of His baptism, during which we know next to nothing of His life. Our text informs us that He returned to Nazareth from the holy city, and was subject to His parents; from another place, where He is called "the carpenter," we learn that He followed that employment; from another still, we learn that His manner was on the Sabbath day to read the Scriptures in the synagogue. These are all the particulars left on record for us belonging to this period of a life more glorious, more eventful, than any other since the world began. Now it is painful to be thus kept in ignorance concerning one who is dear to us. A gap in a great life is like an unfinished place in a picture, or a hiatus in an important manuscript. We lose the sense of a continued existence, and the imagination flutters about in the effort to construct the unknown portions of the great whole after the model of those with which we are acquainted. As the child loves to hear from his father what he did when he was a little boy; as, when he grows older, he wants to take a view of that parent's life in its separate parts, in their connections, in the development of the finished man; so would we all naturally love to know more of Jesus, how He grew up from childhood into youth, how He acted in the family and in the town, how He matured into the Messiah with a perfect idea of His office, such as we behold Him immediately after His Baptism.

But this is not the severe method of Scripture. All it tells is for our use and nothing is for our curiosity. It awakens our minds to higher spiritual knowledge, but refuses to answer a thousand questions that we ask. It gives glimpses, but holds up no broad light reaching from the beginning to the end. It crosses gulfs and leaves the path unknown. It discloses the scattered facts of theology, but gives us no system. It neither aims nor cares to gratify our speculative power, content if it can sway our practical. When it has done with us, more unsolved and insoluble problems arise than before, for as it leads us up from nature to God it shows to us outlines of great mysteries which baffle our reason. So then, when it hides the Lord Jesus from us for a large part of His life in this world, it is consistent with itself and unlike the works of man.

But some one has observed that the reserve, the sacred silence of the Word is richer, fuller of meaning, more teaching than the narratives of ordinary history.* In the spirit of that remark I propose to inquire, as far as can be modestly done, what was the use of the early life of our Lord, and how it bore upon the later periods of His public ministry? Can we not make it strongly probable that a divine wisdom presided over this silent interval, laid up in it treasures of thought and character for His future years, and fitted Him in the stillness and lowliness of the Galilean village for the highest office that man ever filled?

* Trench in his Hulsean Lectures.

And here, before we go further, we need to say a word to those to whom such a subject can be of no benefit, because they do not believe in the normal human development of the Lord Jesus. To such persons He is a simple miracle of existence; one who knew, when a child, whatever He knew when a man; one in whom there was no growth nor advance; always and equally full of God; and by consequence hiding His knowledge from the first, until the occasion came for making use of it. But this is a very false and unscriptural view. It is inconsistent with our text, which tells us that Jesus *increased* in *wisdom* and *in favor with God*. It would, in fact, make the man Jesus a mere appearance, a vehicle for concealing omniscience. It thus presents Him to us, no longer as growing and rising according to the law of incorrupt manhood, but as a prodigy, having nothing in common with man in the movements of His intellect, and therefore incapable of exercising the feelings of a human finite soul. That thus in fact the human in Christ must be destroyed is apparent. Such a view of Him gets no support from the Gospel, nor from ancient faith.

Conceiving of Him then, as in a transition from childhood to manhood, as in a process of training for the highest of works, we ask what lessons are to be gathered from His silent years? And

First, we shall conclude that God qualified His Son, born of a woman, made under the law, for His future office, *by the training of the family state.* "And was subject to his parents."

The family state, we cannot doubt, was most happily devised, according to the original plan of incorrupt human nature, not only for the preservation and physical welfare of the child, but also for the development of all the higher qualities of man. It is the beginning and the condition of society. He who passes out of its healthy training into the larger circle of fellow-citizens or fellow-men, has a foundation already laid for all social sympathies, for the conception of human brotherhood, for the exercise of good will in every form. It is also the condition of, and the preparation for, all law. The dependent being, trained up in it to listen to higher authority and wisdom, to give up self-will and practice self-control, becomes fitted for the loyal life of the citizen, and for obedience to God. Thus it was meant, according to the primeval plan, that the infant mind should be disciplined in the family for a life of law and of love—*law*, which should lead the soul up to the great central Lawgiver of the universe, and *love*, which should embrace the brotherhood of souls, and God, the Father of all. Such was the idea and type of the family which, through the fall of the race, has not been fully realized. But if there should be anywhere a sinless child, brought up by pious, even if imperfect parents, must we not suppose that a large share of the blessings properly belonging to family life would fall to his portion? Where else could there be found such a happy introduction into life, into its responsibilities, its sympathies, its powers of acting in and upon mankind? Here the holy child would grow, not into something angelic, but into a holy man, into a brother in the human family, possessed of recollections and modes of thinking which would give Him superior power in this world to an angel, unless an angel could put off his own nature and his own laws of thought. In short, whatever need there was that the Saviour of men should take humanity upon Him, there was the same need that He should be an entire man, that He should pass through the stages of our nature, learn by experience its relations, grow into perfect manhood under its laws. Thus only could He be a Saviour for man at all, thus only could He become like unto His brethren. It thus became natural for Him to conceive of God as His Father, and natural when He founded a church, to unite its members by the tie of brotherhood. His soul was fitted for its work by entering into the great relations of humanity.

II. Jesus passed through the discipline of *a life of humble industry.* "Is not this the carpenter?" Here we have two things to notice, the discipline of a life of industry upon the Son of Man, and the influence of the lowly position which He thus assumed among His brethren of mankind.

The spirit of the ancient world, owing chiefly to the institution of slavery, undervalued and even despised a life of mechanical or agricultural labor. The same is true of countries in modern times, where an order of nobles, an aristocracy of birth owning the land for the most part, and having the power of society in its hands, keeps the people from rising above a certain level. Now, admitting, as we may, that there is a natural distinction of classes among men, derived from the intellectual requirements of their callings, we must condemn this contempt of labor as vicious and hurtful to society. Why should those callings, which the mass of a race, made in God's image, must fill, be of course degrading? And if a man could unite skill, in manual labor, with highly cultivated thought, would he not be, every way, more of a man for such skill—more of a man than he who is dependent on the labor of slaves, and more of a man than he who is a mere thinker? Would not a pure, incorrupt man, as he worked under God's sun and clouds, or subdued matter into new forms by the tools of skill, be all the while more open to heavenly thought than he who was engrossed by speculation, or occupied among the perplexities of professional study and employment?

We must conceive, then, that during these years of labor as a carpenter, the Son of Man had *time*, even amid His work, *for noble and holy thoughts.* His attention was not so strained, nor His powers of mind so absorbed, that thought could not go and come continually to and from

God. How much better this than to be trained in the little subtleties and formalities of Pharisaic schools; how much truer to nature, and nearer to truth, and nearer to God, such a discipline!

Nor ought we to lay out of account the *patience* which sedulous manual labor would bring along with it. The patience of our Lord gained strength from yet another source, as we shall soon see; but His daily tasks must have cultivated this quality, so important to His future work. For in the mechanical employments there is a certain amount of work which can be done well each day, the quality of which hurry will mar. The spirit of daily industry, then, is a spirit of patience, and the true workman, he who is neither slack from indolence, nor impatient from a desire to get through or to do too much, must be *regular, moderate, even* in his efforts, disposed to work as long, and to wait for the end as long as sound judgment requires.

I may add, that the *helpfulness* of our Lord in His calling tended to strengthen the principle of helpfulness to mankind, or of unwearied benevolence.

The scattered efforts to do good, to which we give ourselves, once a week, or every now and then, are useful, but then, we fall back from them, how often, into a life of indolence or selfishness, collecting our forces as it were, for returning fits of benevolence, because we are not strong enough to do good all the while. Thus, we do but little and grow but little; for our intervals of ease, perhaps of self-indulgence, undermine or obstruct the nobler habit. But the patient helpfulness of Jesus, as He did His work well in and for the family, inured His holy mind to the hard toils of that glorious life of love, in which we learn, on one occasion, that He had not time so much as to eat bread, and gave Himself up to works of mercy so earnestly that His friends thought Him mad. What other training could have equally encouraged His unwearied devotion to the hard, slow work of doing good?

But the *obscurity* of the sphere in which Jesus moved, aided the graces of His character, such as *meekness and lowliness,* and also *enlarged His power of usefulness.* Here we notice only *the last* particular, leaving the others for future remark. It is often thought to add to a man's power among men, if he is born in a high place, and commands the respect of mankind as well by his ancestry and station, as by what he is. But the power to act upon men, so far as it depends on feeling with them, and being felt with by them, is generally abridged by position above the major part of mankind: at least, however high a man rises above his fellows, there should be a chord of common feeling, never forgotten and never extinguished sympathies between him and them, which early life on their level had kindled or strengthened. Hence it is, that those monarchs who have risen from the people can know them better, and come closer to their admiration and their hearts, than such as have inherited the throne. Hence, too, those Reformers are likely to be most successful, who add to other advantages that of a lively interest in and comprehension of the great mass of men, which their birth and early education has encouraged. The son of the miner, at Eisleben, with his homely, earnest peasant-soul, and his manly courage, was fitter to attract and mingle with his countrymen, was better able, when his mind had become enlarged by study, to spread the Protestant Reformation, than if he had been the son of an Emperor of Germany, or one of the princes of the Empire. Such a personage, if he could have understood and preached the Gospel, would have found that a gulf was fixed between him and his people. He would have been to them "a separate star" that "dwelt apart." If he had converted his court, still religion would have been shut up as by a high wall, from the eyes and sympathies of the nation. So, too, it is probable, that the comparatively humble birth of Socrates, contributed not a little toward forming his philosophy. It was human, for it descended from the lofty speculations of earlier philosophers to man himself. It was homely and simple, seeking its illustrations, and drawing its truths from everyday trades and pursuits. An Athenian of the highest birth would have found it much more difficult to commence that reform in philosophy which was the highest achievement of the Grecian mind.

These considerations show, I think, the wisdom of God in selecting such a birth, birth-place, and pursuit for His divine Son. If He was to become one with man in the highest sense, to become able to preach to the poor, and heal the broken-hearted, and mingle with all men, down to publicans and sinners, if, in short, His condition in life was to have any effect on His work, and on His power in it, where else could He have been brought up with more advantage?

III. The silent years at Nazareth enabled Him to *meditate long and deeply on the Scriptures.* A striking characteristic of our Lord, from the first moment of His public ministry onward, is His reverence for and familiarity with the Scriptures. In the wilderness the tempter is rebuked by sentences from the divine word. At the last supper, the words which institute the rite, take their coloring from certain most important passages in the prophets; His words of agony on the cross are in the language of the 22d Psalm; and when the risen Lord appeared to His disciples "He opened their understandings that they might understand the Scriptures." And if we go back beyond the commencement of His public ministry, we find the only habit of life recorded of Him to be that "He went into the synagogue on the Sabbath day and stood up for to read." Here, then, in this sequestered village, away from the emptiness of Pharisaical learning, and from Sadducean skepticism, He was reared on the divine word in its simplicity, was fortified by it against temptation, studied its promises of a coming Messiah, and became ready to apply it to the varying circumstances of practical life.

The wisdom of God in subjecting His Son in the form of a servant to this discipline can easily be made manifest. Why was Jesus born a Jew, of the seed of David according to the flesh, but that He might partake of and hand down the old religion, so far as it was permanent truth and not local, transitory legislation? He might in some other land, by a series of supernatural influences from childhood upwards, have acquired the same truths, without the help of Scripture or any external revelation: but such was not the plan of God. He trained mankind through the Jews; He made His Son a Jew that He might build up on the old foundation the new truths of a religion for the world; and in order that Jesus Himself might be trained up for this work He chose this simple method of placing Him alone with the ancient Scriptures, away from human teachers and comments, that the pure truth of God might fill His mind.

IV. The life of *retirement* which Jesus led at Nazareth was fitted to nourish some of those meek and unpretending graces of character which shone beyond comparison in Him.

I name first *patience*, or willingness to wait until the right time was come. In order to understand fully how in the divine plan, the circumstances of His life trained Him in the exercise of this virtue, we must bear in mind that He had long had glimpses, if nothing more, of some unique relation to the Father, and some work marked out for Him by the Father. "Wist ye not," said He at the age of twelve to His parents, "that I must be about my Father's business?"—or, as it may well be rendered, "in my Father's house." Now it is idle to speculate and impossible to know how much of His great career was opened to Him before His baptism, or by what means it was opened. This, however, we know, that He *increased in wisdom,* and therefore that His comprehension of the Messiah's work must have been far broader and truer at thirty than at twelve. But the great fact for us here is that He knew of a work before Him, whether the outlines were clear or obscure; and that through these eighteen years He waited until the Father should call Him to the field He was to fill. Think how He waited, day after day, year after year, in contentment and peace, while life seemed to be moving no nearer to its goal. Think how this patience was built on simple obedience to the will of God, and prepared Him for the like obedience in the years of trial and suffering which awaited Him, so that His character was summed up in those words of the Psalm, "I delight to do thy will, O my God: yea, thy law is within my heart." Think too how trying it is, as measured by a human standard, when one is conscious of being able and called to do something great, to be obliged to live in obscurity and inaction; how human self-will chafes when its way forward is hedged up; and how sometimes great minds have made a wreck of themselves, and blasphemed God, because their active powers and their feelings could find no suitable theatre. Think how zeal for God itself, and the desire to be doing good to man, would concur in His case with that love of activity which is a principle of the nature He assumed, to spur Him forward and push Him into a more public life. But He dwelt in the lowly village for long years as quietly and contentedly as if He had no outlook on a greater world of sins and wants, and no aspirations for any other sphere; as if His life was to end in the humble employments and lowly condition in which it began. And this patient contentment was not a natural product, the fruit of a perfect temperament, but it was the fruit of piety. It grew out of a union of His will to God, and grew up to its completeness by a long training of His will to obedience in this school of waiting and of trust. When it was complete the time came for Him to appear as the Messiah before the world.

I cannot help stopping here to show the glory of Christ's character, thus ripened, by contrasting it with the principles on which even the best of us are prone to act, when we enter into life. He waited until thirty, and in a little over three years founded a kingdom that shall be universal and eternal. We think no good is done until the work of life is taken hold of. If our work is the ministry, where maturity of judgment, of reason, and of piety should unite, still we often rush forward as if time were our enemy and were robbing us of usefulness. Without treasure of thoughts, without solid convictions, without a feeling of strength, with nothing but feverish haste and that poorest of gifts, the gift of words flattening and belittling borrowed thoughts, some leap into the pulpit, as if it were heroic rather than fool-hardy to take responsibilities to which they were not equal, as if a call consisted of bold desire. How unlike the divine Master! Then too, we seem not to believe in preparation; we seem to be unwilling to get ripe, as if long experience were needed to ripen the apprentice in a handicraft, but in the liberal professions, especially in the sacred one, every one could begin on the stock of small study, and practice would bring up what was wanting. And thus the moral training, so far beyond the intellectual in importance, our years of calm prayerfulness in sight of our fields, our communings with God initiating us into the place He has laid up for us—all this is abridged, or is lost sight of in our fever to begin the race, or postponed until life with its cares shall give our feeble principles no room to grow. When we enter into our callings, too, we are aspiring for some higher sphere;—discontented where we are, we undervalue our usefulness, while perhaps overvaluing our powers; we lose our peace, our motives and our resignation, and wonder what God has in store for us; whereas the quietest nook in His service, if we were led by Him, would be so fraught with spiritual blessings that it would be a haven of joy to us; and if divorced from it at His call, we should thank Him forever afterwards that He called us to such a sanctuary at the beginning. Oh! my brethren, this self-confident, this hurrying, unripe, aspiring character which makes nothing of meditation, this boldness without strength and ardor without depth—let us bring it to the touchstone of our perfect Lord, and see how His character rebukes it.

The same discipline which perfected the patience, perfected also the *calmness* of Jesus. In fact the two graces can scarcely dwell far apart. The calmness of our Lord was not a negative virtue of temperament,—the inability to be strongly moved by anything great, nor was it simply the self-control of a being of large reason, allaying the excitements of the present by a look into the future; but it was, like His patience, a fruit of piety. And as He waited on God, and rested in God, the things of time, as they swept before Him, were not disturbing nor agitating, for God and peace were in His soul; and the more perfect His obedience grew, through His years of waiting, the deeper and *heavenlier* became His calmness.

This discipline of His still years gave strength also to His retiring spirit, or *modesty.* This may seem a wrong term to apply to our Saviour, who never shrank from duty on the open field of public life, nor feared the face of man, nor fell, through diffidence, below the responsibilities of the situation. But by whatever name we call it, there was in Him a quality most opposite to ostentation and love of notoriety, which led Him to prefer, in itself considered, being unknown before public fame, and retirement before crowds of followers. In Him was fulfilled that passage of Isaiah: "He shall not strive, nor cry, nor cause His voice to be heard in the streets." His was the preference of an humble, quiet, lowly life, such as He had led since His infancy, to a life of publicity and renown. It is plain, that such a spirit was as unlike to that which false opinion attributed to the coming of Christ, as it was honorable and glorious to Him who came in the form of a servant. With this spirit He resisted the tempter's suggestions to throw Himself down from the temple, and to receive at his hands the authority of a worldly Messiah. Now, a spirit like this, would be cultivated by the lowliness of His condition at Nazareth, and would be a preparation for meekly wearing the honor and carrying the consciousness of the Messianic office. And they follow Him who are sought by honor and repute rather than seek them, who delight to live in quiet communion with God, who are lost in their work when they enter upon it without wasting thought on themselves or the impression they make, who are not quick to attract attention, and need some discerning person to seek them out and discover them. Such persons, I say, are like Jesus—most like Him, if their character rests on the rock of godliness, and more capable than others of becoming like Him, if it has only a natural foundation.

I only add, that the retirement of Nazareth was fitted to nourish *simplicity of feeling and character*. It has been made a definition of a wise and pure life to live according to nature. Such a mode of living is almost impossible in the most refined states of society, unless that society is equally advanced in Christian culture. The etiquettes, the formalities, the spirit of caste and clique, the tyranny of opinion make it hard for a man to be true to nature and to himself. The soul becomes artificial without knowing it, ceases to think its own thoughts, and forsakes truth for the voice of the governing crowd. How difficult is honesty now, when politeness is a rule committed to memory and not a prompting of nature, when an external standard seizes a man, unless he is made of iron, and moulds him into something unlike his true self, into a thing of shows and artifices,—perhaps of falsehoods. Simplicity and honesty are the gold of character—how hard are they to keep, how rare to find; and when they are kept through the temptations of a conventional life, they exhibit a certain kind of worn and stern aspect—the effect of long and tough resistance to opposing powers.

The simplicity and honesty of the man Christ Jesus were, no doubt, nourished and perfected in a simple, godly family, in a simple village, away from much of the gloss and falsehood which abounded in Judea. We might conceive of divine wisdom taking just the opposite method of calling it forth, that of placing Jesus in close neighborhood to formal and false Pharisees, so that His education should consist in loathing the characters which He should see around Him. That *strength* would come from such a discipline we cannot doubt; and yet the other plan, which was in fact chosen, seems the best for a harmonious perfection of the whole character, and especially for the predominance of the gentler virtues.

I have selected the subject which we have considered, for a reason already hinted at,—because it seemed to me that many excellent persons have very false, or at least, obscure views of the excellence of the man Christ—views which strip Him of a part of the glory of His condescension and rob His example of a great part of its power. They seem to assume that His union with God took Him out of the category of men; He was, so to speak, free no longer, and a man no longer; but absorbed in, and moved by a divine nature which superseded the ordinary laws of humanity. Nothing could be more untrue than such a conception. He was as truly and properly man as He was God. As man, He was subject to the laws of human development and progress; He grew in wisdom, grew in strength of character, grew in consciousness of His exalted relation to the Father. As man, He was subject to the limitations of our nature, except so far as He was specially endowed with a divine power corresponding with His divine office. As man, He had specific traits of character, the assemblage of which in harmony, resting on a foundation of spotless godliness, constituted His perfection. These traits of character were cultivated under the guiding hand of Providence, and the control of godliness; until they reached their highest beauty and excellence. Hence the beauty of His example, hence His nearness to our hearts, and the soft attractiveness of His love.

It has been our endeavor to point out, as far as we could do, how the circumstances of His early life contributed, or at least, to show how they *could* contribute to this result. This is a far *modester* undertaking than to seek to show how His attributes, as a divine being and a human, could co-exist: into that subject of profound mystery, where Scripture holds up no torch, ever so faint, before our eyes, we venture not to intrude. Enough for us, that His Godhead did not prevent His being a suffering man just like ourselves—made in all things like unto His brethren, save without sin. He who cannot believe this, cannot receive Him, in the fulness of His office, as the Mediator between sinful men and God.

SERMON II.

THE TEMPTATION OF CHRIST IN THE WILDERNESS.

MATTHEW iv. 1, 11, (The narrative of the temptation.)

As the first Adam, acting on behalf of his race, was exposed to a trial of his obedience, so it became the second Adam, when He began His mediatorial work, to have His character pass through the fires of temptation. In His private and quiet life before His baptism He must have encountered and overcome temptation, for He could not well have lived in this world to the age of thirty without having excitements of wrong desire present before His mind, and without making His choice between obedience and disobedience. But *now*, when He had received a solemn inauguration by baptism from the forerunner, and a most remarkable testimony from God by a voice from heaven,—now, when publicly and formally He took the place of representative for mankind in the system of grace, and when interests weightier than man had sustained before hung on His conduct,—now, I say, there was a momentous crisis; and the parties most aware of what He might accomplish as the Son of God might well be most active in putting His character to the test. Accordingly the sacred historian tells us that God and Satan, the kingdom of light and the kingdom of darkness, were alike concerned in His temptation. "Then was Jesus," says St. Matthew, "led up by the Spirit into the wilderness to be tempted of the devil."

The first thing that strikes us here is that Jesus was not master of His own movements. An unerring voice, which He knew to be from Heaven, sent Him into the lonely wilderness—the place where no society or communion could disturb the law of development of His character—in order to be tempted in that solitude. He could not have gone thither Himself, aware of the trial before Him, without tempting God; neither the Son of God in the form of a servant, nor any of His followers, would have a right to go uncalled into temptation; but when thus called He could not refuse to go without disobeying the Father, without, in fact, abandoning the office of a Saviour.

The next thing which arrests our attention and, at first, our wonder, is that he was led by the *Spirit* into the wilderness to be tempted of the *devil.* What a fearful and solemn glimpse is here given to us of the moral agencies of the universe. Good and evil, infinite good and absolute evil, good and evil in personal substance, with that intense antipathy to one another that souls of the largest grasp and depth must feel, are in restless action around a human soul. The infinitely good has power not only to baffle His foe, but to destroy and annihilate him; and yet, seeing in the existence and activity of evil some great good for the universe, He allows it free movement, so that its wild waves dash against the very throne of heaven. The absolute evil, on the other hand, knows in its very soul, that no art, force or obstinacy can gain any advantage over God; yea, that its strugglings will enhance His glory; and yet, such is the strength of desperate purpose, so hopeless is the derangement of reason produced by sin, that it must go on its journey through shame and hate, finding its only semblance of happiness in the restless activity of an immortal nature.

And if such parties were concerned in the temptation something of importance must have depended on the result. It cannot have been a mere show presented to the eyes of the universe, a bare form of initiation through which the Son of God, incapable of sinning, had to pass. There are persons who seem to think, because Christ actually did no sin, and because in His nature God and man were joined, that there was no possibility of His sinning, that His innocence was secure by even more than divine help,—by the possession of a divine nature. But such an opinion though it may seem at first to exalt the glory of Christ is a mere inference of the reason and involves disbelief in the simple record of the gospel. Why was He tempted by a sagacious tempter if He could not by any possibility be led into evil? And if He Himself *knew* that He could not sin, what could the transaction have been to Him but a mere formality? How could He learn obedience by the things which He suffered if they could have no action on the strength of His obedience? Or how is He an example for us if His temptation is an unreality? No! they dishonor Christ's work who think thus. When He took on Him the form of a servant He became by His own will subject to everything which can affect human nature—to desires, wants, pains, sorrows, the hiding of God's face, the fear of a cruel death, and death itself—all of which must have been so many motives and trials of character. Faith receives the temptation, as it receives the ascription of divine and human attributes to Christ, on the testimony of revelation: it is not faith, but the want of it, which leads some to question the reality of the temptation, because Christ stood thus alone in His nature.

The next point to which I invite you is the person of the tempter. "Jesus was led into the wilderness to be tempted of the devil." It was not *God who tried Him* by suffering of body or mind, as He often tries His faithful servants; but God *left Him in the hands of an enemy,* whose aim and hope it was to lead Him into sin. Nor could His own sinless soul present inducements to evil to itself, which it must have done had there been concerned in the transaction no personal tempter. For He was not merely innocent, but holy and perfectly holy, with the confirmed character and habits of nearly thirty years,—how then could His own trains of thought, which contained no admixture of sin, originate suggestions to sin. There was then present in this scene a person who united malignant desires with knowledge of man and powers of persuasion, who tempted Adam, and would with the more reason be ready to tempt Christ.

But in *what form,* it may be asked, did this tempter place himself in the way of Jesus? Did he keep to his spiritual incorporeal nature, or take a body, and become visible to eyes of flesh? Was the temptation transacted before the *mind* of Christ, or was its sphere more outward, concerned with bodily phenomena and human language? The first impressions which a reader would draw from the narrative undoubtedly favor its being understood in a literal sense, that Jesus was literally carried through the air to the pinnacle of the temple, and to an exceeding high mountain. In this light, no doubt, has the transaction been commonly regarded. Nevertheless, such a way of understanding the narrative involves us in serious perplexities. For, in the *first place,* the agency of Satan elsewhere, in the New Testament, is that of a spiritual being, and, so far as I am aware, corporeal form is never ascribed to him. In the *second place,* suppose the Saviour to be carried to an exceeding high mountain, yet the spherical form of the earth would allow the eye to take in but a very minute portion of the kingdoms of the world and of their glory. We must, then, either dilute the narrative, as many do, by understanding these expressions in a hyperbolical sense of the little tract of country around Palestine, or must resort to a second miracle, in order to conceive of the broad earth spread outward and upward before our Lord's eye. What need, then, of the high mountain, and why might not the same sight be obtained without leaving the wilderness? In the *third place,* it is noteworthy that the narrative makes no mention of the *return* of Jesus from the temple and from the mountain, just as if, in some sense, He had gone there while he remained in the desert in another. And, in the *fourth place*, if the temptation was addressed to the bodily senses of the Lord, it loses its insidious character, and becomes easier to be resisted. I am constrained, therefore, to believe that the transaction was a spiritual one, a conflict between light and darkness in the region of the mind, in which a real tempter assailed Christ, not through His eyes and ears, but directly through His feelings and imagination. The scenes passed before His soul in *vision*, as we commonly call it, that is, in such an excited state of the conceptive faculty as gives the impression of reality to objects of thought. After the same manner, the prophets of the Old Testament passed through events in vision, of which they speak as we should speak of realities. Thus Jeremiah must have been in prophetic vision when he took the linen girdle to Euphrates to hide it there and went again in quest of it, as also when he took the cup of wrath from God's hand and gave it to the nations to drink. So too Ezekiel was transported from Chaldea to Jerusalem in that remarkable vision, the narrative of which occupies the chapters of his prophecies from the eighth to the eleventh. Hosea, again, it is commonly believed, narrates only a symbolical vision, where he speaks of himself as marrying an adulteress at the command of God. The martyr Stephen, also full of the Holy Ghost, saw Jesus standing at the right hand of God, not in bodily shape, but in a form presented to the mind's eye, and yet expressive of a great reality. And so too the Apostle Paul may have been in vision, as he himself allows us to suppose, when he was caught up to the third heaven. It is not unlikely that the first readers of the Gospel, who were familiar with the prophetic state and language, put no wrong interpretation on the narrative in cases like these.

If, now, the Scriptures allow us to interpret the events of the temptation in this way, we can see that greater strength is thereby given to the suggestions of Satan than if they had been addressed to the bodily organs. The power over the mind of a highly endowed being through the imagination, may indefinitely exceed that which is exerted through the sight. Multitudes have been seduced by that faculty, which paints absent or distant objects in colors of its own, whom no beauty or pleasantness lying in objects of sight could have led into sin. The world of imagination is more fascinating to their elevated mind than this outward world with all its shows and riches. The phantom, which has something heavenly in it, cheats and betrays them, while they turn aside from the obvious snares of visible things. If then, before the mind of Christ the tempter laid a map of the outstretched world, more gorgeously beautiful, more charming to the imagination, than the sights of luxury and pomp of power in the Roman empire, we may suppose that the temptation was thus greatly enhanced, and became more difficult to be contended with.

But we pass on from this point, to a more important and indeed to an essential remark, that the temptations were intended *not for Jesus in His nature as a man, but for Jesus in His official station as the Messiah.* God was not putting it to the test, whether a certain good man or good prophet would yield to evil or conquer it, but whether Jesus was qualified for His office—whether that man whom he had severed from the rest of mankind by a wondrous birth and a union with the divine nature, and who yet stood forth in perfect freedom as a man—whether *He* would remain true to the spiritual idea of the Messiah, or would fall below it under temptation. Nor was the tempter in this case anxious simply to lead a good man into sin, but he was striking at the root of salvation; his aim was to undermine the principles of the kingdom of heaven, to lead the Christ, if possible, by some subtle way into conduct inconsistent with the office to which He had been chosen, and which He had freely accepted. This thought is the key to the story of the temptation. It explains why the temptation occurred when it did, at the commencement of Christ's public work, and shows the greatness of the crisis. The question whether Jesus would be made to adopt the worldly idea of the Messiah's kingdom was one of life and death for mankind. It may be added that the tempter's formula of address, "If thou be the Son of God," shows that the stress of the suggestion bore upon His consciousness of sustaining that relation to God, and not upon His character as a man. The problem to be solved was how He would sustain the Messianic office. Let us bear this in mind while we look at the three several temptations.

Of the first St. Matthew thus speaks (iv. 2–4): "And when he had fasted forty days and forty nights he was afterward an hungered. And when the tempter came to him, he said, If thou be the Son of God, command that these stones be made bread. But he answered, Man shall not live by bread alone, but by every word that proceedeth out of the mouth of God."

It is plain that these suggestions contain an appeal to the innocent desire for food, which now, by long fasting, had become extreme. But the strength of them lay in the ease with which Jesus, as the Son of God, conscious of power over nature, could work a miracle in His own behalf. Perhaps, too, the words contain something of a challenge to put forth that power, and convey a lurking doubt whether it really existed. "Can it be," the tempter might say, "that thou art endowed with such power and authority, whilst yet thou art suffering the severest hunger? Is it the will of thy Father, the bountiful Lord over nature, that His own Son should lack the gifts which are spread before the lowest and the poorest? Has not power over nature been given thee, if thou hast it, in order to relieve the distresses of mankind? Why not, then, relieve thine own? What merit is there in continuing hungry when thou mayest, without harming any man, satisfy thy wants? Is not the starving man bound to use the innocent powers which God has given him to keep off death? Or if he accepts the morsel offered by compassion, why shouldst thou not regard it as the compassion of God that thou shouldst use thy miraculous power for thine own deliverance."

The answer to the tempter contains a refusal to brĕak the fetters of dependence upon God's ordinary providence. God had sent Jesus into this condition of distress, as He sent the Jews into the wilderness, and could sustain Him as He did them, by extraordinary means of his own. Jesus was content to put Himself in the hands of God and await the issue.

Here the mind naturally asks—and shows the subtlety of the temptation by the question—Why our Lord felt Himself bound to endure the pangs of violent hunger when the relief lay within His reach. Why should He feed the five thousand by miracle, we ask, and not provide food for Himself? Did not Elijah partake of the widow's cruse and of the meal which He multiplied? Suppose that one of us could save himself from starvation by a miracle, is there any reason why he should not do it?

The solution of the difficulty lies mainly in the fact, that Christ was tempted as the Messiah. An ordinary man, or a mere prophet, invested with a special, supernatural power, might, for aught we can see, save himself from distress by such agency. But it became the Christ, the founder of a spiritual kingdom, to whom supernatural power was natural, not to place Himself or His followers beyond the reach of pain or sorrow. Had He procured food for Himself by miracle, He would have introduced a principle tending to destroy His kingdom, or wholly to change its nature—just that which the tempter wanted. For if extreme hunger might be relieved, so might that which was not extreme: so might thirst, and cold, and all the ills of poverty: so might affliction be prevented and reproach avoided. And if this might happen in His case, it might in the case of all His followers. Thus His rule and example would have founded a kingdom of earthly ease and comfort, in lieu of one where the hard blows of trial must be met in the spirit of trust and resignation.

And again, had Christ followed the suggestions of the tempter, He could not have taken on Him the work of our salvation. The form of a servant, which He freely assumed, involved subjection to all the physical laws which control our race, and the endurance of all sufferings which the Father should lay upon Him. But if, by His inherent power, He had now relieved His own hunger, He would have escaped from the form of a servant, and even from subjection to the divine will; and, on the same principle, He never could have been obedient to death—even the death of the cross.

We pass on to the second temptation, as it stands in the order of St. Matthew's narrative, or the third in St. Luke's, and of which the former Evangelist speaks as follows (iv. 5, 7): "Then the devil taketh Him up into the holy city, and setteth Him on a pinnacle of the temple, and saith unto Him, If thou be the Son of God cast thyself down; for it is written He shall give His angels charge concerning thee, and in their hands they shall bear thee up, lest at any time thou dash thy foot against a stone. Jesus saith unto him, It is written thou shalt not tempt the Lord thy God."

Here we make a remark in passing on the disagreement upon the order of events between the two gospels. Neither Evangelist in his narrative follows a strict chronological order, so that differences of this kind, which are not of unfrequent occurrence, ought not to surprise us. But the narrative of St. Matthew, as it is fresher and more artless than St. Luke's, so also justifies its superior accuracy in respect to the sequence of the temptations by a psychological probability. It was natural that a real tempter, upon discovering the great strength of trust which Jesus felt, should now endeavor to succeed in his plans by seeking to pervert that trust, by forcing it out of its proper channel into that of presumption. The first two temptations therefore, as given by St. Matthew, have an inward connection, one with the other. The trust of Jesus in His Father naturally suggested to the evil power that He might be successfully tempted to unauthorized confidence. Might not *He* who would put forth no supernatural power even to relieve His own extreme hunger, be led to think that God would suspend the course of nature at His desire and for His sake, when engaged in the divine service? The argument, intended to produce such causeless trust, is drawn from the ninetieth Psalm, and may be thus expressed. The true servants of God enjoy His peculiar protection, and He guards those who trust in Him from all evil. More than all others mayst thou, as His Son, calculate on the special interpositions of His providence. Throw thyself down, in token of being the Messiah, from the pinnacle of the temple, and make trial of what He will do for thee.

The reason why the temple was selected as the scene of this temptation lay in its being the spot of greatest resort, where through the day crowds of Jews would be witnesses of whatever might be remarkable and attractive. To see a man throw himself unharmed from a lofty place of the sacred building, and then claim to be the Messiah, could not fail to draw around him many adherents from among those who were expecting the Lord, the Messenger of the Covenant, to come suddenly to His temple. What could gain greater credence for the Messiah than such an attestation from God, at the thronged and hallowed

2*

centre of His religion. How conspicuous the proof from such a transaction, how quick the admission of it, saving the necessity of long years of contention in comparative obscurity against prejudice and malice!

But to the sophistry of the tempter Christ had a ready reply. "It is written thou shalt not tempt the Lord thy God," that is, "I may not, because entitled to His protection, appeal to it against the laws of His providence, to rescue me from dangers into which I have entered unbidden." As thus viewed, our Lord's reply is given in the same spirit with His former one during the first temptation. He subjected Himself freely to physical law, and His Messiahship depended on His self-chosen humiliation. He could therefore, in consistency with His great object here below, no more supersede physical law or seek to have it superseded in order to secure advantages to Himself than He could escape from moral control. When He took upon Him the form of a servant He entered into this relation to divine providence, that He should be treated as other men are treated, should have no mark of favor shown Him inconsistent with His station; nay, that if God willed, He might frown upon and desert Him. After this it would not be confidence, but presumption, to look for miraculous interpositions on His behalf. If He might not work a miracle *for Himself* to ward off the force of the natural order of things, so too He might not presume upon *the help of God on His behalf* against the laws of His providence. Otherwise a general rule would be established by which His life would cease to be one of humiliation.

And if we admit that Christ resisted the suggestion of the tempter, because it would lead Him to an *ostentatious and superficial way* of making good His claim to be the Messiah, we have fresh proof of His wisdom and of the justness of His conception of His office. It might seem a rapid and certain method of proving that He was the Son of God if He were to make a demonstration of Himself to the public eye, if He should secure notoriety by some great deed. So thought His brethren: If thou do these things show thyself to the world. So have false Christs and false prophets and fanatics very generally thought—that some great spectacle before the face of the world ought to inaugurate their mission. But our Lord's moral instinct and His true idea of the Messiah's office brought Him into complete harmony with that law of the divine government, by which truth comes before men in an unpretending shape, and evidence is never given in such amount as to force assent, but always leaves the prejudiced and the corrupt free to deny its force. If we look through the Gospels, we shall find the same consistent principle running through all the miracles of Christ. He wrought not many mighty works in his own country because of their unbelief. He would give no sign to a wicked and adulterous generation, save the sign of Jonas. He rather shunned observation than coveted it. But when he saw that a feeble, incipient faith could be strengthened by miracles, or when humanity called on Him to put forth extraordinary powers, then, however obscure the scene or the person to be aided, was His time to interpose.

Of the third and last temptation, St. Matthew gives us the following account: "Again the devil taketh Him up into an exceedingly high mountain, and showeth Him all the kingdoms of the world and the glory of them; and saith unto Him, All these things will I give thee if thou wilt fall down and worship me. Then Jesus saith unto him, Get thee hence, Satan; for it is written, thou shalt worship the Lord thy God and Him only shalt thou serve."

The general purpose of this temptation, is obvious. It was an endeavor to divert Jesus from the aim of setting up a spiritual kingdom, and to induce Him to establish such a one as most of His countrymen were wishing for and expecting. It sought also to lead Him to the use of questionable and unauthorized means of building up His kingdom, by which He would secure the co-operation of worldly powers and avoid most of the obstacles which interfered with His success.

Such was the plan of the temptation, which was thwarted by our Lord's just idea of the kingdom of heaven, and by His fixed decision to be loyal to God in the attempt to set up such a kingdom. There are, however, several difficulties in explaining this temptation, which demand our notice. First, why should this temptation come last, when at first blush it seems the easiest of all to be resisted? And again, the boldness and almost impudence of the suggestion to pay homage to Satan, seem unsuited to the character of a sagacious tempter.

We may take off somewhat from the edge of these difficulties, by observing *first* that it could not have been *the love of power* in Jesus, to which the tempter looked for his support. If the love of power is a universal principle of our nature, we may say that it was potentially in *Him* who was like his brethren. And yet I cannot conceive of it as having any strength whatever in His breast. His habits of holy consecration and submission must long before have made it impotent. It would have been folly in the tempter to appeal to it, as a principle of any strength. What was it then, of which the temptation was expected to lay hold? It was the natural and instinctive desire to take an easy road to the kingdom by the means of worldly power, to avoid the humiliation, hardships and agonizing death that lay in the distance before Him if He formed no connection with influences which control the earth. It was to conquer without hard fighting, to reign in glory without conquering, to realize at once the prophetic visions of a world-wide dominion, without fulfilling the twenty-second Psalm and the fifty-third chapter of Isaiah.

The question was not whether the kingdom to be secured would be one of righteousness,—that was a settled point; but whether the means of securing it might not properly pass round the opposition and the suffering which Christ saw in thought before Him. In an exalted worldly position, gained by a single formality of homage, what a power might be wielded by Him for the good of man! what a new order of ages might begin under His sway! what reforms might proceed from His wisdom and illustrious example! His choice of means, however, for securing His kingdom would in the end amount to a choice between two kingdoms, the one, severely spiritual, introduced by moral and religious forces only, the other becoming worldly by its alliance with the world of outward influence and temporal glory. The instinctive shrinking from harm and difficulty, which belongs to us all, would lead Him to choose the worldly way of doing good, would prejudice His mind in favor of the easier and quicker method. But He held on to His spiritual conception of His office, kept His obedience, and triumphed. Thus the dread of pain and of difficulty as well as the prospect of success in another direction gave strength to a temptation where the mere love of power was powerless.

We only add in regard to the proposition that He should worship the tempter, that it must be regarded as an act not of religious worship, but of respect and homage. Yet Jesus saw that if the formality of homage were paid, it would involve subservience to the powers of evil, and become disobedience to God. Thereupon He says, "Thou shalt worship the Lord thy God, and Him only shalt thou serve."

The narrative of the temptation presents the tempter to us as sagacious and crafty, but yet as not having fully penetrated into the nature and character of Christ.

He approached Christ in the belief that he was capable of taking false views of his office, through which he might be led into sin. He does not solicit him with those vulgar traits, by which sensuous, sinful imaginations and wills are drawn like the temptations offered in vision to St. Jerome, but makes suggestions of a kind such as to lead Jesus into conduct which, on a certain theory of the Messianic office, would be right enough, but on a certain other theory would show him to have wholly swerved from the idea. The question to be settled by trial was, whether our Lord's view of his office would be modified by an impression of the difficulties that he would of necessity encounter, or, in other words, whether temptation would blind him, and so lead him astray in regard to the course of life which God's Messiah must take. The tempter then, understood Christ, and did not understand him. He must have supposed that there was a possibility of his sinning, or the temptation was idle; and this supposition was true. He must have wisely regarded the beginning of Christ's public ministry to be the best time for presenting blind influences to his mind and soul. And yet, it would seem, he could not have had a complete view of the grandeur of the Messiah as a redeeming world wide Saviour; otherwise he would have seen the almightiness of God to be pledged to such a work, and all resistance to be of no effect. He knew more of Christ than the Jews did, but less than revelation has disclosed to us. Just so much knowledge accords with what the Scriptures say of the angels, that until Christ ascended on high they did not fully comprehend the plan of redemption. Nor can we doubt, if there be a personal tempter, that many of the followers of Christ actually foil him, in which cases, as in the temptation of the Master, he is ignorant of the result, and, perhaps, like other bad beings, blinded against the probabilities of things by his own deceptive hopes.

Another remark which we desire to make is, that the narrative, as interpreted, shows the subtlety and insinuating character of the temptation. The acts to which Christ was solicited were not sins, so much as misjudgments in regard to the means to be used for gaining the highest and noblest ends. And these misjudgments would consist, not in the use of means plainly and boldly sinful, but of such as involved a departure from the true idea of the Messiah's earthly mission. To remain hungry was no virtue, and to relieve one's own hunger by miracle was not necessarily a sin. To give proof of Messiahship by the miracle of falling from a lofty part of the temple was not, as a matter of course, an act of self-display, nor in itself more a sin than Elijah's proceedings at Carmel, when he put God to the test whether he would show, by the fire consuming the water around the altar, that he was God in Israel. So, too, to make an alliance with earthly powers for the advantage of the kingdom of God may well seem no compromise of principle, if the mind of the friend of God remains true to its work. No selfish feeling need be involved in such conduct, except that which consists in taking an easier instead of a harder road. The sin in these cases is not apparent, and it needs a healthy conscience, an unwarped judgment, a soul sincere in all its parts, to be equal to crises like these.

How many followers of Christ, great in name, have failed on just such occasions. Who among the sons of men is fit to be trusted with miraculous powers without measure, which he can use when and as He will? Therefore we will forever praise our Lord, that he stood amid these insidious suggestions, when we fall before bold and obvious temptations, leading us even to acts of obvious sin. And we will pray Him to keep His people from leaving His path; so that as He was in this world, they may have the quickest moral perception, the absence of all worldly policy, the principle to use gifts and powers not for themselves, not in shortening or smoothing processes of duty, but according to his divine pattern.

The narrative of the temptation, finally, as thus explained, shows itself to have been no myth, or invention of the early Church. The mythical theory draws its general force from an unscientific assumption that there can be no such things as miracle and revelation. In the case before us, its special arguments might be, that Jesus was tempted like Adam, that He was forty days in the wilderness as Moses was forty days on Sinai, and Elijah the same time on his journey to the same mountain chain; and that a part of the narrative, His transportation through the air, was ghostly and marvellous, rather than in accordance with the sobriety of ordinary miracles. The last argument has been already met by a different interpretation. As for the others, which have little intrinsic strength, it is enough to say, that if Christ was the Messiah, there are good reasons why He should be subject to trial at the outset of His work. The temptation is, indeed, no independent proof that He was what He claimed to be, but like His miraculous conception, it is in harmony with His nature and His office.

But it is more important to remark, that the narrative is too refined and too full of a somewhat hidden, but consummate wisdom, to grow out of the imaginings of the early Church. It is no rude picture of assaults which might befall a holy man in solitude, but an intellectual and moral struggle, which put it to the proof whether Christ would be true to the spiritual idea of the Messiah. It involves a conception of the Messiah's kingdom which the early Church did not entertain until some time after the death of our Lord; how then could it be elaborated by crude Galilean disciples of Christ, whose views were full of that earthly mixture which the narrative condemns? It contains, too, we are forced to think, a subtlety of moral discrimination which was far beyond that age, and beyond any age, until it had become enlightened by the Light of the Word. I should sooner say, that Christ Himself invented it, and gave it to some disciple as embodying in an allegorical form the results of His experience. But if He was the Messiah, the temptation is a true narrative. If He was not, He could not have devised a narrative like this, because He could not have understood what pertained to the work of a spiritual Redeemer.

And now to all the tempted, to all who are inclined to gain power by questionable means, to all who can profit for the moment by a departure from the line of principle, to all Christians who are tainted with a spirit of worldly policy, and desert the Master while they profess to be doing service for Him, I commend this story of the temptation. Let us all use it as a means of keeping ourselves in the path of unswerving Christian integrity, that by the help of the Master's trials, we may overcome, and be partakers of His purity and of His glory.

SERMON III.

CHRIST CHARGED WITH BEING BESIDE HIMSELF.

MARK iii. 21. And when his friends heard of it, they went out to lay hold on him; for they said he is beside himself.

IT appears from the narrative, of which this verse is a part, that Jesus had already excited the malignity of the Pharisees on account of a cure performed on the Sabbath, and that they had combined with their enemies, the Herodians, to compass His destruction. Upon this He withdrew to a more secluded place, but could not be hid, for His fame as a teacher and a healer of diseases had already reached beyond Galilee in every direction. After performing many cures among the multitude who pursued Him into His retirement, He withdrew again to a mountainous district, and took care that only certain persons, His disciples in the proper sense who were drawn to Him as their spiritual teacher, should know whither He had betaken Himself. The night, it would appear, was spent in prayer to God. The ensuing morning He organized His church by appointing the twelve apostles, and perhaps delivered the Sermon on the Mount during the same day. Descending again from the hill-country He entered, it is said, into a house, that is, He took up His abode for the time in the city of Capernaum. The people again throng around Him, some to be cured or have their friends cured of outward maladies, some to hear the healing words with which He accompanied His works of love.

It was at this time when the court of the house, with the hall of entrance, was filled full with eager listeners and with people ill of every disease, that His friends went out to lay hold on Him, for they said, "He is beside Himself."

They went out, perhaps, from Nazareth, where their home was, to the neighboring city of Capernaum, for the purpose of seizing and securing Him, on the ground that, according to their judgment or their fears, He was not in His right mind. As we learn from the end of the chapter they could not on account of the crowd enter the door; they send a messenger therefore to call Him out, that thus they may attain their object. Our Saviour knew intuitively what their design was, and reproved it as well as conveyed instruction to the bystanders by the words, "Who is my mother and my brethren?—Behold my mother and my brethren! For whosoever shall do the will of God, the same is my brother, and my sister and mother."

The question now may fairly be asked what led His relatives to the belief or suspicion, that our Lord was disordered in mind, and to the marvellous resolution to attempt to lay hold on Him and keep Him in confinement. The brevity of the record does not enable us to answer this question with confidence, and yet it supplies us with several answers, one or all of which may render this conduct less remarkable.

First, we may suppose that our Lord's relatives regarded His conduct as very strange and unaccountable; that He worked, or was reputed to work, miracles which drew crowds around Him, and declared that He was introducing the kingdom of heaven, while He yet shrank away from publicity and avoided the necessary consequences of being regarded as the Messiah. There may have been here to their minds, as yet involved in unbelief, an inconsistency in His conduct, which they could account for only on the theory that He was not what He claimed to be, but was laboring under a delusion of mind. Such are their feelings towards Christ, as represented to us in the seventh chapter of John's Gospel. "His brethren said unto him," on the approach of the feast of tabernacles, "depart hence, and go into Judea, that thy disciples also may see the works that thou doest. For there is no man that doeth any thing in secret, and he himself seeketh to be known openly. If thou do these things, show thyself to the world. For," adds the apostle, "neither did his brethren believe on him." They could not reconcile His policy with their idea of the Messiah, and of the pomp and splendor with which that office should be ushered in, and therefore explained His conduct, which they knew Him too well to impute to ambition or intentional deception, by the workings of a diseased mind.

Or, again, we may more rationally suppose that they thought Him beside Himself because He seemed to them to be throwing away His life. The Pharisees, they may have learnt as we know it, were already laying plots for His destruction. He was moreover giving Himself up to the good of the crowds which followed Him with an assiduity and a self-sacrifice which were likely to put His life in jeopardy. He appeared to them unaware of His danger and madly regardless of health and safety.

Or, to make one supposition more, the opinion which the Pharisees sought to diffuse, that He worked miracles by demoniac agency, may have influenced them, coming as it did from the teachers of the people. He could not be the Messiah, and yet He worked miracles. He could not be the Messiah, for how could an obscure Galilean, one of their own humble relatives, found the glorious kingdom of heaven, or take such ways to found it as Jesus was taking? He must therefore derive His superhuman power of casting out demons from Beelzebub. He must, as the Jews at Jerusalem afterwards said, have a devil and be mad.

Thus we see that unbelief lay at the bottom of this conduct of Christ's relatives. And it is worthy of notice that in striving to explain His conduct in their state of unbelief, they impute it to no sinful or selfish motive, but to derangement of mind. They show herein a persuasion, founded on acquaintance with His character, that no such motive could be discovered in the Saviour's life.

It is very remarkable, it is even startling, that among these relatives of Christ, who came to lay hands on Him as being insane, His mother is found. How shall we explain this conduct on the part of one who knew His miraculous conception, who had seen His perfect humanity in childhood and maturer years, who without question believed in Him and hoped in Him?

The extreme brevity of the narrative leaves us here again to conjecture. We may suppose that what is imputed to the kinsmen or family of Christ is spoken of them as a body from which Mary is to be excepted. She may have accompanied her unbelieving friends without participating in their feelings, rather to act as a mediator between them and Jesus than to carry out in any degree their views.

But I am quite willing to concede that a cloud of unbelief flitted over her mind; that as John the Baptist, in a moment of disheartening doubt, sent his disciples, to the Lord with the inquiry, "Art thou he that should come or do we look for another,"—an inquiry which shows at once his confidence and his want of confidence—so she, when she saw her Son taking a course unlike what she had attributed to the Messiah, may have been, for a time, overcome by her perplexities, and have not known what to think of Him. Are such doubts stray guests at times, even by the side of confirmed faith? He will not say so who knows what conflicts are going on in many serious minds, nay, what conflicts may arise in many Christian minds, until faith has won a permanent victory. How many minds have hesitated before the amazing doctrine of the *Incarnation*, as if such an interposition and presence in our world were incredible; how many have modified, or rather mutilated the Bible, so as to save the supernatural, and yet reject the divine in Christ; how many have stumbled and fallen over Christ manifest in the flesh; how many have swum to a settled landing-place across the billowing waves of doubt which threatened to engulf them! Was it strange that some kindred struggles should agitate the soul of Mary, if she were at once honest and in a degree unenlightened?

I will only add on this point, that however we explain Mary's participation in the design of her kinsmen, she is included in what is a virtual censure on the part of our Lord. He neither goes out to meet her and her companions, nor admits them into His presence. He exclaims, that His nearest of kin are the children of God, and asks, "Who is my mother and my brethren?" It is thus remarkable, that in the only two instances, until the crucifixion, where Mary figures in the Gospel—the marriage at Cana, and the passage before us—she appears, in order to be reproved by the Saviour, and to be placed, as far as the mere maternal relation is concerned, below obedient servants of God. These passages must be regarded as protests laid up in store against the heathenish eminence which the Roman church assigns to Mary, and especially against that newly established dogma of her being without sin from her birth, which they so signally contradict.

But while Christ was thus charged with losing the guidance of right reason, what had He been doing? Assuming that Mark follows the order of time, and confining ourselves to the events of the few hours before, we notice, *first*, that He had passed the whole night, before His return to Capernaum, in prayer to God. Being about, on the next day, to set on foot great measures, He separated Himself from the crowd which His fame had gathered, and even from His own peculiar followers, in order to commune with Infinite Reason and Infinite Love. On the lonely mountain, with only the stars for witnesses, He strengthened the powers of His soul, and found a refreshment better than that of sleep, in long and close intercourse with His

Father. Of this, indeed, His friend could have known nothing, but it was a natural expression of the piety which shone through His whole life. Was there implied in this any loss of reason? Who would not reasonably go to the ends of the earth, if thus He might experience one hour's communion, such as Christ had in blessedness and purity, with the Father?

Next we notice, that when it was day He set apart the twelve apostles. No step was taken by him, during His ministry, more important than this in its bearings on the future progress of His kingdom. In fact, if we except the two sacraments, this was the only institution which he ever adopted. Its wisdom was demonstrated by the result. The Apostles remained, after His death, as the authority in the Church. They preached the doctrine of Christ. They testified as eye-witnesses to His resurrection. They arranged the order of the gatherings of believers. They transmitted the history of their Lord to coming ages. The consummate wisdom which appeared in this institution, at once so simple and so efficacious, showed the reach of mind, the foreseeing reason of its founder.

And if, in the third place, as Luke seems to declare, the Sermon on the Mount—whether a part or the whole of what Matthew gives us—was delivered the same day, we have in this, too, a proof of the highest exercise of reason. This man, whom His kinsmen pronounced beside Himself, had just been destroying the imperfect system of morals which Jewish wisdom had erected, and had built up a new code, which has reigned through all the ages since; He had announced principles which philosophers, whether believers in Him or not, have united in admiring; and which, if we look at their influence on opinions or on practice, entitle Him to the name of a moral legislator for mankind.

And if, finally, we take into view His deeds of love when He came down from the mountain, how He gave Himself up to works and words of healing, how He bore with patience the importunity of the throng, how He endured fatigue and hunger for their sakes—not having room even to eat bread—we have another trait of a life in which reason and goodness dwell together.

Having thus considered the imputation cast on our Saviour by his relatives that He was out of His right mind, and shown how absurdly false it was by His conduct at the time, we proceed, in the third place, to derive some lessons from this part of the Gospel history.

I. And, *first,* we learn, from the fact that neither the Pharisees nor Christ's near relatives understood His character, how difficult bad men, and oftentimes imperfect good men must find it to comprehend the aims and plans of a person of uncommon goodness.

A person whose mind is not darkened by sin to a degree rarely occurring under the light of the Gospel, will readily admit, in the abstract, the leading obligations of practical religion and morality. He will confess that men ought to devote themselves to the service of God in the spirit of supreme, self-sacrificing love, and to the welfare of mankind, without looking at their own ease, comfort, or reputation. He will even approve or condemn persons living in a past age by such a standard.

But when men come to judge of measures and of principles, as they appear in the life of men, they will be apt to fall into one of the two following faults:

First, if they are low-minded and selfish themselves, they will impute the best conduct of the best men to motives as base as their own. This is, in part, a simple application of the rules derived from experience to a new case. The man is conscious of nothing noble or exalted: he sees in himself no impulse, no capacity to act under the sway of the better class of motives, such as zeal for God and love to man. All his friends, with whom fellow-feeling unites him, have the same low standard, and must take the same view of the conduct of others. The opinion in the whole society will be, that all men have the same governing principles at bottom; that benevolent concern for the welfare of men is either a pretense or the weakness of a character peculiarly constituted; that the semblance of religious zeal is hypocrisy. Within the experience of the whole society no character has risen above the vulgar level of selfishness. Within their observation, no conduct has occurred which cannot somehow be accounted for on the meanest principles. Thus we see that the selfish cannot comprehend disinterested goodness, that the impure cannot believe in purity and chastity, that low-minded politicians believe that all men can be bought, that unscrupulous merchants hold that every man will violate the law of usury or the laws for the revenue, if sure of impunity. Our judgments find it hard to rise above the level of our character. We bring men down to our own principles, if we cannot raise ourselves, in our conceit and imagination, up to theirs.

This philosophy of experience, if so it may be called, commends and insinuates itself into the mind by the comfort it imparts. If there is no more exalted standard of character than that low one which such persons adopt, there is no occasion for self-condemnation; they can walk with the head erect, and look on the noblest souls as their equals; they need feel no impulse to reform, and painful aspirations for something beyond their reach are repressed. Such self-complacent comfort can stand the attacks of abstract moral or religious convictions with tolerable security. But when a *life* shines before it, constructed on other principles, a life that commands respect, and tells "how awful goodness is," then this poor pride of character quails and feels its beggarliness, and gives place to self-reproach and self-contempt. To avoid the beginning of such a change of feeling, the life of the good must be interpreted amiss, and reduced below its real standard.

Was it then to be wondered at that goodness like that

of Jesus was misunderstood and maligned by Pharisees? Was it strange that they who knew of nothing within their own experience but selfishness and hypocrisy, who would have been condemned at heart by the light of divine excellence like Christ's, should seek a solution of His wonder-working power in Satanic agency,—should call "the master of the house Beelzebub?"

But *again,* persons like the *relatives* of Christ, who have no especial prejudice to warp their judgment, nay, even good men, are liable to misunderstand an exalted character. The explanation here is in part the same as in the former case. Their own deficient standard, the opinion which controls the society in which they move, supplies them with the rule of estimating the conduct of others; and they would be painfully reproved if they traced that conduct back to the highest principles of action. But their judgments are by no means so unjust as those of the prejudiced and the unprincipled. They do not put the worst interpretation on the best actions; they are not apt to malign motives; nor does their own consciousness carry them to the baser part of human nature, as explaining the lives of all men alike. But it is possible for men, they find, to be one-sided, and to overlook considerations drawn from expediency or prudence. It is possible to seek to accomplish too much all at once without committing the seeds of effort to future time. It is possible in attempting to gain one good to throw away another, to sacrifice quiet unduly to truth, to undertake some reform without taking into account the opposition it may excite or even strengthen. Multitudes of mistakes, of failures, of abortive enterprises which delay the cause of humanity and virtue for a generation, do actually arise from sources like these. All admit this when they criticise other men's measures, and weigh other men's hopes. Now is it not quite possible, when a person of exalted self-sacrifice, of godlike love, of earnest zeal, appears within the horizon of minds not in entire sympathy with him or unable to comprehend him, that they will apply these rules of judgment in his case? Does even true zeal for God of necessity exempt men from miscalculations? May not such a man aim at that which is unattainable? May he not waste his powers with a self-consuming zeal? May he not entertain hopes which are chimerical,—or in short by some excess or defect may he not depart from the line of right reason?

Thus even good men may misunderstand and misinterpret exalted virtue. But to this it should be added that our judgments *concerning what is practicable*—which must always influence our opinion of men—are in part of a *subjective* character; they vary with our desires, with our feeling of the importance of the object, with our moral characteristics, as much as with our intellectual. It cannot fail then, that measures which an earnest, self-sacrificing, godly man regards as practicable, must appear to a person of an opposite nature to be just the reverse, and to indicate a want of sound judgment or even of sound reason.

Thus a man needs to be thoroughly good himself, if he would comprehend and do justice to those who are truly good. It is not enough that a man has fine powers of mind and great practical discernment. His powers of mind will but quicken his ingenuity in finding causes for conduct which are not the true ones; his discernment will discern impassable obstacles in the noblest effort, if he is not in sympathy with goodness.

An illustration of what we have said may be found in the names of reproach which pass current among the unthinking, and are applied oftentimes to the best of men. Christ, as we have seen, was no exception to this. The honored name of Christian was at first, it is probable, a term of contempt. Paul was a man that turned the world upside down. Puritan and Methodist were originated as words of scorn. All new enterprises of benevolence are exposed to the charge of enthusiasm or of fanaticism. Whenever, in an ungodly community, some one breaks away from the bondage of reigning sin, the slaves of it call him mad. The friends of evangelical light in a part of Switzerland are now called *momiers* or hypocrites. The friends of oppressed men are among us stigmatized as *fanatics.*

In a world where light and darkness are contending, we cannot do good prudently without having such missiles cast at us by the unthinking or the malevolent; we cannot, as we are apt to do, pass the line of prudence, without furnishing them with a pretext for so treating us; we cannot mingle resentment with our zeal without justifying them in their opprobrium not only of ourselves, but of our cause.

But if we would be like Christ and do good service in the world, these names which are bugbears to many of the weak and lukewarm need not disturb us. A name of reproach is a rod of terror in the eyes of him who has no opinion on great questions, or no sympathy and power of generous emotion, or no courage and self-reliance. But if a man can rise to a higher level, reproach will only quicken him; he will feel that to be hated by the weak and wicked is one proof that he is right. A man, whose soul was on the side of freedom in our struggle for independence, was not much frightened by being called a *rebel;* a man who is on the side of Christ will only feel the more deeply the need the world has of being made over, when he is called a *fanatic.*

If we are misunderstood and depreciated let us remember what happened to Christ. "Therefore the world knoweth us not," said the disciple of love, "because it knew Him not." If we are misunderstood because we are like Him, the better for us and the worse for them who wrongly judge us.

II. Christ by His life on earth has done much to show that true enthusiasm in the cause of God is truly reasonable.

We have said that men, even good men, often fail to comprehend the noblest purposes and characters. But Christ by His glorious life on earth has enlightened mankind in this respect. It is more difficult than it once was to deny the reality and the reasonableness of Christian virtue. A higher standard of judging and of acting has been set up in the mind of the world.

Our Lord has not only purified man's abstract conceptions of virtue, but He has taught us what to admire and approve in life and action. He has lived a life, the principles of which are an everlasting protest against the misjudgments of men arising from their low standards. He has shown us the highest human excellence misunderstood, the highest reason pronounced a derangement of reason, and thus has put us on our guard against similar mistakes. He has shown us that men with far-reaching plans without noise or show are too deep for worldly minds to fathom; so that it is not safe for us to rely with confidence on the practical judgments of the world. He has shown us a plan, which in its *weakness* was imputed to a person beside Himself, in its maturity crowned with more than human glory. In Him we see the true measure of what is right, and what is practical in conduct, of what in the end must commend itself to the rectified judgment of the world.

Let us think of this, my friends, more than we do when we lay plans and pass judgments concerning life. It was an inconceivably mighty undertaking to set up the kingdom of God, and yet an obscure, unpatronized man undertook it and did it. *That is practical and that is practicable* which commends itself to a sound soul, to a calm, trustful, courageous soul in unison with Christ, which commends itself to a faith that overcomes the world, to a love that is capable of self-sacrifice. Undertakings will not suffer shipwreck, however maligned or scorned, into which men who have His spirit enter.

III. It is a little matter if we are misunderstood as long as God understands us. Christ too was misunderstood, but God understood Him.

For a while, the bad and the foolish in their use of names have it all their own way. The man of earnest Christian effort cannot pay them back in their own coin if he would, and he has too much to do to revile. Quietly working under God's smile he trusts to Him who is in sympathy with what worldlings hate, and despises what they highly esteem, who knows the essence and the results of things. God's own plan, which embraces those of His servants, includes immeasurable ages, and works itself out by resistless laws. What can a generation do—what can names of reproach, invented by a generation, do against God and His counsels? What can they do against those whom He favors?

Moreover time is God's minister, and this minister of God is constantly sitting in judgment on human opinions to approve or condemn. What enormous mistakes, often condensed in terms of censure, cannot Time tell of! There was a man to whom a crazed reason, to whom Satanic agency was imputed, and He now has a name above every name. There were men called Christians in contempt, and now it is the highest honor to be called a Christian. There was a party sneered at for uncourtly faults, disliked for rigorous precision, against whom every quill was dipped in gall, who were called Puritans by the impure, and now they are a landmark of history, one primary source of civil and religious freedom among men. "They are the people," said the politic Pepys in his diary, "that at last will be found wisest." * There was a sect,

* Pepys' Diary under Sept. 4, 1668.

or rather company of ministers who preached a warmer, truer gospel to a loose generation. They were laughed at by the witlings, were pelted with stones by the profane, were eschewed by the decorously cold; the name Methodist was a name of opprobrium. And what have they done? They have revived the religious life of England, kept piety from going out among the poor, and are now one of the strongest bodies of Christians in two great lands.

Thus good men often outlive their bad names. They conquer by God's help a place of honor for themselves in the judgment of coming times. Posterity garnishes the sepulchres of those who were reproached by the fathers. Honor is done, late indeed but long, to God's standard of principles and measures. The enthusiasts of one age may be found in the next to have first hit upon some great secrets; and instead of idly dreaming, as they were charged with doing, to have uttered prophetic voices. The fanatics, at whom men interested in vile traffics and wrong institutions gnash their teeth, may turn out at last to be friends of mankind. As the heathen of the first age who called Christians the enemies of the human race were grievously in an error, so it has been since; the world's supposed enemies have been its true friends, and are owned as such, when the tongues that maligned them have been silenced by death, and the reputations that were built on their disparagement are blasted.

Thus time, God's minister, corrects mistakes. But still all unjust reproaches, all depreciations are not corrected. There are especially multitudes of private persons, who die forgotten with no defender in the future against the reproaches of the past. Now for such as these there is still another court open. The last account will put each character in its right place, and keep it there forever. Forgotten goodness will be called into notice again, misunderstood character be commended; men called mad, but not such, will be shown to have drunk at the well of infinite reason; each will be restored to the rights which he had in the sight of truth and of God. It will be then no loss to have played a *small* part *well.* "Whosoever shall give to drink unto one of these little ones a cup of cold water only in the name of a disciple, verily I say unto you, he shall in no wise lose his reward."

Let us, my friends, in the great conflicts of opinion in which we cannot but partake, and while virulent epithets are freely applied to us, remember this great, this last reversal of former wrong judgments. Let us live with it before our eye, and in a manner appeal to it from the sentence of mankind. Let it inspire us with courage, so that mockery and imputations of unworthy motives will not be able to warp us. Let it fill us with cheerful hope, for if, at the end of a reproached, calumniated life, the judge shall write upon us the name of God, and His own new name, will it not be an ample reward?

SERMON IV.

NEUTRALITY IN REGARD TO CHRIST IMPOSSIBLE.

MATTHEW xii. 30. He that is not with me is against me.

THE man who uttered these words wandered up and down in Judea and Galilee, without a place where to lay His head, poor in this world's goods, indebted to the charity of His friends for a subsistence. He had no advantages of family or education; He never sought to become known, nor courted notoriety; He came from an obscure place of a despised part of Palestine. He preached chiefly to the poor, died three years, or a little more, after He began His preachings, and made a few hundred disciples. His life, from an earthly point of view, would be called a failure. Such was the man who said, He that is not with me is against me, as if He *were* something, and *taught* something about which men could not help taking sides; as if in spite of His lowness and insignificance in the eyes of men, they would have to form an opinion against Him or in His favor; as if He would force Himself upon their notice and compel them, all unpretending and lonely as He was, not to be indifferent to Him and to His message.

Suppose one of the great thinkers of antiquity had used these words. Let Plato or Aristotle have said, "He that is not with me is against me;" the reply of derision might have been, "There are thousands, in all generations, who will never hear of you; there are other thousands who will be supremely indifferent to what you write, and by and by you will become a name, awakening some respect perhaps in a few minds, but lost gradually in the forgetfulness which hides past ages from the view of man."

And yet this strange man, who never wrote a book, never taught a scheme of philosophy, and was only half understood, while He lived, by His disciples—this strange man, I say, used no words of assumption or arrogance, when He said, "He that is not with me is against me!" Nothing is more apparent through the world's history, than that He has been pushed, if I may not already say has been pushing Himself, upon men's notice, in wider and wider circles, ever uttering through the generations the same language, so that what once was marvellous to be heard, seems to us neither strange nor unaccountable—and that now the question of questions for the world, turns on Christ, and men everywhere more and more are summoned to take His side, or to be against Him.

These words of Christ were dictated by vast assumption, or by truthful consciousness. You might say that He was a deranged man, who, like many in their insanity, thought Himself God, or God's inspired messenger; but His wisdom, His consistency, the impression He made on His disciples, the absence of all evidence of derangement show the contrary with such force, that very few have been willing to resort to this hypothesis. You might say that He imposed on men consciously by His assumptions, but when you find it to be psychologically certain, that false claims would have demoralized Him, and can discover no flaw in His life, you have to abandon this position. You are compelled to admit that He told what was true, when He said: "For judgment came I into this world, that they which see not might see, and that they which see might remain blind!" And so you have to admit, also, that He understood Himself, and the world, and His relation to the world better than all men besides did; that He looked down the ages with an eye of foresight which none else had. And for this, you must account as you can.

But my object is not now to show that the claim of Christ implied in our text, is true, but that what He said turned out, during his life-time, and has been turning out ever since, to be an historical fact. Men then, men now, are forced to consider his claims, to accept or to oppose them.

The Apostle John, in a tragic sentence, says: "He came unto His own, and His own received Him not." The record in His life-time was chiefly of those who sided against Him. If numbers, dignity of station, loud voices of dislike and contempt, ought to weigh in such a matter, His memory ought scarcely to have survived His life-time. Still there were a few who received and loved Him. Let us look at those who were for Him, and then at the opposite and larger party.

In general, you find those who were for Him, and whom He, by His attractive power, forced to declare themselves His disciples, to have belonged to the least esteemed, the obscurest and humblest classes of society. But among His adherents from these classes, He sought to excite no partizan or class-feeling in His favor. He dreaded making friends by appeals to any popular feeling. He preferred not to present His claims, rather than to win proselytes by political and worldly hopes. When He had reason to believe, that those in whose behalf He multiplied the loaves of bread, would come by force and make Him a king, He hid Himself from their view. And when a part of the same throng met Him afterward in Capernaum, He gave them such instruction in regard to His person and work, that they deserted Him in great crowds, so as to leave only a few friends at His side. He forced multitudes thus into opposition by what a political man would have called the most maladroit of all methods. Instead of winning them and pledging them to His person by His great miracle, after which, as one might think, He could have schooled and purified them, He taught them such hard truth as to come into conflict with the prejudices of thousands. Thus, as might be expected, nearly all forsook Him.

There was a noticeable quality in His preaching, which ought here to be taken into account. In the midst of His pity and kindness, He asked for no man's good opinion or adhesion to His cause, who did not give it out of love to Himself, or on some purely spiritual ground. He wanted no disciple, humble or lofty, who had any by-ends, any expectations of preferment, any hopes which were fastened on this world. Hence, very many, even of the common people, were displeased and rejected Him. And just such treatment He expected; He was prepared for it and was not disappointed when it came.

Of those who were for Him, there were two classes, both made friends of by some peculiar attraction toward Him, both comparatively ignorant, yet differing widely in their earlier life and habits.

One of these classes was composed of simple Galilean peasants, unlettered, but by no means wholly ignorant; full of the national prejudices and false opinions of their countrymen, yet moral and religious. This class, the best part of the Jewish people and the most hopeful, evidently excited the strongest interest of Christ. Around them the war between Him and His enemies was the most active, for whoever gained them gained the nation. He lodged in this class, wherever He preached, such impressions of His power and goodness, and of His prophetic mission, that if He had gone further even a single step, if He had humored in the least their crude earthly notions of the Messiah, He might have gained large masses from this class and moved at the head of an army to Jerusalem. But He would not. He purposely ran entirely athwart their prejudices; He forced them to be against Him. And thus there was left a small body of disciples drawn to Him by love rather than by intelligence, yet so loyal, with such rudiments in their souls of a life after His pattern and His wishes, that few as they were, they were the fit germ for the coming kingdom of God.

There was another class from which, in a very remarkable way, Christ drew friends and followers, although beyond doubt, many who belonged to it, shut—as would be natural for them—their hearts to His message. They were publicans and sinners, those who had lost their character by their unpatriotic acceptance of office as tax-gatherers under Roman farmers of the revenue, and those of either sex, especially of the female, who lived on the vices of society and were the most abandoned among the people. A philosopher passes by this sort of persons in contempt or in hopelessness. The laws of States only brand them with infamy and harden them. Society abhors and dreads them, regarding even to be seen in their company as a disgrace. Yet with this class Christ mingled so openly, that Pharisees reproached Him for it, and on this low level He called for contrite and loving hearts. He made publicans and harlots choose whether they would be for Him or against Him. I will not stop to inquire why He did what seemed so out of the common rule to the Pharisees, nor to show that this wonderful approach of the purest and noblest of beings to the lowest and vilest was an attestation to His sincerity and His strength of character: it is what resulted from His mingling with them that interests us now. They heard Him gladly. They were, or at least, some of them were filled with wonder and awe, as He told them of a better life. They forsook their sins and loved Him. A woman that was a sinner, as she stood weeping and washing His feet with ointment, received as high an approval from Him as He ever gave to any mortal. He said to the uncivil, hard Pharisee, whose table He honored, she has had much forgiven, and therefore she loveth much. He brought to such persons the transformation of their souls by a new love and new hopes, and into this character personal attachment to Himself led the way.

One of this class of persons affords us a remarkable illustration of the way in which Christ sometimes forced Himself upon men's attention, as if He were determined to make them decide whether they would be for or against Him. He sees a man, of wealth indeed, but of bad reputation, one of those publicans, who was supposed to have got his money by extortion, watching Him from a tree, as He passed in a crowd through the streets of Jericho. At once He invited Himself to be his guest. He was taken home, and the next day the man made his profession of repentance, and Christ testified that salvation had come to this house of the sinner. And this He did amid censures and evil speakings, preferring to make the acquaintance of the publican rather than to lodge with the most immaculate Pharisee.

But most of those who sought Him, or whom He sought, especially if they belonged to the more intelligent classes, were not thus affected by their interviews with Him. Whether they came indifferent, out of bare curiosity, or came with a favorable bias, it generally happened that in the end they were repelled from Him. Let us now look at the kinds of men and the particular instances of men with whom He fell into contact, and we shall find that they could not go away from Him as they came. If they came indifferent, they went away generally displeased or hostile; if they came hostile, they were apt to go away more hostile; if they came favorably impressed, very often what He said altered their temper, and they passed over to the ranks of avowed enemies.

The Pharisees, as a class, rejected Him, and finally procured His death. Their hostile attitude is shown all along through the narratives, and He, on His part, took no pains to propitiate them, either by lowering the tone of His claims, or by looking with a venial eye on their faults, or by abating their fears of political evil from the regards of the people toward Him. At the same time He gave such evidence of extraordinary power that they had to account for His works of healing on principles which both proved and increased their malignity. It is plain that they narrowly watched Him; they sent spies to entangle Him in His talk, and members of the great council, belonging to this party, seem to have gone as far as Galilee to examine and report on His life and conduct. While He would doubtless have gladly gained them as converts on His own terms, it is strange to see how superior He stood to their patronage, and how He tried to plant truth in their minds, which made them reject Him with animosity. It is striking, too, to perceive how meanly He thought of this class of men. In His eyes they were hypocrites, covetous, blind, of hurtful influence on the common people, and He took pains to show by His own different views of the Sabbath and of the law how unlike His doctrine was to theirs. He thus offended the whole sect, saving some few better souls who saw greatness in His lowliness, and wisdom in His words, but who yet rather mourned for Him when He was crucified than confessed Him while He lived. Nicodemus, the seeker with eyes half opened, Joseph of Arimathæa, the wealthy friend who even dared to raise a point of justice on His behalf in the council, will show that in this sifting and winnowing process of Christ's some few of those who were most receptive of faith in Him did yet regard Him with kindly eyes, although not courageous enough to be enrolled among His disciples.

The Sadducees drew the notice of Christ to themselves less than the Pharisees, for they formed a sect which had less control over the people. But even they could not remain indifferent to Him. Pleased as they might have been with the rebukes which He poured out against their rivals, they heard Him overthrow their own dogmas, they must have consented to His death, and they appear afterwards as the leaders of the party against the apostles.

But let us leave these classes of persons and look at

single persons whom Christ forced to take sides for or against Him. Here the young ruler, who asked Him the great question how he might inherit eternal life, shall head our catalogue. Another mode of treatment, a few polite words, making the yoke easy and the burden light at the first, might have attached this person to the cause of Christ. Why was such a burden laid on him in the very beginning, as few from among the wealthy class could have born at a maturer stage of discipleship? Does it not seem harsh to repel him as Christ did? Why he was put to this test we may understand better at another time; at present I seek to show that our Lord did what He knew would drive the rich young man away, unless he were willing to bear all trials and go all lengths in the good Master's service. He put such conditions before him, as, if refused, could hardly fail to make him an enemy at last. Thus He wanted positive friends or positive foes. He purposely tested characters and dispositions at their weakest point.

More fearful still was the trial to which Judas was subject. I stop, not to inquire why the Master admitted this unworthy man into his nearest intimacy, why He did not drive him away in the early part of his ministry, when such words as, "Have I not chosen you twelve, and one of you is a devil," show how He looked into Judas' heart. Instead of doing that He kept Him by His side; He put the common purse into the hands of the man whom covetousness might turn into a thief; He trusted him, as if offering him a chance to act the traitor; in short He treated Judas so that he could not help becoming a thoroughly good man on Christ's side, or the basest of villains. Oh, why, we may ask, as we contemplate him while he is becoming steeped in guilt under the very eye of Christ,—Oh, why was he brought to choose between heaven and hell; why exposed to temptation by the confidence and the purity of Christ, when his first offers of service might have been rejected and he have remained in comparative ignorance and indifference? Whatever we say to that, one thing is clear, that Judas could not help being a sure friend, or a vile and hollow enemy of the Master.

And as we draw near the cross, we see the truth put into still clearer light that Christ forced people to take sides in respect to Him. First, Herod comes to view, the very man who had killed John, and whom Christ for a long time avoided. He had heard of Christ in his hall of guilty pleasures; his remorse had suggested that John his victim had risen from the dead, and was working miracles under the name of Jesus; but he had had no personal interview, no occasion to reject the claims of the remarkable man. Now, however, at the very last, an opportunity was given to him of showing his friendship or his opposition. And how does he use it? First to gratify a curiosity so strong that he is represented as exceedingly glad to see Him; then, when he found that no miracle was to be expected, and no answer to inquisitive questions to be got from Jesus, the soul of the cruel, cowardly, man turned into mockery; he sat Him at nought and arrayed him in a gorgeous robe. He fell in with the vehement accusations of chief priests and scribes. Thus to him also it was given to be with Christ or against Him, and he chose in conformity with his character.

Still more remarkable was the position of positive hostility into which Pilate was forced. This rapacious, unprincipled Roman moved in a sphere so unlike that of Christ, and was brought into contact with Jewish ideas at so few points, that it would have been perfectly natural for him to feel supreme indifference in the case. What could he care about the squabbles of Jews whom he despised and disliked? And, at least, no sympathy with the reigning opinion of the Jewish Council could have influenced him. But, he too, was forced to take sides for or against Christ, and that after a personal interview, in which the words and demeanor of our Lord made a strong impression upon him. He tried, perhaps, in the first moments of the examination, to be indifferent, but could not. There are certain persons whom you cannot keep your eyes off from, who attract and yet over-awe you. Pilate seems to have seen something strange and unique in the prisoner at his judgment-seat. He became, ere long, convinced that Christ was innocent. His knowledge of men assured him of the fact. Nay, there was something great and grand about the prisoner. Surely he could be no ordinary man. Pilate was without prejudices—in the best condition to intervene between the prisoner and the party calling for his death. He wanted to take His side. But the clamors of the great men of the Jews made him afraid, and he wavered.

Next he tried to avoid taking sides, by throwing the responsibility on the enemies of Christ. But they told him what he knew well, that the Romans had taken away the right of life and death from the Jewish Council, so that the decision rested with him alone. Then, as if a formality could clear him from guilt, he took water and washed his hands before the multitude, saying, I am innocent of the blood of this just person; see ye to it. All the effect of this was to make them more deliberate in their guilt. They took sides indeed when they said His blood be upon us and on our children. And he sided against Christ, when, out of policy, he stifled his own sense of justice and gave Him up. He did this when he felt that Christ actually pitied him as being put in a place by Divine Providence for which he was unequal, when the sin of the chief priest, a greater sinner, dragged him along into guilt beyond what could naturally have fallen on him.

Next we have a most striking narrative of two men alike in crime, one of whom justified Christ, and the other mocked Him. The two malefactors, just before the darkness of death and on the very cross of their agony, as well as on their way to the cross, observed and watched the wonderful man. The one was struck with the conviction that He was innocent, and true, and worthy to be trusted; the other, jeeringly and without a particle of trust, called on Him to save Himself and them, if He could. Strange, fearful contrast between an open soul and a closed soul at this dread hour, between the ingenuous penitent, who saw the light from Christ at the darkest moment, and the hardened one who wanted to be saved from death, but wanted no Saviour.

There was but one other occasion after this, during the life of the Lord, for taking sides. The soldiers, cruel, brutal, yet ignorant, had mocked Him, spit upon Him, took the side that such men, who believe in sin but not in goodness, would naturally take, but there was a heathen officer appointed to watch at the cross, whose mind the scene affected very differently. He may have known very little of our Lord before, but when the earthquake strangely accompanied the last breath of Christ, his awe-struck soul, no doubt prepared to admit the innocence of Christ before, took His side while He hung there as a malefactor. "Verily," said he, "this was a righteous man; truly this was the Son of God."

The method which Christ took to bring His claims before men, and to test them in manifold ways, is a subject full of instruction and of argument for the reality of the claims themselves. Some of this instruction I hope to be permitted, by Divine Providence, to lay before you at another time. At present, I will not pursue that train of thought, but confine myself to a remark which naturally follows and completes what has been said: it is, that the Gospel still carries on the same method of presenting Christ to men, and of pressing His personal claims to their love and obedience. All things else almost have changed, in the external aspect of religion, since Christ was on earth; established order has taken the place of a nascent church, form has succeeded to the simple oral preaching of the first teachers, doctrine fixed by men has interpreted, and almost stifled the unsystematic Gospel of the New Testament, but in and above all change Christ appears, pressing Himself upon our notice, demanding that we adhere to Him in personal devotion, and putting it to the proof, oftentimes, by tests hard to be endured, whether we will forsake all and follow Him, or whether we will forsake Him and follow the Pharisees and the Priests, the Pilate and Herod of the New Testament, the hardened thief and the Apostle that betrayed Him. He might, as I have said before, take another way to win us. He might use fair words with us, leave out of view the hardships, the oppositions we may encounter, and tell us of nothing but flowers and smooth roads and delightful prospects. But this way of treating *us* He no more adopts than He condescended to smooth the road into religion to the men of his day. Whatever there is of severity in His exclusive claim to supremacy over our hearts, He will not abate one jot of. We may think Him severe, but He repeats the old message, He cleaves to the old principle. He wants disciples, but He wants such only as have counted the cost, and have determined to forsake everything else but Him, such as are ready to love parents and all nearest kinsmen with a love that may be called hatred, so far does it fall below the height of love to Him. He tries us perhaps at the very point where we are most tender, most likely to estimate His service a hardship. To one He says, "Let the dead bury the dead, but go thou and preach the Gospel." To another, "Sell all thou hast and give it to the poor, and thou shalt have treasure in heaven, and come follow me." To another, "Whoso looketh on a woman to lust after her hath committed adultery with her in his heart. And if thy right eye offend thee, pluck it out and cast it from thee." To another, "Whosoever will save his life shall lose it." To another, "If ye forgive not men their trespasses, neither will your Father in heaven forgive your trespasses." And to another, "Except thou be converted and become as a little child, thou shalt not enter into the kingdom of heaven." Thus He approaches the delaying, the worldly, the covetous, the lustful, the selfish, the unforgiving, and the proud at the very point, where sin is dearest and conscience has been most drugged: He says to them, I ask you to give up that sin for My sake; other things are to be done afterwards, but that sacrifice I call for now. Oh how many poor, imbecile wills, how many longing hearts would have been calmed for the time, if He could have consented to take another course, if He had been willing to touch with His probe, not the sorest wound, but the one half healed, to take the out-works, and not drive right at the citadel. And oh! how many resist and fall away, and will have nothing to do with Christ, just because He requires so much at first. Could not—our hearts ask—could not our characters, by some other process, have gathered strength by yielding in little things to yield finally in great? But such is not the way into the kingdom of God, and so we turn away from Christ and from His offers.

It is remarkable, too, how now—more in fact now than for many ages—Christ forces Himself upon the notice of those *who believe Him not.* When they speculate about religion, when they trace human culture back through history, Christ stands right in their way; doctrines of men, claims of churches, moral codes they might pass by; but they cannot pass Christ by; He confronts them with a revered, yet not welcome presence. They cannot be indifferent to Him; they must examine His pretensions; He perplexes them like some problem hard to be solved. They say to Him, "Thou who hast killed the old religions, Thou who hast divided history in twain, and begun a new order of ages, and hast struck Thy roots into all human interests, who art Thou? Give us more proof of Thy rights over us than Gospels, and their fruits in the world afford." Like Herod, they long to see some miracle done by Him. But

He keeps a dead silence, only bidding them forsake their sins. They raise this and that objection, they pare down the Gospel, they lop off myths, but still there He stands to be accounted for, and claims of them that they follow Him. And so He puts them to a hard proof, calling on them for all those works and sentiments that make up a perfect life, while yet they will not draw strength from Him for the great conflict with evil. They must be for Him or against Him; for His side, whoever He be, is the side of all virtue. They cannot be neutral, even when they deny that He has any right over them, for whatever else He has done or not done, He has set up a kingdom of love and well-doing in the world; every one that loveth, and doeth well, must be for Him, every one who loveth not, and doeth evil, is against Him.

SERMON V.

THE SELF-PROPAGATING POWER OF SIN.

PROVERBS, v. 22. His own iniquities shall take the wicked himself, and he shall be holden with the cords of his sins.

IT is very common in the Scriptures to bring divine providence and the results of sin into immediate and close connection with each other, as if the pain attendant on sin were a direct act of God. But there are other passages where sin is looked at, as bringing its own punishment with it by a law of the world analogous to the physical laws of nature. Each of these ways of stating the doctrine of retribution has its advantages: the one makes a vivid appeal to our feelings by setting God as a person of infinite holiness directly before us; the other represents the punishment of sin to be such an essential part of the system of things, such an unalterable law of the moral universe, that nothing but divine grace, making exceptions to law, and bringing in remedies unknown to law, can prevent its infliction.

In the text the results of sin are represented as taking place in the natural order of things. The sinner thinks that sin is over and gone when it is once committed. But wisdom says no! It has consequences from which he cannot escape; it throws its cords around him, and takes hold of him so that he cannot get away. If you put a divine punisher of sin out of sight, sin does the work of the executioner on the sinner. "He shall die without instruction, and in the greatness of his folly he shall go astray."

Among these consequences of sin certain ones are often insisted upon,—such as bodily evils, loss of temporal advantages, fear of the wrath of God,—which show the displeasure of the Creator on the natural side, as connecting sin and pain together. But there is a far more awful view of sin, when we look at it on the moral side, as propagating itself, becoming more intense, tending to blacken and corrupt the whole character, and to annihilate the hopes and the powers of the soul. It is to this aspect of sin that I invite your attention in the present discourse. It is one which is very affecting and impressive in itself, and it has to do, you will observe, not with the purpose of God, but with facts, as old as mankind and as lasting as the soul; with facts which any heathen sage might notice, and which Christianity does not create; with facts as awful as any punishment of sin through the body and the sensitive powers of the human being. You may call these consequences of sin, as you like, retributive or not; you may say or deny that sin punishes the sinner by making him more and more morally corrupt. I care not for the terms used,—the fact, the dark fact, as a part of the system of things, remains unaltered.

Let us now turn our minds to some of the general classes of facts or laws of character to which these consequences of sin can be reduced.

I. The first of these laws of character which we notice, is the *direct* power of sin to propagate itself in the individual soul. If each act of sin stood alone by itself, and when committed brought nothing with it but its positive punishment, then half its sting would be taken away. It may be that in that case punishment would be strictly remedial, for the innocent soul, enticed into evil and speedily tasting the bitter fruits, would have ample power to return into the ways of life, for sin, by the supposition, had made no impress on the character. The soul might recover, as the body now recovers after a scratch or a bruise. But alas it is not so. Sin is the fruitfullest of all parents; each new sin is a new ever flowing source of corruption, and there is no limit to the issue of death.

1. The first illustration of this power of sin which we notice is that exceedingly familiar one *of the law of habit*, or the *tendency of a certain kind of sin to produce another of the same kind*. The law of habit, which applies alike to all our physical, mental and moral actions, must be regarded in its design as a truly benevolent one; for what greater blessing could the new-made immortal have, who must at all events encounter temptation, than to be strengthened by resistance, and thus to acquire such a degree of virtue, that temptation at length would no longer be needed or be feared if it came nigh. But the law of habit, when the soul yields to sin, works death to the sinner:—like the pillar of the cloud which made day to Israel, and was darkness to the Egyptians, so this law, which is bright to the well-doer, sheds night upon the path of the sinner until he is plunged into the sea of death. It reigns over every act, quality, and state of the soul, to render the sinful act easier, to intensify the desire, to destroy the impression of danger, to increase the spirit of neglect and delay. Take the *internal* affection of envy for an example of the *ease* of sin. The soul separated from God becomes unhappy and discontented. In its discontent the sight of the enjoyments of others gives it pain by making it aware continually of the void within, and this is what we call *envy*. Now the tendency has become such that every good whatever, pertaining to another, by this revival of the feeling of unrest will give the soul pain; and thus it places itself at war with all the joy in the universe, and this, although it bleeds under the stings of envy at every pore. Why does it not cast off this tormentor in some desperate struggle as if for eternal life? Alas! the law of character is stronger than the soul; the soul must envy if away from God, and must envy more and more, and on less and less provocation, the farther it flees from

its true rest. It must in the end acquire the impression that all the happiness or prosperity of others is inconsistent with its own.

Or, take an *external* habit—such as some sensual appetite, for an example. An appetite, we are told, answers to some end for which man was made, and the pleasure attending it is a wise provision for fulfilling the end. Under the law of reason and of God, therefore, any appetite would be innocent and harmless; none of them would interfere with the claims of God or of man, of the soul or of the body; none would be clamorous for instantaneous gratification, nor stir up an agitation in the soul, nor demand to be gratified at the wrong time or in the wrong degree. And as if to prevent the formation of evil habits, God has made the pain and the shame and the loss from excess so obvious in the world, that every new transgressor is forewarned by the shipwrecks of others if not by the voice of conscience. When now these barriers are past, which are placed in the way of sin by the law of God imprinted on human nature, law parts company with the sinner, and turns into his enemy—not indeed into his enemy in *this* sense that it hands him over to hopeless punishment, but in *this*, that it shows him, by what he is *now* bringing on himself, what he will *one day* bring on himself, when all his powers of resistance to temptation are weakened, and his leaning to unlawful pleasure has grown strong. For by yielding to sinful desire he changes the current of his thought, so that a new object seizes on the trains of thought and bends them from their old direction; he discovers new facilities for indulgence, and new ways of keeping it secret; he invents excuses for it, which rise in their sophistry and their wide-reaching extent, until every pleasure, however base, could be justified on the same ground; he increases the strength of desire until it becomes his main purpose to live for its gratification;—yes, when it has become so strong that its intensity has grown into an awful hunger, and when nature has become so blunt that all pleasure from it is killed out, desire rages still the more fiercely, and the aim now is to put an end to an ever returning torment, rather than to supply *new* pleasure to a sated soul. Oh! ye drunkards, who drink now to still a gnawing on the vitals which you liken to the fires of hell, and who yet are so holden by the cords of your sins that you are incurable; oh! ye degraded libertines, who have abused your natures in the indulgence of brutish lusts, until intellect is wasted and the body is diseased all over; oh! ye tenants of hospitals, who in catering to some vice have not been able to stop, until the divine ray of a soul is buried in hopeless idiocy, rise up in your dreadful legions, and testify to these young souls who are forming their habits, what the tendency is of indulged sins; bear witness if your own iniquities have not taken you and you are not holden by the cords of your sins—bear witness if sin must not be a vast evil, when it leads to such an end.

2. But another illustration of the self-propagating power of sin is found *in the tendency of a sin of one kind to produce sins of* ANOTHER *kind.* We supposed a little while since that each act of sin stood by itself, without having any fruits or results within the soul. Suppose now that each kind of sin stood alone, with no tendency to bring on any other. If this were so, how much would the poison of sin be qualified, how much of self-restorative power would be still left to the sinner. For by the supposition he has not undermined *character;* all his moral perceptions, his dispositions, his native tendencies to virtue remain unimpaired; and it may be these will prove stronger than the rebellious desire which has risen up to destroy the peace and break the confederacy of harmonious powers within the soul. And thus perhaps the disorders caused by this one inordinate impulse, when every thing is tamed down and brought back into place again, may be a landmark in the soul's history in favor of lasting union and peace. But alas! the supposition is a dream relating

to a possible kind of nature, and does not apply to the character of man. The confederacy of powers in him admits of no separate action of any one wayward impulse, but as soon as evil in one shape appears, it tends to corrupt all the parts of the soul, to disorganize, to reduce other powers under its own control, to weaken those which resist, until the most harmonious of structures becomes a wreck, the fairest of temples lies on the ground, with its walls parted and its pillars broken, a hopeless ruin. And could it well be otherwise, if sin be a divorce of the soul from God? Ought not some awful confusion naturally to ensue, when the soul, at war within, at war with the laws of its nature, must be conceived of as being at war with its God also?

The first point we notice here is, that *one sort of sin puts the body or soul, or both, into such a state, that another sort becomes more easy and natural.* Thus there is an *affinity between bodily lusts,* they are relations who introduce one another into the quarter they have occupied—*and, again, any one of them* tends to derange the soul *by a loss of inward peace.* In this way, drunkenness, for instance, may be the forerunner, not only of other base indulgences, but even of envy, distant as their province seems; for the loss of comfort, or of a good name, which drunkenness brings with it, may make the prosperity of another a source of anguish. By an opposite process, the loss of inward quiet, which an internal sin, like envy or inordinate worldly care occasions, may drive the man into degrading pleasures in quest of something to satisfy or stupefy the soul. *Still further* it will seem natural, if not necessary, *that one wrong affection should render another easier,* if not give birth to it, as anger may give rise to detraction, revenge, and all the hateful brood that herd with them, or pride, after blunting the edge of the sympathies, may open the door to the same malevolent traits of character. *And even an absorbing master passion,* like covetousness or ambition, when it has grown so great as to domineer over the enslaved soul, *although it may exclude some other inconsistent passion, does not reign alone,* but has around and behind it a gloomy train of satellites, which are little tyrants in turn. Covetousness—let it sway the soul, and suspicion, fraud, falsehood, discontent, envy, malice, will get as firm a foothold as the master demon himself, and no power of his can afterwards drive them from his company. The miser cannot be also a prodigal, but he must have spirits of hate and death in his soul. So ambition may exclude covetousness from the throne, but it has another train of its own familiars, as greedy, if not as base, as those of covetousness. When the spirit of evil conquers a man, "it taketh to itself seven other spirits, and they enter in and dwell there, and the last state of that man is worse than the first."

But, again, *a more striking example* of the connection *between different kinds of sins is seen, when a man resorts to a new kind of sin to save himself from the effects of the first.* The general explanation of this fact in character is simple enough. According to God's merciful system in this world—under which many are kept back from sins, or at least from gross ones, after a warning of experience—sin is generally attended with evil consequences, which are sufficiently annoying. Now, when a soul has gone far enough on in its evil career to perceive what is coming, two paths are open to it. One is to confess its fault to God, and seek peace and union with Him; the other is to devise some mode of concealing sin, or of supplying the wants which its commission in the past has occasioned. This last is the ordinary way, in which human nature endeavors to avoid the cords of its sins, when they begin to hold it tight. And in this way the reign of sin is extended over the character, and reaches on through all the lengths of time.

Thus let a man by vicious practice have brought himself into fear of want, he lies under a fearful temptation to steal or rob or peculate or commit forgery, according to his condition of life, his facility of gaining his end, and his qualities of character. I need not say that the number of those comparatively innocent thieves, who "steal to satisfy the soul when they are hungry," bears a small ratio to those whom guilt drives onward into deeper guilt; or that the plunderers and defrauders of more genteel society are almost all of them led into their new crimes in order to repair the ruin with which old ones had threatened them.

But the painfullest view of our life suggested by these considerations, is that by the process of sin just described *falsehood* is introduced into the world and spread to an infinite extent. Every sin needs a falsehood, some concealment or pretense or profession, to support it, and thus the sinner knows that in the case of each new sin he can resort to a new lie to save himself from immediate evil. Think what a deadly fountain is opened here, which, but for previous sinning, would never have sent forth its poisonous waters over the world, and what an awful temptation comes upon the sinner's soul from the success and ease of its past concealments and lies. Virtue needs no cloak nor borrowed garb. There never would be an act of insincerity, or even of dissimulation in a virtuous world—not a tone or gesture or hint tending to deceive or misguide. All the boundless numbers of all the forms of untruthfulness, whose very names show their frequency, insincerities, prevarications, equivocations, falsehoods, lies, concealments of truths, pretenses, hypocrisies, treacheries, perjuries, and the rest,—all these are the supports, and the resorts of sin, generated by sin, generating sin. And thus, if the sin that gave birth to the falsehood tempts the soul no longer, the falsehood still sets up its tent in the soul. In the impressive language of the prophet, "that which the palmer worm hath left, hath the locust eaten, and that which the locust hath left hath the canker worm eaten, and that which the canker worm hath left hath the caterpillar eaten." It is as with a burning house: whom the flame consumes not the smoke suffocates.

Nor can I forbear to mention in this place that another dark shade is thrown over the malignity of sin, from the fact, that it so often makes use *of innocent motives* to propagate its power over the soul. The fear of danger or evil is a good thing, for it quickens the mind in its efforts to avoid danger, and lead us into the path of virtue which is the path of safety. The love of esteem is a social principle most happily put into us that it may aid the virtue of the one by the approbation of the many. But see how, the moment that sin reigns within us, these innocent principles become sources of temptation and ministers of death to the soul. The fear of danger or of want, impels into new crimes as an escape from the results of old ones. The love of esteem is the handmaid of all falsehood and hypocrisy. What a picture this gives of the baneful power of sin—that it can undermine and corrupt the soul by the help of the very affections which were made to be the servants of virtue—that what can be used to build up everything good, it uses only to destroy.

II. Another law of character by which the propagation and strength of sin is secured, is the tendency of sin to produce moral blindness. Our Saviour has stated the leading thought here in these words: "Every one that doeth evil hateth the light, neither cometh to the light, lest his deeds should be reproved." Sin freely chosen must needs seek for some justification or palliation; otherwise the moral sense is aroused, and the soul is filled with pain and alarm. Such justification cannot be found in moral or religious truth, and of this the soul is more or less distinctly aware. Hence an instinctive dread of truth, and a willingness to receive and embrace plausible, unsound excuses for sin, which neutralize or destroy its power. And in the process, inasmuch as there is a moral if not a logical affinity between all truths, and the same between all falsehoods, when one untruth is embraced it brings another in its train, and yet another, until a whole system is constructed, on which the mind relies the more, because it has the compactness and strength of a system. Of course, the system of truth is driven out, and a hostility grows up in the soul towards it, because it is perceived to be a destroyer of present comfort and peace. "Lest his deeds should be reproved." They who know how annoying is the fault-finder, and how irritating sometimes is even the reproof of a friend given in kindness, will estimate what the feeling would be towards truth when it came into the soul while falsehood was building up its castle, and sought to pull it down; what a bitter war would ensue, a war which might reach beyond truth itself to all that love it, to all that preach it, to the book which professes to contain it, to the author of it Himself. In short the opposition is fitly expressed by that great physical contrast of light with darkness, which our Saviour uses in His illustration.

Now the ways in which this overthrow of unperverted moral judgments, this rejection of light tends to strengthen the power of sin, are manifold. It decreases the restraining and remedial power of conscience; it kills the sense of danger and even adds hopefulness to sin; it destroys any influence which the beauty and glory of truth could put forth; in short, it removes those checks from prudence, from the moral powers, and from the character of God, which retard the career of sin. If sin reigned before, how much more tyrannical its reign when falsehood is become its prime minister.

III. Closely connected with this blinding power of sin is another law of character—that sin tends to benumb and root out the sensibilities,—by which process again, its power over the soul is anew increased. "Who, being past feeling, have given themselves over to lasciviousness, to work all uncleanness with greediness." We may perhaps reduce such a law, if it shall be found to exist, under the general law of habit, for where there is a long-continued check on the exercise of a feeling, it loses its power by habitual neglect, or suppression, just as it gains power by exercise. Now that such a law does exist, we may almost assume: it is acknowledged, and its workings are seen on every hand. It is seen in the acquired cruelty of men of blood. "What difference do one hundred thousand men dead or alive make to me?" said Napoleon, when an Austrian statesman urged the loss of life which his measures would involve. It is seen in the horrible want of pity of the miser; it is seen in that deadness to conscience, produced by long sinning, to which we have alluded above; in that sinking down below the sense of character which the drunkard carries, as it were, on his face; in the disregard of rights which the prodigal manifests; in the extinction of the family affections; in the astonishing selfishness of the seducer; in the destruction almost complete of the religious sense of the blasphemer.

And this view of sin shows it in its true light as a perverter of nature; an overturner of all those particular traits, the union of which under love to God makes the harmony and beauty of the soul. Sin tends to destroy even those qualities which in a brute awaken our deep interest, and to put into their place a lead-colored monotonous selfishness, which is not properly human nature, but its wreck and overthrow. Oh! when selfishness, from being an instinct, becomes a law, a reign, a tyranny over the soul, when this corruption has absorbed and assimilated to itself all the feelings and affections, must not the power of sin be greatly augmented?

IV. Another of the self-perpetuating processes of sin consists in its crippling the power of the will to undertake a reform. The will itself, indeed, as a faculty, cannot suffer extinction, any more than the soul. It must continue through thousands of years of sinning, and may show a fearful energy against the enemies of sin: it may even consent to what looks like disinterested sacrifices, out of mere hostility to goodness. But I refer to those cases, very frequent in life, which show a will so long overcome by the strength of sin and by ill-success in opposing it, that the purpose of reform is abandoned in despair. Here the infirmity of the will depends not on deficiency of intellect, nor on natural weakness of the faculty, nor on constitutional want of hope, but on a practical estimate of the chances of success derived from experience. The man has fallen into a bad habit and struggles like a captive to set himself free. He undertakes the task with a firm purpose, and a strong hope, but there are two things he has not taken into account—the temporary excitement and even recklessness which desire can introduce into the soul, and the fallacious pleas by which it attempts to pacify conscience. At the moment of temptation, therefore, he loses his strength and will to resist, and is again caught and claimed by the kidnappers of the soul. The power of habit, now known to him by experience, increases the probabilities of being overcome again, and he goes back to this work of resistance with less hope than before. And so, repeated failures prostrate him, he owns himself vanquished, foresees no better times ahead, and yields as a slave to sin. Must not sin now have a heavier dominion over him than at first—yea, if he fall into some new kind of sin, will not this sense of weakness go with him, and help on the conquests of the new master? Oh wretched man that he is, who shall deliver him from the body of this death? Who but that very Ransomer from whom sin keeps him far away?

The outcries of human nature under this bondage to sin are tragic indeed; no scene of murdered helplessness is more lamentable. Hear how Coleridge writes during that part of his life when he was a slave of opium, from which at length divine grace rescued him. The words are from a letter to Mr. Cottle: "Had I but a few hundred pounds, but two hundred, half to send to Mrs. Coleridge, and half to place myself in a private mad-house, where I could procure nothing but what a physician thought proper, and where a medical attendant could be constantly with me for two or three months (in less than that time life or death would be determined), then there might be hope. Now there is none! O God! how willingly would I place myself under Dr. Fox, in his establishment; for my case is a species of madness, only that it is a derangement, an utter impotence of the volition, and not of the intellectual faculties. You bid me rouse myself! go bid a paralytic in both arms to rub them briskly together, and that will cure him. 'Alas!' he would reply, 'that I cannot move my arms is my complaint, and my misery.'"

I knew a man once, now dead, a learned lawyer and a fine Greek scholar, but a drunkard. At his death his journal was found, and there, from day to day, he recorded his lapses, his lamentations, his hopes, or his want of hopes; and the dreary record went on until he died without reform. It suggested to me the analogy of an officer in a weak fortress writing down the successes of the enemy. Now they are on the esplanade, now upon the glacis, now they have taken a bastion, now the resisting soldiers are slain, and now a half-completed sentence shows that he, too, is dead. Oh, when sin takes our will away and our hope, what is left to resist its power?

V. Sin propagates itself by means of the tendency of men to associate with persons of like character and to avoid the company of persons of an opposite character. The good and the bad, the farther their characters diverge, have the less fellowship with one another, until their tastes judgments, pleasures, and purposes, become diametrically opposite. It is indeed a merciful provision that ten thousand ties of kindred, neighborhood, business, mutual dependence, bind men of all characters and lives to one another. And by the constitution of this earthly being of ours, good and evil being in the germ and not having attained their full growth, cannot take the attitude of full opposition, because they cannot appear to each other as they really are. There is, moreover, a constant possibility of reform in a world of grace. But even here, in this world of confused and imperfect characters, what a separation takes place between the opposite principles, between the men of honor who shrink from the contact of the base, and the men of dishonor who dread seeing themselves in the light of noble deeds, and dread coming to a discovery of their own shame; between the women of purity, and the forlorn ones who have cast character and hope away; between the servant of God, and him who believes in no God or keeps at a distance from His face. But this separation, effected by sin, is far from keeping the sinner alone. He needs company the more, the less he is able to find resources, comfort, support within himself. Thus there are, in fact, two societies in spite of the binding forces among mankind, and if each of us, my friends, could live long enough to carry out the tendencies in us to their perfection, if this world consisted of old inhabitants who had time to develop their qualities in full, then there would be as wide a separation between men of opposite lives as if they dwelt in different planets.

In the operation of this law of companionship, if I may so call it, the evil have a power and an increasing power over each other. The worst maxims and the worst opinions prevail, for they are a logical result of evil characters. Separated from the good, the evil have no check on their mutual influence. The older corrupt the younger. Can you doubt that every perversion of truth, every depraved habit, must have full sweep in such a society?

Can you question the power of sin to propagate, to intensify itself, where the social principle itself is in the service of evil? O, what a blessing it is that in this system of grace such societies are of limited dimensions, are broken up by various causes, and that remedial influences from rejected grace shine sometimes with life-giving power into these chambers of death. Blessed be God that the full fruits of sin are not gathered in this world, for the tendencies, even when partially counteracted, and manifested but in their beginnings, are beyond measure appalling.

In conclusion, now, I have to say that with the justice or goodness of this system, I have at present nothing to do. The Bible did not set it on foot, the Bible does not fully explain it, but only looks at it as a dark fact. Nor can I stop to discuss the question whether men who are thus under the sway of moral death, are so wholly by their own fault, or partly by their misfortune. Somehow or other mankind, ready as they are to palliate sin, are unanimous through all their races and generations and forms of life, in feeling and owning a load of sinfulness. But suppose mankind in this wholly wrong, I ask whether it does any good, when you have the pestilence, to inquire whom you took it from, or whether you were to blame in catching it, rather than whether it can be cured? Nor finally, will I refute the unfounded suggestion, that sin may be a stage of being through which we all must pass toward a higher. At least, sin does not cure itself or pave the way toward truth and right. The question then still is, is there any cure? There is no cure certainly in continuing to sin. Sin no more destroys its own sway over the soul than Satan casts out Satan. If there be any cure it must be found outside of the region which sin governs, either from some law of character, if there be any, over which sin has not gotten the mastery, or from some divine strength which is to be sought with all possible earnestness.

Tell me, then, my hearer, is sin or is it not a great evil, one which no pains to oppose or to cure, are too great? Do you say that you are not sensible of the greatness of the evil, that the tendencies which have been told of are seen in extreme cases only? But if the tendencies are inseparable from sin; if it sometimes fails to work out its full task, because some influence outside of the man controls it in part; if you can see its devastations in all ages and climes; if even the one vice of drunkenness has slain more victims than pestilence and war, what then? Is it not fair to point out such inevitable tendencies, is it not wise to dread them, is it not consistent with truth to use them as the measure of the power of sin?

I call on you then to find out for yourself a cure. I offer you one, Christ and His gracious Spirit. But if you do not believe in it, or dislike it, choose for yourself some other. Be a Pharisee, or an ascetic, fight against sin, crucify it in your own fashion. Get rid of it in some new way of your own if you can, *no matter how,* provided only you are freed effectually from this self-spreading and self-continuing curse. Oh, my friends, the poor self-tormenting Hindoo Faquir may be wrong in his means, but his end is a nobler one than you can ever reach, while you neglect your character. Yes! all, in every land, Pagans or Christians, clowns or philosophers, who, in whatever way have fought against or wept over the grand evil, will rise up in the judgment and condemn you because you have thought so lightly of this dread malady of your soul,

SERMON VI.

SIN UNNATURAL.

JER. ii. 12, 13. Be astonished, O ye heavens at this and be horribly afraid, be ye very desolate, saith the Lord. For my people have committed two evils; they have forsaken me, the fountain of living waters, and have hewed them out cisterns, broken cisterns, that can hold no water.

THE heavens and all their host obey the law of their nature with unchanging regularity. But man, another of the works of God, commits two evils; he forsakes the fountain of living waters, and hews out for himself broken cisterns that can hold no water. In thus deserting the waters of life he is untrue to his own nature. If the heavens had a soul and could notice this unnatural conduct, so unlike to their conformity to the law of their being, they would be astonished and horribly afraid. The whole universe under physical law would cry out against man's strange disobedience to moral law, his swerving from his nature, his disloyalty to the author of his nature.

It is this aspect of man as a sinner and this quality of his sin, for which I bespeak your attention at the present time. There is something unaccountable and unnatural about sin, which, if we were not the victims of its power every day, would startle *us* also and make us horribly afraid. If we merely heard of it as existing in some other of God's worlds, we should doubt whether the report of it that reached our ears could be true. We should demand more than the usual amount of testimony, as in the case of a miracle, before believing so unnatural a story, and when it was proved, should not cease to wonder, and to ask what cause beyond our experience had brought to pass a thing so marvellous.

This view of sin as being unnatural is quite unlike that which men are apt to take. It is not strange, they think, to cheat or lie or get drunk, but to lead a perfectly sober, truthful, honest life is wonderful. To remain in a state of sin is quite natural, but to become a true Christian by a hearty reception of the Gospel is regarded as so unnatural, that many who profess to believe in Christianity refuse their faith to the reality of conversion, and many others describe it as the infusion of a new nature, as if the very seeds and capabilities of goodness had been lost out of the human soul.

This is explained in part by the fact that man, as fallen, is in an abnormal or unnatural state, so that he wonders, when he sees the normal condition of his nature. The very description of this state as a *fall* implies that it is unnatural, that it is a departure from a type or character properly belonging to mankind, a sinking down from a level where we had been placed, or a separation from God with whom we were for a time in harmony. And yet we are so removed in character and in experience from the higher, holier life which is our birth-right, that such a life startles us as something not human. Men stare at goodness, as if it had no right to be here on earth, or suspect it as unreal. Even Christ, a practical life and not an idea of the mind, Christ all instinct with living goodness, is a marvel in His perfection, so that some seek for flaws in His character, and others cannot believe that such goodness existed in the shape of man, and others still refer his perfection to the God within Him; and yet He was, as a perfect man, a sample of a regular unfolding of our nature. The regular irregularity of man is the wonder. There is none like it in the material world. The asteroids, the deformities, and unwonted misgrowths of animals, and even double flowers, are strange, but they are exceptions. So it is also with deranged reason. But here the abnormal is the order of things, the conformity to nature is the exception almost unheard of.

Among the marvels or mysteries of sin, we name as the *first*—

That it prevents men from pursuing what they own to be the highest good.

There is an often quoted passage of the poet Ovid * where a person in a conflict between reason and desire is made to say, "Video meliora proboque, deteriora sequor;" and in a like strain we hear the apostle Paul, or rather the man made aware of the bondage of sin saying through him, "That which I do, I allow not: for what I would, that do I not, but what I hate, that do I." And so true to human nature such words are, that no one ever thought of them as being misrepresentations of the real state of man. No! man everywhere, by every kind of confession, uttered or unuttered, makes known that he has an idea of duty, right, good, within him to which he fails to conform, that he does this by no constraint, but prefers the known *worse* to the known *better*, that in so acting he sacrifices what he verily believes to be his highest happiness even in this world, casting another world out of account. And everywhere we see examples of this sacrifice of a higher good to a lower, of acknowledged greater happiness to less, of the improvement of the mind to the enjoyments of the body, of future hopes to present pleasure, of an object of desire felt to be praiseworthy and exalted to one which is base and low and sure to be followed by remorse. We find this cleaving to the best of men and to the wisest: the influences of the gospel may weaken but never remove this tendency. It belongs to mankind.

But if any thing can be inferred from our nature and capacities, it is certain, that an estimate of the compara-

* Metam. vii., 20, 21.

tive values of things desirable is implanted in our minds, in order that we may choose the superior good and refuse the inferior. When we fail to do this, we reproach ourselves with folly or with sin. When we look back upon past choices and pathways in life, we feel remorse or self-approbation, or at least, respect or despise ourselves, in proportion as we have been true or false to our estimates and convictions in our choices between objects of desire. This is inevitable, whether we make the true good to consist in happiness, or in obedience to the law of duty, or in being like God, or under *whatever* aspect we view that which we believe to be the highest object of desire. Thus there is a universal preference of a lower good to a higher in the life of men, a universal power of comparing goods with tolerable accuracy, and a universal condemnation lying on the race for not being true to its estimates and standards.

Is there not, now, something very strange in this fatal proclivity toward the low, in this constant, wide-spread, unalterable folly of choosing wrong within the moral sphere of action? Suppose that we found the same obliquity of judgment and choice elsewhere—that, for instance, a scholar, aware what was the right meaning of a passage according to the laws of thought and language, deliberately chose a wrong meaning; or a merchant, acquainted with the laws of trade, undertook an adventure with his eyes open, from which only ruin was to be expected; or a general, patriotic and discerning, adopted a plan of battle which all his experience had condemned as sure to end in his defeat; should we not regard such a person, if we could conceive he had thus acted, as a kind of moral prodigy, as fit to be put away in a museum of morbid psychology among the deranged men who have believed themselves to be two persons, or that their souls had gone from their bodies? Do you say that this is a perverted use of freedom? But is there nothing strange in a perversion, which sacrifices a known good? Or do you say that it is a fatal, hopeless want of freedom? But is there nothing strange in such fatality, if a creature of God is made to choose what he condemns; and if there were no God, would it not be equally strange that man, the offspring of chance, should regularly condemn what he chooses? Or will you say that by some internal excitement of desire the present inferior good or even the present evil puts on fair colors, takes a false dress, and with a half conscious connivance of the soul deceives it into sin? Very well, but why cannot the superior good which is in itself all beauty and in its fruits all enjoyment,—why cannot *this* take its proper place before the mind, and act with its proper strength? Is there nothing strange in this —that falsehood should have such power of fascination, such constant power, and truth show itself so feeble, at the very time when we discern them both, and own the force of obligation? Must we not, when we reflect what man was made for, what the law of his nature is, what his harmonies and his true life are, wonder that he should make such choices in the sunlight of truth, with great risks and threatened evils attending a wrong choice, with conscience not yet seared, with his soul craving the better portion, and *often, very often*, witnessing against him that he is preferring death to life? Here then is a marvel of our nature: sin is something unnatural and monstrous; its sway is not according to the true law of the soul's constitution but against it.

II. Another marvel, connected with the sway of sin is, that it is not dependent on a weak capacity, but that the very highest intellects are often employed in its service.

It is indeed true, that sagacity and folly will differ in their ways of sinning and of escaping detection. An absurd, or ill-contrived crime, will be committed by a boy or a half-witted person, and not by a man of shrewdness. Whence it may happen, that the criminals in a penitentiary may be, in the average, below the ordinary range of intellect. In other words, the vigor of mind will show itself, either by abstaining from certain crimes, or by committing them in such a way that they will not be brought to light. But we do not find that the highest abilities keep men from sinning, from a life of pleasure, from deadly selfishness, from feelings which carry with them their own sting. Great minds lie like wrecks all along the course of life; either they disbelieve against evidence, or give themselves up to monstrous pleasures, or destroy the welfare of society by their self-will, or gnaw upon themselves with a deadly hatred of others. If they are sometimes philosophers, or great inventors, or philanthropists, they are at other times in the front ranks of wickedness. There have been great infidels, as well as great Christians. There have been great conquerors, scourges of men, as well as great philanthropists. And, on the other hand, persons of feeble capacity are oftentimes good ; better than many—if not than any—of the great men of their times. Nay, so often have intellect and morals been out of harmony, that many persons think knavery a *prima facie* evidence of talent,—confessing thus, that in their opinion, men are likely to employ their powers of mind in a wrong and foolish way.

Now is there not something very strange in this? We do not wonder when we hear that an idiot, or half-idiot, has committed a crime; and a court will not punish him, because he has not mind enough to balance his native strength of passion. He will be shut up as a dangerous person, but not punished as a criminal. Ought it not to be strange, on the other hand, that intellect is used by so many, not to check desires, which end in crime, but to enlarge the plans of sinning, and to purchase impunity? And if a moderate intellect will fit a man for the business of this world, ought we not to expect, if there is not something abnormal in our condition, that the Cæsars and Napoleons, that the great statesmen, and poets, and artists, should be pre-eminently the men of God; men for whose minds this world was too small, who shook off its fetters and soared away towards the Great Mind that filleth the universe? But who among them turns his thoughts thus upward, and forms his plans on a scale as grand as his own mind? It does not surprise us to see the very ablest men slaves of drunkenness or impurity, or to see them filled with intense hate; their intellects, so far from looking ahead and warning them against dangers, are ministering to their lusts, and putting fuel on the flame, like the engineers in a steamer, when it is running on the rocks. And, therefore, moralists have made tirades against the weakness of the human intellect, because great men have rushed into all follies to their own ruin. Whereas the intellect is not at fault—it can scale the heavens, and travel through eternity, it can search all depths of science, and is equal to all things with which our nature has to do;—why should it then not mitigate, why should it carry forward the great malady of sin?

III. Another marvel of sin is that its existence involves the contradiction of the freedom and the slavery of the will. This is but another aspect of the truth which we have already considered—that the soul steadily chooses in some strange way an inferior good before a superior; but it is too important a view of our nature not to be noticed by itself. Mankind in choosing the evil, have been an enigma to themselves, and to the philosophers who have studied human nature. On the one hand, duty implies power to do what is required, freedom to yield to a given motive or reject it; on the other hand, the experience of the soul points to a bondage under sin, in which the freedom natural and essential to it is obstructed, and the man is as much a slave, as if he never gave his assent. So helpless man appears, so fruitless are his unaided efforts to escape from evil habit, and above all to yield himself to God his rightful ruler, that the unexercised freedom seems unreal to many, and they deny its existence. Some hold that the will is swayed by laws as sure and almost as mechanical as those of the outer world. Others quiet their consciences by the plea that they are not responsible. But after all, the faith in human freedom comes back and falls into conflict with the certain awful fact of the bondage of our nature under sin. We see our nature exercise its freedom in various ways—choosing now a higher good in preference to a lower, and now a lower before a higher,—doing this over and over within the sphere of earthly things, yet when it looks the supreme good full in the face unable to choose Him, unable to love Him, until, in some great crisis which we call conversion, and which is as marvellous as sin is, we find the soul acting with recovered power, acting out itself, and soaring in love to the fountain and life of its being. Oh, who can deny this to be marvellous, that all good things, save the truest good, are accepted or rejected *ad libitum,* while that which alone deserves to be called good, is avoided and disliked constantly. Ye philosophers, tell us if there be any marvel in nature like this. It is as if a balance should tell every small weight with minutest accuracy, and when a large weight was put on, should refuse to move at all. It is as if the planets should feel each other's attraction but be insensible to the force of the central sun. Is not sin then as unaccountable as it is deep-seated and spreading in our nature?

IV. But, fourthly, the same mystery of sin appears, when we consider that it has a power of resisting all known motives to a better life. This, again, is only another form of the remark, that we are kept by sin from pursuing our highest good; but under this last head we view man as opposing God's plan for his salvation, while the other is more general. Here we see how causeless and unreasonable are the movements of sin, even when its bitterness has been experienced, and the way of recovery been made known. If there had been no higher life disclosed to us in the Gospel, it would not seem so very strange that the calls of earthly prudence should be disregarded, that between motives not vastly different in power, a weaker should prevail over a stronger, that earthly interests should be sacrificed to earthly pleasure; for earth is but a point, and if we lose in the continuance of our enjoyment, when we are deaf to the voice of prudence and listen to pleasure, we yet gain in the intensity of it, we crowd more into a moment. But the marvel is, that the Gospel, with its mighty motives, appeals in vain to thousands who profess to have no doubt that it is from God. There is surely no such crowd of motives and reasons attendant on any other question as on that of the reception of Christianity. It is a question between life and death, in which our highest interests are concerned, which appeals to our hopes and fears, our consciences, our aspirations after a better life, our gratitude and love. It founds its appeals on the most remarkable facts in the universe, on the love of God to sinners, on the incarnation and death of Christ. We have the offer of pardon, peace, help to raise us up to God, deliverance from fear, support in death, and a blessed immortality. The way in which the Gospel comes to us is the most inviting possible—through a person who lived a life like ours on earth, and came into tender sympathy with us; through a concrete exhibition of everything true and good, not through doctrine and abstract statement. It has been the religion of our fathers, and of the holy in all time. It is venerable in our eyes. It is God's voice to us. Where else can so many motives, such power of persuasion be found; and yet where else, in what other sphere where motives operate, is there so little success? Even Christians who have given themselves to the Gospel, confess that all these weighty considerations often fail to move them; that they stand still or turn backwards a great part of their lives, rather than make progress. So marvellous is the power of sin to deaden the force of motives to virtue, even in the minds of the best persons the world contains.

Nor will the force of these considerations be escaped by saying that the motives fail to act because the Gospel which presents them is not believed. If by belief is meant faith in its divine origin, thousands have that faith, and would highly resent the charge of being without it, who are as little governed by the motives to which it appeals, as the professed infidel. Or if by belief is meant such an impression of the reality of the Gospel as makes its facts and truths motives of action, that is the very marvel of which we speak, that this dread assemblage of truths can be accepted as real, without exerting a motive power upon the soul, without awaking it from its dreams of worldliness.

And, again, if one should say that the marvel is lessened by the consideration that man is a creature of sense, over whom spiritual, intangible realities can have no power, or that he must be educated up by a long process to a capacity for spiritual life, I reply, that as far as we admit this we see another of the marvels of sin. Here is a creature, formed in God's image, yet sunk so low that his brutish nature has almost forgotten its relationship to its author; the noblest, most essential powers of his soul lie so latent that they seem to be extinct. Is there not something very strange in this degradation, this locking up of the spirit, this unnatural fall? But man is not a creature of sense with the spiritual powers wholly unexercised. All religions with their appeals to invisible gods, all ascetic and mystical efforts to become virtuous, the love of fame creating a world for the author or warrior after his death, all affection for the departed, all systems of philosophy, all standards of duty above that of the Epicurean, show another capacity in man, that, namely, to which the Gospel speaks, when it invites the soul to a fellowship with God and an inheritance in eternal life. That this capacity is so inactive and feeble under the Gospel, that is the wonder. Our *nature* can not explain this; it can be referred only to the unnatural state of man as a sinner.

V. Another of the marvels of sin is, that it can blind the mind to truth and evidence. Of this we see numberless examples in daily life. We see men who have been accustomed to judge of evidence within the same sphere in which religion moves, that of moral and historical proof, rejecting the Gospel, and afterwards acknowledging that they were wilfully prejudiced, that their objections ought to have had no weight with a candid mind. We see prejudice against the Gospel lurking under some plausible but false plea, which the man has never taken the pains to examine, although immense personal interests are involved. We see men rejecting the Gospel unthinkingly, repeating some stale argument scarcely worth refutation, as if a great matter like the welfare of the soul might be trifled with, and made light of. We see men in a state of skepticism half their lives, resting on nothing, and willing so to live, rather than to make up their minds on the truth or the falsehood of Christianity. We see men claiming that they have sifted evidence with all candor, yet starting with an assumption to the prejudice of the Gospel which is obviously false.

It is strange too, how quick the change is, when for some reason the moral or religious sensibilities are awakened after long slumber, how quick, I say, the change is from skepticism, or denial of the Gospel, or even hostility, to a state of belief. Multitudes of intelligent men have passed through such a conversion, and have felt ever afterwards that truth and evidence were sufficient, but that their souls were in a dishonest state. Now how is this? Is this a new prejudice which has seized upon them, at their conversion, and has their candid skepticism given way to dishonest faith; or did sin,—that which in a thousand ways, through hope and fear, through indolence, through malignity, through love of pleasure, blinds and stupefies, did sin destroy their power of being candid before?

The power of sin to prevent the force of truth seems marvellous, especially when we consider the greatness of the risk run in rejecting the truth. It is possible that belief and the favor of God may go together. It is quite possible that character and happiness forever may depend upon receiving the truth and the motives which it carries in its train; thus personal interests, welfare, the possibility of virtue, God's enduring smile, all may depend upon belief in the Gospel. It certainly claims so much importance for its truth. Is now the state of that mind, which is thoughtless of its own interests for eternity, while it is alive to the smallest interests of time, a state of the highest candor and impartiality, or is it a state of prejudice or of lethargy so deep that nothing, not even the hazards of a future life, can shake it off? And is not this a strange, unnatural state, when a soul that is made to watch over its own welfare a great way on; a soul that can plan for ages after death; a soul whose very selfishness ought to make it more intensely anxious to know what is the way of life; that such a soul can treat truth like a play-thing; that a man of intellect can grow old without sifting the evidence of the Gospel; that many shrewd men can die with their hostility to it unquenched, as if it were the great foe of their peace?

VI. I only add, that the inconsistency of sin is marvellous in *this* respect; that we allow and excuse in ourselves what we condemn in others. Men seem sometimes to have no moral sense, so open are their violations of morality, and so false their justifications of their conduct. And yet, when they come to pass censure upon others, they show such a quickness to discern little faults, such an acquaintance with the rule of duty, such an unwillingness to make allowances, that you would think a new faculty had been imparted to their minds. These severe critics of others are all the while laying up decisions and precedents against themselves, yet when their cases come on, the judges reverse their own judgments. They condemn men unsparingly for sins to which *they* are not tempted, although the radical principle in their own and in other's sins is confessedly the same. They blame and hate others for heart sins, such as envy, when they feel no compunction for this, the commonest of sins, in their own hearts. They complain of detraction and evil speaking, when they are injuring the good name and aspersing the character of others continually. Perhaps, after they have fallen into a sin which they had condemned in others before, they become, in that particular, somewhat milder censors. There is, however, in other cases, a very constant condemnation and justification, by turns, of the very same sins. Marvellous inconsistency! Strange that the same mind balances between two standards of conduct so long. Why does not the man, whose own rules condemn himself, begin to sentence himself, or to excuse and pardon others? Is not this an unnatural state of mind; impossible, save on the supposition that it is effected by some strange perversion of its judgments?

Such are some of the points of view from which sin looks unnatural, a breach of the order of things, a monstrous innovation introduced into the world. But we have not exhausted the subject. If we take a view, for an instant, of some of the affections and sentiments, the same thing may be made apparent. We have the feeling of reverence within us to lead us to worship, and yet while all false and foul divinities are worshiped, man flees from the face of the infinitely holy and beautiful God. We are endowed with sympathy, that we may rejoice in the joy, and grieve at the pain of others; yet, what seems more natural, or is more common in the world than envy which grieves at the joy, and even malice, which rejoices at the pain of men? It may be shown, that every sentiment under the control of principle and right reason, which are the natural condition of man, would harmonize with every other. But the social principles are all taken hold of by sin, and so disharmony seems to be written on our souls, and on society. Shame leads us to do things that are in reality shameful, and a sense of honor, things that are dishonorable. Selfishness reigning supreme, brings the individuals of society into hostility, and one society into hostility to another. Fear, covetousness, love of superiority, suspicion, and their kindred, make a state of disorder in the world seem so natural, that war, according to some thinkers, is the normal condition of man.

We have thus looked at some of the phenomena which take place among men under the sway of sin, phenomena common enough—alas! far too common—but not natural nor regular actings of our souls. And this strangeness has always been felt to exist. Some have talked of two souls with different characteristics. Some, of opposite spiritual powers, leading a soul different ways. Some have done violence to their primary convictions, by denying the existence of sin, as if man became less of an enigma on that supposition; but sin remains, and the strange perversion remains, which it brings into the system of motives and into the intellectual state! Perversion! Do not words like this, and like *wrong*, that is something wrung or twisted, and many others, indicate the judgment which has been passed on sin by the makers of language, that is by human minds, as something opposed to the right, the good, and the true?

And if sin is thus unnatural, thus strange in its workings, true faith in Christ, true godliness, union with God, on the other hand, is natural, is regular, is in harmony with truth and reason. We become the followers of Christ, and in proportion as we are so, we pursue the highest good; every good thing takes its place in our regard according to its importance; our wills no longer remain under bondage to sin, while conscious of freedom; every motive has its due sway over us; every truth is sure of admission to our hearts; we have the same standard for ourselves and for others, only throwing something into the scale in their favor as a make-weight to our own selfishness. We are brought, in short, into harmony with God, and thus put forth our natural powers in their natural direction. Then, as we look back on the old pathway of sin, it seems a delusion, a bondage, a marvel; we are astonished at it, and conversion seems the only reasonable, the only natural thing. And when we look at a world under the control of sin, strange, inexplicable, sad, as its mysterious *introduction* among us seems, its fearful, unreasonable, all perverting *power* is the strange thing which ought to affect us most. Redemption, too, is strange. It is marvellous. But if sin has been discovered by us to be so perverse and marvellous a thing, we shall not estimate the outlay of divine power in redemption as too great. Christ and His cross are in proportion to sin; and when we come to think of it, we shall sometimes feel as if the incarnation of the Son of God was not more wonderful than that free, responsible men, to whom their own interests are so valuable, should act without regard for every thing true and good; that above all, they should reject this very redemption which Christ has provided for them.*

* Compare Augustin de Civit. Dei xi. Cap. 17.

"Sine dubio, ubi esset vitium malitiæ, natura non vitiata præcessit, vitium autem ita contra naturam est, ut non possit nisi nocere naturæ. Non itaque esset vitium recedere a Deo, nisi naturæ, cujus id vitium est, potius competeret esse cum Deo. Quapropter etiam voluntas mala grande testimonium est naturæ bonæ."

And again, Lib. xii. Cap. 3:

"Naturæ illæ, quæ ex malæ voluntatis vitio vitiatæ sunt, in quantum vitiosæ sunt, malæ sunt; in quantum autem naturæ sunt, bonæ sunt."

SERMON VII.

SIN NOT SELF-REFORMATORY.

ISAIAH i. 5. Why should ye be stricken any more? Ye will revolt more and more: the whole head is sick, and the whole heart faint.

I HAVE lately called your attention to two aspects of sin, to its dreadful power of propagating itself, and to its being a violence against nature. I invite your attention to-day, to a third aspect, that there is no tendency in sin to cure itself, or that sin has in itself and its consequences no self-reforming power.

It might seem, if sin can be called unnatural and monstrous, that nature could shake it off, and return to her own law. It might seem also, that the results of sin would cure the sinner of his evil tendencies, and send him back on the path of wisdom. Do we not learn continually by our mistakes? Are not men made better by the faults they have committed and the evils they have suffered? What is more common than that the beginning of a religious life proceeds from some out-breaking sin, which shows to a man for the first time his true weakness of character, and leads him in humble shame to the grace of the Gospel?

We grant that a man in a state of sin may be led to abandon some sin, or some excess of sin, from considerations of prudence. We grant also that affliction softens many characters which it fails to lead to sincere repentance, by lowering their pride, or by sobering their views of life. We have no doubt that the seeds of a better life are sown amid the storms and floods of calamity. And for the Christian it is certain that sorrow is a principal means of growth in holiness. Nay, it may even happen that a sin committed by a Christian may in the end make him a better man, as Peter, after his denial of Christ and the knowledge he thus gained of his feebleness, grew in real strength as much as he declined in self-confidence, and was able the better to strengthen his brethren.

We admit, also, and rejoice to admit, that a life of sin, being a life of unrest and disappointment, cannot fail of being felt to be such, so that a sense of inward want, a longing for redemption, enters into the feelings of many hearts that are not willing to confess it. Many persons who have not reached the true peace of the Gospel, sigh for it; many feel the weakness of the disease, without applying to the physician; many reform their lives in Pharisaical strictness, without coming to Christ: and many come to Christ, being led to Him by this inward unrest, this inward void which a life of sin has produced.

But all this does not oppose the view which we take of sin, that it *contains within itself* no radical cure, no real reformation. Man is not led by sin into holiness. The means of recovery lie outside of the region of sin, beyond the reach of experience,—they lie in the free grace of God, which sin very often opposes and rejects, when it comes with its healing medicines and its assurances of deliverance. The most which prudence can do, acting in view of the experienced consequences of sin, is to plaster over the exterior, to avoid dangerous habits, to choose deep-seated sins in lieu of such as lie on the surface. Exchanging thus Pharisaical pride for vice, respectable sin for vulgar sin, sin that does not injure for sin that injures body and good name, it seems to the unthinking to have worked a marvellous cure. But there is no true reformation, no giving of a new form to the soul, in the case. The physician has changed the seat of the malady, he has not driven it out of the constitution.

Now that sin works out no cure of itself, that sin by no

process, direct or indirect, can purify the character, will appear

First, from the self-propagating nature of sin, to which your attention was called some time since. If sin has the nature to spread and strengthen its power, if by repetition habits are formed which are hard to be broken, if habits of indulgence in one kind of sin pave the way for other kinds, if the blindness of mind which supervenes adds to the ease of sinning, and takes away from the force of reformatory motives, if discouragement and the feeling that all moral strength is gone render return upon one's step more difficult, if sin spreading from one person to another increases the evil of society, and therefore reduces the power of each one of its members to rise above the general corruption, do not *all these considerations* show that sin provides no cure for itself, that there is, without divine intervention, no remedy for it at all? If sin at once extends its sway in the soul, and weakens the power of existing motives, whence can a cure come, unless from new motives and from influences of a divine origin? Can any one show that there is any maximum of strength in sin, so that after some length of continuance, after the round of experiences is run over, after wisdom is gained, its force abates, and the soul enters on a work of self-restoration? Alas! this does not verify itself in the life of men. Is it the nature of virtue after long persistence to chop round like the wind, and give place to vice? Can vice be shown from what we see of character to have a contrary quality?

II. The same thing will appear from the fact, that the *mass* of the persons who are truly recovered from sin, ascribe their cure to some *external* cause,—nay, I should say to some *extraordinary* cause, which sin had nothing to do with bringing into existence. Ask any one who seems to you to have a sincere principle of godliness, what it was that wrought the change in his case, by which he forsook his old sins. Will he tell you that it was sin leading him round, by the experience of its baneful effects, to a life of holiness? Will he even refer it to sense of obligation awakened by the law of God? Or will he not rather ascribe it to the perception of God's love in pardoning sinners through His Son? Nor will he stop there; he will go beyond the outward motive of truth to the inward operation of a Divine Spirit. Somehow religious persons agree in attributing the change of their life to a cause as remote as possible from sin. Sin, by no means, wrought the transformation. Law did not. Even the unaided truth of the Gospel did not. But if sin *could* cure, if it *did* cure itself, we should find another conviction in the minds of those who were under its treatment; we should not see this unanimity. You cannot make those who have spent the most thought, and had the deepest experience of the quality of sin, admit, that spiritual death of itself works a spiritual resurrection.

Moreover, were it so, you could not admit the necessity of the Gospel. What is the use of medicine, if the disease, after running its course, strengthens the constitution, so as to secure it against maladies in the future? Can truth, with all its motives, do as much? If, then, the experience of sin, by some wonderful law of nature, is fraught with such a benign efficacy, the Gospel is officious in its offers of help; it were better that the human race be left alone, until it find itself, through its sins, advanced to a position of superior virtue.

To this it may be added, that the prescriptions of the Gospel themselves often fail to cure the soul: not half of those who are brought up under the Gospel, are truly Christians. This again shows how hard the cure of sin is. For the motives drawn from the Gospel do not operate against nature, but with it, and if nature has of itself a restorative power, they ought only to accelerate the process. Why should nature reject them? Why should they fail in any case? Is it not a proof of the severity of the disease of sin, that they often have no good effect whatever?

III. We do not find that inordinate desire is rendered moderate by the experience that it fails to satisfy the soul. A most important class of sins are those of excited desire, or, as the Scriptures call them, of lust. The extravagance of our desires—the fact that they grow into undue strength, and reach after wrong objects, is owing to our state of sin itself, to the want of a regulative principle of godliness. When the spirit of love and obedience is absent, something must take its place, or there will be a vacuum in the soul, which is abhorrent to our nature. Our individual natures determine what this master-passion shall be. Is it the love of money? This love, indulged, grows in strength, and grasps at more than it ever possesses. But, inasmuch as no such gratification can fill the soul, inasmuch as man was made to be nourished by angels' food, and not by the husks which the swine do eat, there must come a time of dissatisfaction, a feeling of emptiness, an apprehension of coming want. How is it now with the soul which has thus pampered its earthly desires, and starved its heavenly? Does it cure itself of its misplaced affections? If it could, all the warnings and contemplations of the moral philosophers might be thrown to the winds, and we should only need to preach intemperance in order to secure temperance; to feed the fire of excess, that it might the more speedily burn out; to place temptations in the way of the youth, that he might become a *roué* at his prime, and so have an old age of moderation before him? But who would risk such an experiment? Does the aged miser relax his hold on his money-bags, and settle down on the lees of benevolence? Does the worn-out voluptuary, even when his senses are blunted, shake off his vices and become a new man? Is this the natural process? Is it so common as to be looked on without wonder? Or, rather, when the grace of God—a cause from without and extraordinary—

penetrates into the heart of such a man, do not men look on his change with suspicion, as a kind of compulsory divorce from his vices; or, if he is admitted to be a sincere penitent, is it not regarded as among the marvellous results of Divine grace?

No! my friends, think not that nature or some law of the mind breaks the chains of desire so easily, when a life or long years of a life have hardened the bondage. Christ knew of no such thing when He said "How hardly shall they that have riches enter into the kingdom of God." Calculate not too confidently on the moral powers of a mind which has spent all its strength on sinful desires. It is not so very easy a thing for a supremely selfish man to renounce himself, even with the offers of the Gospel before his eyes. The soul must take a leap almost in the dark; must in its own apprehension run the risk of being stripped of every thing without gaining anything. "Give up my supreme good? Why not ask me to annihilate myself? How do I know, who have never had it in my bosom, that this new affection, this love of God to which you call me, is not as much smoke as that old desire which has reigned in my members?" Such are some of the suspicions with which a jaded, sated soul will look on the invitations of the Gospel, even while it owns its want of inward peace. *Without* the gospel what promise of good is sufficient to stem or alter the desires of such a soul?

IV. The pain or loss, endured as a fruit of sin, is not, of itself, reformatory. I have already said that under the Gospel such wages of sin are often made use of by the divine Spirit to sober, subdue, and renovate the character. Many have been enabled to say that before they were afflicted they went astray, but that now they keep God's word. And this benefit from afflictions is by no means confined to those trials which are properly the direct consequences of sin, but belongs to all the sufferings of this earthly state, whatever be their source. But even under the Gospel, how many, instead of being reformed by the punishment of their sins, are hardened, embittered, filled with complaints against divine justice and human law. The tenants of prisons, under the old system of stern infliction, were rather corrupted than made better by confinement, by every display of the justice and indignation of society. The Jewish system was one where justice preponderated, yet although grace was not there excluded, we find continual complaints on the part of the prophets that the people remained hardened through all the discipline of God, although it was *fatherly* chastisement, which held out hope of restoration to the divine favor. "Why should you be stricken any more? ye will revolt more and more," says Isaiah in the words of our text. But a passage from the prophet Amos may stand instead of all others. "I have given you cleanness of teeth in all your cities, and want of bread in all your places, yet ye have not turned unto Me, saith the Lord. And also I have withholden the rain from you when there were yet three months to the harvest—yet have ye not returned unto Me, saith the Lord. I have smitten you with blasting and mildew; when your gardens and your vineyards and your olive trees increased, the palmer worm devoured them; yet have ye not returned unto Me, saith the Lord. I have sent among you the pestilence after the manner of Egypt—yet have ye not returned unto Me, saith the Lord. I have overthrown some of you, as God overthrew Sodom and Gomorrah, and ye were as a fire-brand plucked out of the burning; yet have ye not returned unto Me, saith the Lord. Therefore thus will I do to thee, O Israel; and because I will do this unto thee, prepare to meet thy God, O Israel."

Such was a large experience of the efficacy of punishment under the Jewish economy. Turn now to a state of things where the divine clemency is wholly unknown or seen only in its feeblest glimmerings. Will naked law, will pure justice work a reform to which divine clemency is unequal?

V. Remorse of conscience is not reformatory. Perhaps we ought to say that remorse in its design was put into the soul as a safeguard against sin, in order to prevent the new offender from repeating his transgressions. But in the present state of man remorse has no such power for the following reasons:

First, it is dependent for its power, and even for its existence, *on the truth* of which the mind is in possession. Of itself it teaches nothing; it infers no general rules of morality from single instances, no law of action from separate actions; it rather obeys the truth which is before the mind at the time. If now the mind lies within the reach of any means by which it can ward off the force of truth or put falsehood in the place of truth, sin will get the better of remorse, the dread of remorse will cease to set the soul upon its guard.

We say, *secondly,* that every sinner has such means of warding off the force of truth, and so of weakening the power of self-condemnation, at his command. The sophistries which a sinful soul plays off upon itself, the excuses which palliate, if they do not justify transgression, are innumerable. Admit the plea that a strong temptation renders sin venial, or that a man has no freedom to do otherwise than he has done, or that pleasure is the end of existence, or that inconsideration is an excuse for wrongdoing, and what becomes of remorse? It has for the present lost its sting. The guilty soul learns to trifle with it.

But, *again,* remorse according to the operation of the law of habit is a sentiment which loses its strength as the sinner continues to sin. It is benumbed like other sensibilities which are violated, like pity, which is blunted by acts of cruelty, or sympathy, which is undermined by the indulgence of envy: when we injure the powers of our souls in their legitimate exercise, they take a terrible revenge upon us by neglecting to do their work; the sentinels have been tampered with by a traitor within, and the camp is open to the enemy. What good are you to get from the voice of conscience, if you have enfeebled its power so that it can be scarcely heard? Will the whisper of reproof reform you when the loud thunder could not?

But, *once more*, suppose that all this benumbing of conscience is temporary, as indeed it may well be; suppose that through these years of sinning it has silently gathered its electric power, but, when the soul is hackneyed in sin and life is in the dregs, will give a terrible shock—will *this* work reform? Will remorse then take its seat as an admonisher, and not rather as a judge and a doomster in the great criminal court of God? Will there be courage to undertake a work then for which the best hopes, the greatest strength of resolution, and the help of God are wanted? No! discouragement then must prevent reform. The sorrow of the world worketh death. The most hopeless of all persons is he who has put darkness for light, and stupefied his conscience for years with success, until some crisis, some danger of death comes. Then the cry will generally be, even under a Gospel of mercy—"It is too late."

VI. Finally, the experience of sin brings the soul no nearer to religious truth. Truth is the treasury from which our active powers draw their instruments or motives for the government of the life. Now if sin, as we learned its nature and results by experience, brought us nearer and nearer to the truth which can regulate our character, and deepened the impressions which our condition here below ought to make upon us, then the gray-haired sinner of a life-time were worthy of all envy, and sin would contain in itself, instead of a sting at the last, a Gospel of mercy. But it is not so, as is plain from what we see of life and know of our own selves.

For sin, amongst other of its effects, makes us more afraid of God or more indifferent to Him. The first inward change wrought by sin is to beget a feeling of separation from God; we have, by sinning, severed our interests from those of the moral universe over which God reigns, and we know that the good of the universe cannot be sacrificed to our wishes;—nay more, we perceive that our selfish desires oppose that good and the will of the great Ruler. We may not have reached this feeling by our reason, but from the first movements of remorse it is a feeling, almost a moral instinct with us. Adam and his wife, as soon as they sinned, hid themselves from God, among the trees of the garden.

This being so, how are we to attain to a true knowledge of religion? Is there any method, without taking into account God, the great factor? But the sinful soul turns from Him in fear with an instinctive feeling that He is an enemy. Must not, then, almost of necessity, a false system concerning God and man be embraced rather than a true? And when such a system takes possession of the mind, will it not be harder to find out the truth, than it was before? Perhaps now one great point is gained, namely that the dread of God is abated:—will it be easy to break up such pleasant slumbers and acknowledge the terrible truth, that neither God nor the order of the world can fail to be an enemy to the man who clings to his sins?

Or suppose what happens under the Gospel, when sin and the purpose of future repentance live together in a worldly life, that a person has become quite indifferent to God; he *is not afraid of God* because the Gospel of mercy shines upon the world; *he does not love God*, because all higher love is buried under a load of sin,—he is a *neutral.* Is this a state where the experience of sin will teach the truth? Must we not say here, as in the last case, that this attitude is taken in order to have quiet in sin, and that it requires the strongest motives, the strongest impressions to break up this false peace? Or if we should say that a real hostility lies concealed under this indifference we should only make the case worse. The soul incurs the guilt of opposition to God, but continues to escape the conviction of it. This is plainly no good condition for exercising honesty of mind in view of the truth.

To this we may add that a habit of skepticism is contracted in a course of sinning, which it is exceedingly hard to lay aside. It became necessary in order to palliate sin and render self-reproach less bitter, as we have already seen, to devise excuses for the indulgence of wrong desires. These pretexts are half believed, they are not simply taken up at the moment of sin and then laid aside, but they acquire some positive influence over the mind, they fill it at least with doubts of which sin has the benefit. In this way there grows up a skepticism in regard to the great rules of conduct. But there is no stopping at this point. We cannot doubt concerning the rules of morality, without stretching these doubts into religious truth, both natural and revealed. The skepticism then must run through all those classes of truth which can furnish moral and religious motives. Is then such a habit easy to be shaken off? Is it easy, when habits of sin have brought on habits of skepticism, to become perfectly candid, and to throw aside the doubts of a life-time, which are often specious and in a certain sense honestly entertained? Will it not be hard to break up the partnership between the mind and the heart, between falsehood and sin, so long as each supports the other? The Scriptures teach us that "evil men and seducers wax worse and worse, deceiving and being deceived." They deceive themselves and are deceived by themselves as well as deceive others. Thus they cut off the power of motives. We cannot reach truth by the experience of sin any more than we can make good legislators out of law-breakers and culprits.

The blindness of the mind is the best security against reformation.

From the course of thought in this discourse *it appears in the first place* that our present life shows no favor to the opinion that sin is a necessary stage in the development of character towards perfection. This opinion draws so little support from what we know of man that it deserves to be called a chimera, a bare theory devised to get rid of a difficulty in the system of the world, to wit, the permission of evil. No reason can be given, which is valid, why a finite being cannot remain innocent and holy, as the holy angels are, and as we are assured by the Scriptures that Christ was. No argument can be derived from experience to prove that sin, when once begun, works out its own cure. The cures of it, which have seemed radical, have come from abroad, from a system of grace, from the free act of God, or at least from a belief in the divine forgiveness. The tendency of sin, as life shows, is to grow blinder, more insensible, less open to truth, less capable of goodness. If, then, any one should say that in spite of all this the soul in some other life will turn right about on its course, we shall not argue with him, any more than if he should say that the spirits of the blessed will have wings or will inhabit the sun.

And *again* the experience of this world throws light, or, I should rather say, darkness, on the condition of the sinner who dies impenitent. There is no tendency in the experience of his whole life towards reform. How can it be shown that there will be hereafter? If he has contracted guilt, and Divine justice reigns over him, will not his circumstances be worse then than now; more unpropitious for knowing the truth, more fitted to indurate him in sin? In this world Divine compassion in Christ shines on men, and wins many over from sin; but mercy in its very idea is a free act which may have a limit: who can tell us that death is not that limit? The sinner goes away from the world with a perverted will, with selfish affections predominant, in the full tide of his ungodliness? Who can tell that these are not a part of his soul, and who cannot tell, that with such a soul, whether he sees the full blaze of truth or wanders in new errors, he must be miserable?

Then, *lastly,* our subject points, as with a finger that can be seen, to the best time for getting rid of sin. All we have said, is but a commentary on that text, "exhort one another *daily while it is called to-day,* lest any of you be hardened by the deceitfulness of sin." Do not think that the swearer will become reverent from the practice of profanity, or the drunkard, sober from the thirst he has acquired for strong drink and the evils he falls into, or the revengeful, forgiving from the torment of his vindictiveness, or the selfish man, benevolent from the indulgence of evil affections, or the ungodly man, godly from neglecting and disobeying God. Do not think, you who are young, that a little more acquaintance with the evil of life will be of use to you. Far from this, it will lead you, like Adam, to try to hide from God. You will lose your innocence, lose your peace, lose your soul, and for what? To discover how easy is the course of sin, and how fast it grows when you run into temptation. O, that Divine grace would make its own use of your past sins—to humble you and show you that their end is death, before your standard of character has fallen too low, and the blindness of sin is too great for recovery. Sin is now shaping your character; he is adding stroke after stroke for the final countenance and form. If you wait, all will be fixed; his work will be done.

SERMON VIII.

SIN MEASURED BY THE DISPOSITION, NOT BY THE ACT.

1 John iii. 15. Whoso hateth his brother is a murderer.

These are harsh words, some will say, and many will deny that they are just. "I hate such a one, it is true, but I would not harm him for the world. There is surely a wide interval between the feeling of rancor or even the bitter lasting quarrel, and the act of Cain who was of that wicked one and slew his brother. Why come to a reader or hearer who is consciously incapable of acts of injury, and say to him such severe things, as if on purpose to make him odious to himself, if he puts faith in them, and so to render him desperate?"

As for the spirit of the words it is enough to say at present that they proceed from the apostle of love, and that, if true, they ought to be known. Moreover, if you find fault with him, you must find the same fault with Him from whom he learned his religion. Does not Christ say that "whosoever looketh on a woman to lust after her hath committed adultery with her already in his heart?" The measure of the desire or imagination is the sinful indulgence to which it can lead, as in the other case the measure of the hatred is the injury to a brother man.

But besides this, our feeling that we are incapable of this or that sin is not to be entirely trusted, so that we ought to be slow before we reproach passages like this with being unfair descriptions of our nature and of ourselves. There was a man once to whom a prophet foretold that he would be king over Syria and would do immense evil to the children of Israel. "Is thy servant a dog," he replied, that "I should do this great thing?" But on the morrow he murdered his sovereign, and reigned in his stead. So too our great poet portrays to us a man, loyal, upright hitherto, conscious of no secret treachery, into whose mind the infernal powers sent the thought, that he, now Thane of Cawdor, should be king hereafter. The thought ripened into a wish, the wish into a plan: he murdered his king, when asleep and a guest under the protection of the rights of hospitality, and from this dark beginning he waded on through blood, to retain what he had grasped, until he worked out his own ruin.

So then, let us calmly look at the words of the apostle, without taxing them hastily with harshness. Let us feel that they may represent human nature under a true light, and may apply to us, unless ours is an exceptional case.

The apostle says not that all hatred will end in murder, —far from it—nor that all hatred is equally intense and equally reckless, nor that hatred which bursts out into great crime may not imply a worse state of soul than such as remains within, and does no obvious harm to others. *Nor does he intend to confine the murderous quality to positive hatred.* Want of love, hardened selfishness, acting on calculation with no rage or wrath in it, may be as deadly, as murderous, as malignity or revenge. He had just said, " he that loveth not his brother abideth in death." He might have said with truth " he that loveth not his brother is a murderer," for want of love and hatred are only forms of one common character, which in the one case has excited feeling in its company, and in the other shows itself as bald self-interest.

The Apostle teaches us in these words, *that evil lies in the heart, and that the evil there, which meets with some temporary or some lasting hindrance, differs not in kind from that which is ripened by opportunity.* It may be forever dormant as far as the notice of man is concerned. It may never burst forth into the poisonous flower of wicked action, yet the hatred within and the hatred in the wicked action are one and the same, one quality runs through both. The powder that is explosive and the powder that explodes do not differ.

Need I show the justness of this teaching which John borrows from his Lord? *Unless evil begins only when the feeling bursts into action;* unless there is no inward sin and no other form of sin besides particular intended acts of it; unless the quality of the feeling and of the desire, however excited or inordinate, is neither good nor evil until a resolution is made to commit outward transgressions; there must be evil tempers, vicious propensities, wrong desires, a bad heart. The hatred or the lust may be repressed, and that is a praiseworthy discipline. But if there be no principle reigning in the soul, which will introduce love instead of hatred and change the nature of the soul itself, the thought and the act will be both evil, *and the act will be the measure of the thought.* And this is the doctrine of all moralists, however they may differ about the essential character and moral power of human nature. They hold that the way to prevent crime is to bring a new set of thoughts or motives before the soul, that by an abhorrence of evil, or by a sense of the beauty of virtue, or in some other way the forms of crime may be prevented. And they all teach that nothing effectual is secured for the improvement of human character, until the soul itself is conformed to a perfect standard.

It is true, notwithstanding what we have said, that the *strength* of an active principle in human nature, such as hatred leading to revenge or lust leading to self-indulgence, is *measured—somewhat rudely it may be—by its outbreak into forms of sin which conscience and society condemn.* It is just as we measure the power of a flood by its breaking down a dam or transporting heavy masses to a distance. There are restraining influences which secure human society from the explosion of injurious passions, so that such a crime as murder, common enough, if you gather up all the instances of it in a year, will excite wonder and awe in the place where it is committed. It seems, as men contemplate the injury, as they judge of it by the rage of the wicked mind, by the want of an impulse they find within themselves to a similar deed, by the vastness of the wrong, or by the terrible condition of a society where such crimes are of daily frequency, that it is out of the common course of things, and that it presents human nature to us in a new light. And in truth, it is in an important sense, an extraordinary crime, that is, a crime which is not produced by the ordinary state of human souls. But so is an earthquake in one sense an extraordinary phenomenon, while yet the forces which shake the world are not new but as old and as natural as the earth itself. We may calculate with certainty that the greater part of the malignity and revenge in human breasts will not lead to murder, for we know what obstructions sin encounters before it finds a vent in enormous crimes. We know that fear of consequences, conscience, respect for public opinion, pity, are as permanent and universal as sin itself is, and that they are the dam and the banks which keep the stream of unregulated selfishness from sweeping over society. Yet though we call the crime extraordinary, whenever it occurs we trace it back to some principle or habit. That man who committed homicide was subject to great fits of rage which he took no pains to restrain, or his natural heat was increased by strong drink, or he had such a covetous temper that he was tempted by it into robbery and murder. All this is obviously just.

But with all this, we have a right to say, that the limit to which a passion, such as hatred or lust, leads, is a fair measure of its general power. When hatred leads to murder, it is no exceptional case. The extreme limit is the measure of its tendency and its natural strength. This is the measure which the Apostle applies to it: he that hateth is a murderer, because hatred destroys all the happiness of others that is in its way, whether the happiness consist in a good name, or in riches, or in life. Hatred has that in itself that it rejoices in the evil of others, and, in certain circumstances, will assuredly occasion that evil.

We apply to the strength of hatred, or some other evil passion, the same measurement which we apply to the capacities of the mind. A man of genius seems at one time to be inert and without creative power: at another, he will produce a poem or a picture that the world admires. We measure his genius by his best productions, by what he does in the most favorable circumstances, not by the vacancy of his dreamy or inactive hours, where thought is gathering strength for a new flight. Why not judge of sin, and especially of hatred, after the same fashion? What it can do in its unimpeded moments, when the chains are off its neck, and the fetters and manacles are cast from hand and foot, is the measure of its deranged power. It lay inactive, half asleep, until the fatal moment came, when all temptations seemed to plead at once, and all restraining voices were silent. Now it shows what it can do, what its true strength is. Now we see it in its simple, unchecked energy, while, for the most part, it lay before in a kind of chemical union with the other principles that govern mankind.

The justness of the Apostle's words is shown by the awful quickness with which resolutions are sometimes taken to commit great crimes. Nothing is more fearful and awful about our nature than this rapid rush of a human soul from seeming innocence to full-blown guilt. With one bound the soul leaps over all those blessed restraints that tie us to outward virtue and to the respect of mankind. We flee into crime, as if the dogs of sinful desire were on us, and we sought the outward act as a relief from the agitation and war within the soul. So strange do some such historical crimes appear, that they look like the sway of destiny. A divine *Nemesis*, or *Ate*, urged the man into self-ruin. The tragedy of life was not accomplished by his own free will. And when the deed is done, unthinking men will ascribe it to the force of circumstances, as if circumstances could have any effect, independently of the passion or selfish desire itself. And the criminal himself may think that he was hardly a moral agent in the deed; that his own power of resistance was destroyed by temptation against his will; or, that others, the most respectable men in his society, would do the same. To all of which, we reply, that the consent of his soul was his sin; that his sin was weakness; that if he had wanted strength really, and prayed for it, it would have come down out of heaven, and that whether others would have acted like him or not is a point of no importance. Perhaps they would. We do not charge him with being so much worse than others, as his murder, or his lust, is enormous beyond their acts. We charge on human nature, when it hates, the same quality of guilt it would have when its hate bursts into act. We charge this on all who hate, or do not love, in order that they may know what they are, and may come to the Divine Christ, whose love is the life of the world.

I will illustrate this leap of a soul into sin by a single case, the particulars of which I may not repeat with entire accuracy, having to trust to a somewhat imperfect recollection. There was in London, a few years since, a German tailor, who was, probably, not more dissolute than hundreds of others in such a vast city, a mild, inoffensive man, whom nobody thought capable of dark deeds of wickedness. He found himself in a car of an underground railroad, in company with a wealthy man. They were alone, and yet, as the cars had a number of stopping-places in their five or six miles' course, every few minutes a new passenger might come into their compartment. They were alone, I say, for a passenger had left them, and the door was shut. Now, in the interval of three or four minutes, this man had murdered the wealthy man by his side, had seized his purse and watch, and in the hurry taken his hat by mistake, and had left the train the instant it reached the next station. He fled to this country, was seized on his landing, was found to have the dead man's hat and watch, was handed over to the English authorities, carried back, tried, and sent to his execution. How terrible was this speed of crime! No whirlwind or water-spout, no thunder-cloud flying through mid-heaven could represent its swiftness, and yet here there was nothing unaccountable, nothing monstrous. He himself had been no prodigy of sin, nor was he now. The crime was an epitome of his life, a condensed extract of his character. We may safely say, that what took a moment to resolve and to execute, was not the growth of those moments. It lay in his soul, in its selfishness, that was all ready to sacrifice the rights, the life, of a brother man, for the gratification of a wicked desire. You or I would not have done this, my hearer, but we have that within us, perhaps, that might lead to the doing of it. We are of the same clay.

And again, the Apostle's principle is vindicated by the rapid deterioration which we often observe in the lives of particular men. There are some who seem to remain at a fixed point all their lives, growing neither worse nor better, and meeting all the demands which the laws of social life impose upon them. There are others, who, with no external change, are growing better within, are more under the sway of principle and of right emotions. There is a third class, whose lives resemble a gentle stream, that suddenly pours over rocks; the outward manifestations of character have become wholly new. From a life of temperance, or purity, or peace, they run over into one of intemperance, lewdness, or violence. It seems as if they had only covered up their sins before, as if an evil life could not begin, all of a sudden, but the habits of sin must have been suppressed, perhaps, for a long period. *But it is not so. They have not grown suddenly worse,* but some natural motives, which swayed them before, have given way to other natural motives which were for a time counteracted. Self-indulgence was counteracted by prudence or by conscience, hatred was kept down or shut up in the breast by public opinion. Meanwhile changes of life, more liberty of action, greater means of self-gratification, new forms of society, new sentiments and opinions, make the road of temptation leading to outward sin easier. I do not deny that an outbreak of sin also has a tendency to deteriorate character still further, as we see especially in the case of drunkards, who, losing their own respect and that of their society, become desperate and reckless, weighing the pleasure of drinking against that which they have lost, and resorting to that pleasure to still the regrets of their souls. But what I wish to say is, that the deterioration went on in silence before the act of outward sin, or was the result of a choice of sin, against known and estimated motives for right-doing. The sin, when it appeared in a palpable shape, was not of a new kind. Their characters had not become monstrous, and borne fruit, of which before they were incapable. They were not new men, as men are said to be when they put forth new love towards God, when they return to Him from a life of sin in the spirit of obedience. But all happened in the regular way of development, not by a fated pre-arranged plan which would excuse them, and take them out of the ranks of responsible beings, but by a development in which their own free choice went with the laws of character.

According to this view of man, there is nothing strange when hatred culminates in murder, there is no new principle injected, there is, in reality, no sudden worsening of the character. It is natural, not monstrous or morbid, that he who indulges hatred in his heart should yield, when he is tempted to manifest it in the life. The deed is the expression of the feeling, as words are of thoughts. There may be a long silence of passion, and the first you know of it, it may cry aloud, it may hurry into publicity as full-grown crime.

I add, again, that if in any given case it were certain that sinful affections would be suppressed and be prevented from going out into sinful deeds, the apostle's principle would still be true. There are thousands of people who indulge malignant passions and commit no murder, to one who is actually led to this extremity of crime. It is wholly improbable that the well-educated, the intelligent, the prudent, the compassionate, will be led into any outrageous violence towards their fellow-men, even if they allow malevolent emotions, such as envy and pride, to have dominion over them. But this is quite consistent with the words of John. The spirit of the extreme crime is in the unblamed malice or the unobserved envy. It is neutralized, as the oxygen of air is by nitrogen. The two in mechanical union form an innocuous atmosphere, and yet we know that oxygen alone would be a principle of death. So hate in the heart is a deadly affection although counteracted, and although it may be always counteracted.

1. In closing this discourse *I wish to remark in the first place, that sin deceives us until it comes into manifestation.* Men are apt to think that they are good enough, because no indications of a corrupt character are shown in their lives. And then, when the time of trial comes and they yield, they excuse themselves because temptation is so strong and so sudden. In neither case does their moral judgment conform to the true state of things. Principle *means that which will stand the test, when native characteristics which were on its side have turned against it.* The measure of principle is the strength of resistance to

attacks of temptation, and if hatred or lust is a cherished feeling of the heart, there is no possibility of resistance when circumstances turn so as to favor sin. How deceitful then and how false the judgments from a mere absence of outward sin! And these judgments are contradicted by continual experience, for *we are obliged to admit that characters full of open faults,* and even stained by manifest sins, *are often more estimable than those in which the fault never comes to the surface.* Peter, who denied his Master and yet really loved Him, would have been less worthy of regard, if he had loved less although he never had denied. His sin was a revelation of what sin is, but not of the comparative worth of his character. So too the great crimes of David show that sin in the form of strong desire leads to enormous wickedness, even to so heinous a crime as murder, while yet in the judgment of God and of man, many a person would stand far below David in character, who had lived an outwardly unspotted life.

And this shows the importance of the disclosures of our character which positive acts of sin make to ourselves. We live in self-ignorance. Our selfishness or our malevolence is so calm, so constant, so quiet, that it makes no impression even on ourselves who ought to be conscious of the internal temper. By and by there arrives a crisis of trial; a storm of temptation blows down our prudence; selfishness in one form prevails over selfishness in another—the stormy wind over the gentle steady breeze. Now we discover what we can do, and if we are wise, our weakness becomes manifest, our pride of character is gone; we humble and distrust ourselves, and seek strength from that celestial source which is ever open for us.

2. *Sins committed by others may fairly suggest to us what we ourselves can do,* and so, in a certain sense we may be humbled by them, when we apply them as the measuring line of the deep possibilities of sin within ourselves. We

belong to the same race with the most grievous offender who has violated social law, and hurt his own soul. We have the same propensities. Circumstances, part of which he did not create for himself, have caused much, if not all of the difference between him and us. We see in him a picture of ourselves, drawn indeed in dark colors, but a veritable resemblance. Perhaps, viewed by the eyes of God, he is even better than you or I. And in the same way, all the crimes of our race, as we read of them in the history of the past, or hear from time to time of dreadful corruptions in the present, ought to be mementos to us what we are capable of doing, of what we have been saved from, not by our natural virtue, but by the restraints of a merciful God. *We ought to have, in this direction as well as in others, a sympathy with man.* As we admire him in the manifestations of his powers, his wisdom, his genius, his goodness, so we ought to follow him in his depths of ruin, with a fellow-feeling drawn from the consciousness of having the same seeds of guilt in us. As we say with exultation in the first case "I also am a man," we should feel the sympathy of a brother, together with the humbling sense of a common weakness, in the other case also. It was no cant when John Bradford, the English clergyman and martyr under Mary, said, as he saw a man going to Tyburn to be hanged for crime, "There, but for the grace of God, goes John Bradford." Many a Pharisee, if he had heard it, would have said that the man was making a hypocritical confession according to the formula of a certain school, in which the plan is to make human nature as bad as possible, in order that Scriptural grace may be exalted. But Bradford died for Christ, whereas the Pharisee would doubtless have recanted. And Bradford was in the right of it. He knew by a proving of his own heart, which the Pharisee was a stranger to, how desire or feeling leads to sin. He knew by a sympathy with the most unworthy, what was hidden from the

Pharisee, that men are alike to a greater degree than they are different. He did not magnify his sins, and liability to great sins, in order to magnify the grace of God, but he magnified the grace of God, because he felt and found within himself the same sinful nature which he saw in the unworthiest. He read himself in the history of his fallen and guilty brother.

And so we see that the Apostle's words, "He that hateth his brother is a murderer," *are a protest against all Pharisaism,* all overvaluation of ourselves, all undervaluation of others. They cherish pity for the erring, and without some such principle as the words involve, we should despise the faults, rather than compassionate. At the same time we condemn the sin. The apostle's words are the strongest possible condemnation of hatred. Christ's words, already cited, are the strongest possible condemnation of lust. As soon as we receive them and make them the rule of our judgment, we bring ourselves and the open offender against morality or the rights of men to the same standard. The same hatred which lay unexpressed in us, uttered itself by an act of murder in him. Our feeling did no obvious harm as his did, but the wrong was the same. We stand then on a common level,—he being more hardened perhaps by his career of sin than we,—we need a common redemption, and if that redemption has come to me, it has opened my mind at once to the frightful possibilities of crime within my human nature, and the glorious possibilities of even divine excellence to which divine strength enables me to attain. I do not thank God that I am not as other men are, but I own that I am like other men, except so far as power above me has lifted me above my old self. And the lifting up has consisted, if it is real, not in simply keeping me from murder or lust, but in helping me to entertain the spirit of love instead of that of self and hatred.

3. *Finally, we see what an uncompromising principle*

love is. The apostle John abounds in such incisive remarks as, "He that hateth his brother is a murderer;" "He that loveth not his brother abideth in death;" "He that loveth not knoweth not God;" "If a man say, I love God, and hateth his brother, he is a liar." Some seem to think that love is a state of mind in which all moral sentiment disappears, the most loving having an indiscriminate good-will towards all of every character. But a man of such a nature would be a monster whom none could respect, without strength of soul, without adaptation for the society of mankind. *He* has no true love who does not feel within him the same aversion from all the forms of wickedness which Christ and His apostles showed, in their words and in their lives. He has no true love, no complacency in goodness, who does not from the soul condemn every thing that is evil. There is no benevolence any where in any moral being, which is not instinctively opposed to selfishness in all its forms. One may say with truth *love hates malevolence*, hates all that is opposed to itself in the feelings or the manifestations of the inner life. The conception of it as consisting in a weak good nature which is indifferent to character has no foundation in the word of God or in the lives of men whom we cannot help revering. Love is an element of a strong character which views men as they are in all their sins, which feels no favor towards the principles by which the worldly, the selfish, the proud are governed. And thus as it looks on moral evil in all its deformity, it can feel intense pity toward the blind in sin, the misguided, the fallen, the unworthy, and is ever ready to sacrifice its own interests for their good. This is the sign of love that it is capable of self-sacrifice. But no true self-sacrifice can exist without a sense of the misery of sin. Even the lower forms of love hardly deserve to be called by the name, when the motive is mere compassion, without a sense of the greatest evil in human nature. He who can relieve misery but is indifferent to the sin he sees around him, who only excuses it or makes light of it, he is not, to say the least, made perfect in love. The possibility is, that he has no true love at all.

Let us remember then, that the love conceived of by the apostle, the love that dwelt in Christ is something more than instinctive benevolence, good nature and compassion; that it is a moral quality of the highest order, implying in the soul repugnance to sin, to selfishness, to malevolence, to ungodliness; and that it is prompted, in the effort of doing away with sin and of reforming sinners, to all compassionate, self-sacrificing efforts. This is the love that enlarged the soul of the apostle John, causing him to utter his strong language on the evil of hatred; this is the love that made Christ at once hate sin with all intensity, and seek to redeem sinners by the highest act of pity and self-sacrifice. This is the love of God, who sent His Son to be the Saviour of the world, because sin was in His eye the greatest of evils.

SERMON IX.

THE BLINDNESS OF MEN, AND THE NEARNESS OF THE SPIRITUAL WORLD.

2 Kings vi. 17. And Elisha prayed, and said, Lord, I pray Thee, open his eyes, that he may see. And the Lord opened the eyes of the young man, and he saw: and, behold, the mountain was full of horses and chariots of fire round about Elisha.

To THE eye of unbelief, and of distrust, this visible, outward world is everything. Its value is the only assignable value; its history the only true history; its dangers the only dangers to be shunned; its help the only help to be sought. The servant of Elisha, until his eye was divinely opened, saw nothing but the hosts of the enemy surrounding Dothan and cutting off escape; but as soon as divine light fell on him, he beheld a new spiritual world. There were more on his side than against him, and mightier. He lifted up his eye, and behold the mountain around the city was full of horses and chariots of fire, sent there for the protection of Elisha. He was now the enlightened one, the man of opened eyes; while the Syrians, who gloried in their strength, were smitten with blindness, and led captive by a single unarmed man. His mind had drawn in a great lesson. The chariots of fire, indeed, and horses of fire, were, in one sense, unreal; that is, they were not of flesh, nor obvious to human sense: they were unearthly powers, who assumed a form by which they could make an impression of truth on the distrustful, fleshly mind of the prophet's servant. There were no chariots there, nor horses; but there were spiritual hosts, who showed themselves before the imagination of the young man to be more than a match for the army of besiegers. Thus a great truth from heaven, a reality as lasting and as wide as the universe, was taught him, that, beyond our eyes and ears, a majestic, spiritual world is moving on in silence; that an unseen God has infinite, unseen resources; that the causes and issue of things lie outside of the horizon of the senses; that immense agencies may be at work in all stillness and without the slightest show, of which the worldly mind does not so much as dream. If there are hosts of foes of God, there is a God of hosts above them. If there is a throne of iniquity, which frameth mischief by a law, there is a higher throne of righteousness. "If thou seest the oppression of the poor, and violent perverting of judgment and justice in a province, marvel not at the matter, for He that is higher than the highest regardeth, and there be higher than they."

Let us take up the vision presented to the young man in the text, as a rebuke to *distrust,* and generally to *unbelief,* that worldly state of mind, content with the outside of things, from which, in an hour of danger, distrust proceeds. The unbelieving man, we are taught, is a superficial man, and a blind man. There are things the most momentous in the whole world, which he cannot perceive, nor apprehend. There is a world around him, in him, larger, mightier, more enduring, than the earth's rocky base, with bearings on life and destiny of untold importance, a world which meets him on every hand, follows him along while he travels through this world, into the noiseless workings of which he is unable to penetrate, the existence of which, therefore, enters not into his plans, nor affects his desires. Is he not blind in such thick unbelief? Or, if he admits into his mind the existence of such a world, and is continually falling back into distrust, so that goodness seems to him to have no power on its side, is he not still but a blear-eyed man, whose eye needs to be opened in order to see the array of spiritual forces that are under the command of God?

1. Let us apply the text first to that particular form of unbelief, namely *distrust*, which is especially referred to. The blindness and sinfulness of distrust will be apparent, when we take into view the plans and resources of the invisible world. It is a part of the plan that this invisible world does not manifest itself by obvious interferences in the present order of things: everything which we can touch, taste, see or hear, goes on by law and process as much as if there were no God. It is another part, that, although evil has entered into the system, and although there is an everlasting conflict between evil and good, yet no act of power is put forth by *Him*, who must be conceived to side with goodness and to love it with all his heart. Such being the case, while, on the whole, and in the end, the right side will conquer, it is often depressed and defeated; its progress is so slow that for days and years it seems to stand still. This is true of the cause of God in the world, and, to a degree, is true of the same cause in the heart of the single person. Thus it will often happen, that distrustful hearts will send up a cry like that of Elisha's servant in the text, "Alas master! what shall we do?" The distrustful good man will say with the Psalmist, "God has forgotten to be gracious. He hath, in anger, shut up His tender mercies."

Now the blindness of such distrust is made apparent, from considerations already hinted at and implied in our text.

First, God is ever active, and has an intense sympathy with what is good and true. Between this and atheism, there is no middle ground, for the distrustful man of this day will not fall into the Epicurean's belief, that God is indifferent to human things, and indisposed to interfere, or into the Manichean belief, that there is an equal contest waging between light and darkness. Such being the case, we say *secondly*, that God must have a plan, and that the plan may consist partly in leaving the subordinate combatants on the sides of good and evil to themselves, without divine interference in favor of what God must love. It is as if the general of an army, whose troops were raw and needed to be inured by long discipline to military hardships and military skill, suffered them to undergo partial defeats until they were ripe for some great movements of decisive battle. Must such a general, of necessity, be hard-hearted, or devoid of love to his country and his cause? So God may suffer the conflicts of this world to go on in order to fasten the hearts of His loyal people to Himself; He may let His cause in the world go backward seemingly; He may let single souls grapple with doubt and temptation, in order at last to bring forward a well-trained army of faithful friends, and make ready for a decisive triumph. Is there anything absurd in such an explanation of God's plan? If it were only a supposition, will it not remove difficulties, and is not the distrustful man blind not to know that God's plans, which embrace boundless ages, may, like the paths of the planets, be apparently retrograde, while really, they are tending towards a glorious consummation?

But *thirdly*, the power of divine help may be nigh and ready, if an act of trust be put forth. The chariots and horses of fire are near by, but it may be that according to God's plan or according to the constitution of the mind, they will give no aid, as long as the soul or the church loses its confidence. We have put this forward as a possibility, but it becomes probable, if not certain, when the plan of co-operation between the spiritual powers and man here below is properly considered. Every thing moves forward on a system of partnership, if I may so call it, between divine and human agency. If the divine did everything, man would be a machine, or an idle, useless part of the universe. If man did everything, God would disappear from His own world, and man could lay claim to everything. Such being the case, man must be nerved to action, and among the strengthening influences there must be trust in his divine partner. How without this can he undertake with courage, persevere with hope, or accomplish with humility? How can the true relation be discerned between God and His finite creature, or how can the creature keep his right position in the universe, without trust which recognizes at once his dependence and the presence of a helping God?

2. But we pass on to consider the attitude which *unbelief* takes in regard to spiritual power and presence. There is a more radical and deadly form of doubt than *distrust.* Distrust believes and disbelieves at once, or passes to and fro in its various moods of courage and apprehension, from one state of mind to its opposite, but there is an unbelief which is fixed and unbroken by any fits of belief, which recognizes no spiritual agency or none affecting the conduct. Distrust catches a glimpse now and then of the horses and chariots of fire, and again loses the sight, as we lose the sight of a star or distant mountain on the horizon; but unbelief sees and hears nothing except the sights and sounds of this material world. Let us look for the rest of this discourse at this unbelief, at its blindness, at the greatness of its blindness.

I. Here we may notice first that unbelief must in fact admit, while it denies, the existence of some kind of spiritual world. The unbeliever, though he may be a materialist and a sensualist, recognizes those immaterial forces which we call the human soul. He feels himself to be governed by desires or by reason, and to have a power of choice between the objects which he regards as being in different degrees good. He uses motives to persuade others, and cannot help making a wide distinction in his own mind between the power which gives direction to the body or confines its motion, and the power which moves the soul. He admits the existence of invisible social principles, which imply a reference of each individual to a community-life; and the existence of a feeling of justice which seems intended to preside over such a society, distributing to each of its members what is due to him, and binding the whole body together by the feeling of obligation expressed in law and penalty. He beholds the nations of the world bound together by the same feeling of justice, and amid all their crimes and follies appealing to the sense of obligation as pervading mankind. Nay more, he finds in the lives of men and in history, possibly within himself, an indelible sense of sin, a sense of ill-desert as old as the world, and with it, going through the whole course of history numberless efforts to propitiate some invisible God above the soul, who is felt to be offended by evil doing. All this the unbeliever has to recognize, however he may account for it all; and thus his mind must have created for itself a world full of life and movement, connected by many cords with the world of sight, but as different from it as possible. This world out of sight, moreover, is of exceedingly great importance, he finds, to himself. His welfare depends on it. His happiness is bound up with it. Regrets for remediless evil, a sense of injury from others, their contempt or malice, has more of gall in it than anything he can taste, and the pleasures drawn from an invisible world, more of sweetness. He is thus forced to regard the external world as a mere minister to these strange forces which we call *soul;* and yet he is blind, it may be, to the existence of such a thing, or if he believes in soul, he lives for sense, as really as if soul were nothing.

II. In this invisible spiritual world, even if we confine it to mankind, great and most remarkable events are going forward, which the unbelieving man is too blind to perceive, or to which he fails to give their true value.

He reads the history of the earth's surface, of human

progress, of states in their rise or fall, but he forgets that there is another kind of history more internal, governed by spiritual ideas, and by influences most mighty although invisible. That human character should be tried, formed, improved or depraved; that multitudes of minds with the idea of obligation and the sense of sin should be contending with sin or should have become its prostrate victims; that a faith in eternal realities and in a divine revelation should have become a settled principle in countless breasts;—these certainly, unless it can be proved that the soul is to die with the body, are events of deep significance, rising in their weight beyond earthquakes or flaring comets or victories or revolutions of states. Nay more, all the external history of man is modified by these spiritual powers, so that to be blind to them is to be blind not only to one of the worlds with which our being is connected, but to history and to life itself.

Let us look at some of these events or classes of events which belong to this spiritual kingdom, in order to estimate their importance, and the blindness of him who takes no account of them.

We refer first to the life of a man once obscure and unnoticed in an obscure nation, who by the force of His life and of His character has swayed more souls and done more for man's inner life than all other human beings put together. What would the external manifestations of man's nature, manners, morals, law, art, science, government, be at this day apart from Jesus Christ; and yet His peculiar province is the invisible region of the soul. Listen to the words in which a noted novelist of Germany, Jean Paul, speaks of Him: "Jesus, the purest among the mighty, the mightiest among the pure, with His pierced hand lifted kingdoms off their hinges, the stream of centuries out of its bed, and still rules the ages on their course. An individual once trod on the earth, who by moral omnipotence alone controlled other times and founded an eternity of

His own; one, who, soft-blooming and easily drawn as a sun-flower, burning and attracting as a sun, still, in His mild form, moved and turned Himself and nations and centuries together towards the all enlightening primal sun: it is that still spirit, which we call Jesus Christ. If He existed, either there is a Providence, or He is that Providence. Only quiet teaching and quiet dying were the notes wherewith this higher Orpheus tamed men-beasts, and turned rocks by His music into cities." *

The power, then, by which this wonderful life of Jesus fed itself, was wholly of the spiritual world. He lived in communion with the highest conceptions of virtue; he lived in intimacy with the infinite Father, or at least, as the unbeliever must admit, with a God who to Him was a reality; He had a deep theory of human nature in the ruin of its spiritual capacity, which, joined with His deeper love, moved Him to what He regarded as a life for man's redemption. And the result of His spiritual life and thinking has been the alteration of the world—changes which no laws, nor wars, nor arts could have effected.

And by what instruments has He worked so mightily on human hearts and characters? By spiritual ones, by the feeling of guilt, the longing for purity and peace of soul, by offering pardon and the promises of life-giving assistance to the contrite, by a life and example of united love and holiness, by unveiling God and the soul's unending life. Such are the means by which He has set up His throne over mankind, pushing His sway beyond souls into every thing which pertains to man. And yet the unbeliever sees nothing great or wonderful or spiritual in Him; he accounts for Christ as for some natural phenomenon, as for a meteoric stone from the skies; acknowledging perhaps that he cannot explain Him entirely, but

* From the Dämmerungen für Deutschland, vol. 33, pp. 6, 16 of his works, Berlin, 1827.

persuaded that He had no connection with a higher spiritual world.

Passing away from this great, unique fact, let us look at classes of spiritual facts to which the unbeliever will give no heed, which are of continual occurrence, and which may follow one another in the life of one and the same human being.

We begin with a condition of a human soul when it is grappling with great and strong doubts concerning spiritual realities, or when the dark shadow of guilt has fallen upon it. How it heaves one with sorrow, and arouses all our sympathy, to see that soul struggling against billows of skepticism, willing to give up all earthly hopes to solve the great mysteries of God, sin, redemption, and eternity, crying to heaven and to man to help it on its way, crying like Ajax to give it light if only to die in. O, what outward events can compare in importance or interest with such passages as this in the life of a soul!

Or look at another state of a human soul, which is much more common. There is a conflict of long standing between desire on the one hand, and the voice of duty together with aspirations after an honorable and a perfect life on the other. The soul has been often bowed down to the dust by defeat; but so intense is its conviction of the necessity of resistance, so real and practical before its eyes the great idea of duty, that it will sooner yield up its existence than forsake the struggling. The smile or frown of the world without is now nothing in its esteem. Invisible things are the forces which arouse it to action. Now, whether it shall rise or fall, is in this struggle of no importance? Is the supreme worth which is attached to *character* in such a mind undeserving of notice? Say you who are worldly and unspiritual, or rather, when you estimate the power of mind thrown into the struggle, or the possible results in the direction of hope or despair, is any contest of material forces, however vast, of weight enough to be placed by its side?

But there is another and a more advanced class of spiritual facts. Great multitudes think that they have got beyond the first and hardest encounters of such a conflict; and have made headway principally, because the great thoughts of a holy God and of a redemption from sin somehow threw strength into their souls, and helped them to rise out of the atmosphere of spiritual death. Henceforth they are engaged in leading a life of virtue, of intercourse with a divine and spiritual helper, of faith in an endless life. Their aim is to fit their characters for such endless life by becoming on earth as much like God as possible. And as they proceed on their way, imperfectly indeed, but as successfully as is the lot of human strivings, hope of spiritual good in prospect cheers them, the favor of an invisible God brightens their path, all unseen things become more real and all seen things more unsubstantial. There is, thus, a spiritual life led by great numbers of men on earth, a life of resistance to sin, a life of love. a life of faith in those divine things, which, whether they can be proved true or not, form the most noble characters.

But as we watch these persons longer, and behold them at the termination of their earthly lives, we meet with another group of spiritual facts, which are of almost hourly occurrence These persons, as they leave this world, rather grow than wane in the conviction that what has had the chief power over their lives has been a profound reality. Hope instead of expiring at death grows brighter. Sin, instead of seeming a small thing to be watched and striven against, seems darker and more terrible. God now is ineffably true, redemption ineffably valuable. They die, giving every proof that these spiritual ideas are enstamped on their souls, have moulded their characters, and have fitted them for a spiritual, holy world, if there be any such place.

Facts such as these are occurring in countless instances, while the unbeliever is reading his newspaper, driving his trade, enjoying life like an animal, with no inquiry whether there be a spiritual world, and with no interest in the success or disappointment of this nobler class of minds. Oh! are there not among mankind two different kinds of worlds? While some are acting as if right and wrong, life and soul and God are dead realities, others cleave to the dust like the serpent's brood; while some devote their lives to the attainment of virtue, the improvement of character, the preparation for death, others eat, drink, live, think, wish, as if the earth enclosed and satisfied man. "Some, to their everlasting home this solemn moment fly," on wings of hope, while others have no more than a brute's concern about death, and a transient dread of some possibility beyond it. What a contrast, if the vast throng of spiritual ones could be mustered over against the vaster throng of unbelievers. What a difference of character and of main purpose, what a difference of thoughts reigning in the intellect and over the heart. Could two worlds of material substance, made by the hand of God, differ so widely? If the unbelievers are enlightened, the others are benighted; if the world of spiritual minds are in the light, the other world is blind and in darkness, "and in love with darkness."

III. These events of the spiritual world *among* mankind depend on the existence and presence of a spiritual world *above* mankind. This is indeed obvious, and has come into view as we looked at the life of Christ and of those who followed Him in a spiritual life. If the unbeliever is on true, safe ground, there is nothing that ought to rule the life except the material earth and its laws, the desires, chiefly the animal ones, and some few of the social principles. If the spiritual man is right, there is a higher world, beyond the laws of matter, desire, and society. The exercise of his reason, conscience, and affections has introduced him among a different set of realities, which themselves involve the existence of real personalities above man. He now acknowledges the laws of a moral universe—laws made to regulate thought, and therefore emanating from a *being* who has *planned* and *thought.* Sin itself, felt in his conscience, conducts down upon him the justice of the universe. When once God is admitted to be a reality, there is a system centering at His throne; let him for a moment, in thought, conceive of God as not existing, and the spiritual world *among men* becomes darkly and inexplicably incomplete. Whether the process is logical or not, he finds he must deny moral and spiritual realities among men, or carry them upward until they fill the universe. Thus he cannot stop short of a personal God, of a world of real beings of which He is the centre, or he must give up everything. And so, from the opposite quarter, the unbeliever must strand on atheism.

IV. If, now, there is such a world with God for its centre, it is the height of blindness not to see it. This is obvious from a great variety of considerations. If there is such a world, it must be of infinite importance compared with the world of matter; the interests of the soul are bound up with it, and to live as if they depended upon the earth must be self-ruin. If God exists, His existence must, in various ways, be of boundless moment to the soul, and especially must the thought of God, and faith in Him, be of the greatest weight in moving and directing the character. The life passed under the power of spiritual realities is as different from a life according to the course of this world, as Heaven is from hell. If sin is a fact, it is a very weighty, a very dreadful fact. If there be such a thing as recovery from sin possible, it is the pearl of great price. And if all this be so, and the unbeliever shuts his eye to it, how great must be his blindness, how deserving is his state of being called a state of spiritual darkness and death!

V. Such blindness needs to be overcome by a divine act of opening the eyes. Men may well pray "Lord, open his eyes that he may see." And the unbeliever himself, if a glimmering of light falls on him, may well pray for help from the God of light. If there is such an entire contrast between the worlds of which we have spoken, it must needs be that old habits of thought, strengthened through an unspiritual life, must render spiritual apprehension exceedingly difficult; that the intense reality which has gathered around worldly objects must make objects of faith seem spectral and misty; that inordinate desire, gravitating toward the ground, must make all upward movement of the soul next to impossible; that speculative difficulties must block up the path, if the soul should try to break away from the prison of sensual things; that the dawn of faith must be overhung with clouds of distrust; that the soul must feel itself without strength to use faculties which have been so long asleep. How can belief grow up in a mind full of skepticism, in a soul almost without the power to trust? Can argument produce belief in spiritual realities? But where the power of appreciating moral truth is nearly gone, where conscience is blunt, and the affections almost extinct, argument can have no force, for it runs back to convictions which are either dead, or too weak to arouse to action. If the unbeliever had never had his attention called to spiritual things, his slumbering powers that have a sympathy with the invisible might possibly be awakened; but now, long use, long love of the earth, has enfeebled and deadened him. He cannot catch hold of divine realities and lift himself upward. The hardest step is the first, and this costs almost superhuman effort.

Is his case then hopeless? No, not hopeless, if you

take into account the resources of the invisible world, but only hopeless, if you look at this world of outward things, at his present strength, at the character which a life of unbelief and worldliness has formed. Weak as he is, the spiritual world is as near him and as powerful as ever, possessed of means to awaken and enlighten him. The most interesting of thoughts in his case is that these superior powers are at work on man, as is shown by the throng who have come out of sin, have seen the light of God, and received a spiritual life. All praise be to the enlightening Spirit which has opened so many blind eyes—he too may see. The chariots and horses of fire may present themselves to him also. Under the influences of the new spiritual sight, he may become a new man, and the novel things of the invisible world may fill him with joy.

SERMON X.

UNION OF JUSTICE AND GRACE IN GOD.

EXODUS XXXIV. 7. **Forgiving iniquity and transgression and sin, and that will by no means clear the guilty.**

ROMANS III. 26. **That he might be just, and the justifier of him which believeth in Jesus.**

THERE is an agreement in the spirit of these two most important passages of scripture. The one proclaims the union in the character of God of forgiveness and holiness. The other declares that when God, in His plan of salvation through Christ, treats sinners as if they had never offended, He is at the same time just. He was not willing to exercise His highest act of forgiveness, without at the same time and in the same transaction showing that He has as sincere and strong an aversion to sin, as if He had not cleared the guilty but allowed the law to take its course.

It is not my purpose at this time to treat theologically of this union of qualities that may be called opposites in the divine government, nor chiefly to seek to show how they were manifested in Christ's work and passion; but my object is to show *how* the human race is *prepared* for such a twofold exhibition of the divine character, and *how* the exhibition *trains men up* in those excellencies of character which would be defects if they existed apart. "Behold the goodness and severity of God," says the Apostle Paul. In most cases the *goodness* is illustrated by *one kind of events* and the *severity by another*, but in Christ's work the same event of His death displayed the two sides of God's character alike and at once, and thus pardon was never offered to the guilty without a loud protest against sin. Now the pains taken to *inculcate both these qualities* through the entire scriptures seem to point at something in man, *some conception of character which he needs to have impressed* upon him and *which he ought to realize* in his own life. We may go farther and say that this two-sided view of God meets man's conceptions *already* awakened by the actings of his own nature, and thus strikes a chord in man which is in harmony with the scriptures and especially with the gospel.

I. And in pursuing this subject we remark first that among men he who is capable of exercising only hard, unrelenting justice is held to be far from perfection, and *cannot be loved;* while on the other hand a character in which bare kindness or goodness is the only noticeable trait *secures no respect.* Only where we see the two qualities *united* can we feel decided confidence and attachment.

Let us look first at several manifestations of bare justice in character or temper, and then at mere kindness or goodness, in order to see whether this be not so.

First we notice *sternness,* which is the attribute of one who has a strict rule of duty or of propriety in his mind, and measures the conduct of men by *inflexible rules of right.* He *condemns* and *approves* for good cause. He has no favorites and pays no respect to persons, but approves or condemns by the same severe rule *all alike,* whether friends or foes. He notices *all* departures from the standards: *a little* one does not escape his penetrating eye; *a great* one meets with its proportionate censure. In short, morals and manners are estimated by him with impartiality, and deviations from the right rule are blamed as strictly as if he had no other feeling but that of justice, and were not a man. When this character runs into excess, so that a man rates defects at more than their just weight, we call him *harsh* or *severe,* and when he takes pleasure in discovering defects we call him *censorious,* and these characters we dislike by an instinct of nature. But let the man *be simply stern*—is he loved for this quality? Certainly not, if the trait throws others which are fitted to give relief to it into the shade. And this dislike, assuredly, is owing, not to the unwillingness of fallen men to be narrowly scanned, but to the distorted picture of human nature which is presented by a character, in which simple justice predominates in the temper and the life.

Again, we will call up before us the quality of *indignation*, and conceive all the manifestations of the life within to run in that channel. Indignation is the expression, especially the *sudden* expression, of displeasure at what is regarded as unworthy of a man. Like *sternness*, it implies the recognition of a standard supposed to be righteous, united to a strict judgment according to the standard and to displeasure at short-comings. Indignation is a virtue of character, and no character can be perfect if it be absent. It is a sense of justice carried into the *soul* and kindling it up into anger. It is the resistance of human sensibility against wrong doing. In indignation there is properly no selfish element, any more than in justice, of which indignation is the hand-maid. We may add that indignation serves the *sympathies* of our nature; it takes under the protection of its just wrath public wrongs, wrongs done to the defenceless and the humble. It is a *generous* emotion, for it breathes defiance to arbitrary power, to whatever exalts itself against humanity; it draws its sword against tyrannical public sentiment; it shelters the rights of the minority and the despised under its wing. Thus there is no noble soul in which this is not found a guest. But suppose now that indignation gives the key note to character; suppose that a man, like a mastiff at the door of righteousness, is forever growling at injustice; that his eye is sharp to see wrong which ordinary senses cannot discover; and suppose also in its favor, that its strength is duly proportioned to the strength of the wrong perceived, so that it is neither excited on the wrong occasion nor runs over the line of justice;—even then, we ask, will such a man be loved? Certainly not. He will be *respected* for his fidelity to justice, but *loved* he cannot be. No one likes to take a storm home to his bosom, or feels gladness when the lightning is playing before his eyes. The reformer, whose soul is continually on fire with just wrath against social or political sins, is perhaps the most useful man in a community, and yet he is apt to have but few instalments of love paid to him. Even the quiet and the loving among his advocates like to stand a little way beyond the hearing of his denunciations. And yet he is the truest servant of justice.

I mention but one more of those traits of character which partake of the quality of justice—it is *dutifulness.* What is more praised and honored in the world than this quality, which in its lower forms of *legality* constitutes the honest citizen, and in its higher the man of unshaken fidelity to conscience and to God? Moreover, dutifulness, in its wider sense, embraces the feelings and affections which are due to those who are near to us, so that it occupies a field from which love is not shut out. But look at it as consisting *in the mere discharge* of *obligations,* as the naked inclination of the soul to do what is commanded by lawful authority, and you will see that it excites no love, draws no sympathy towards itself, is no bond of union between minds. And it is so with the lawgiver as with the subject: maintenance of law, like loyalty to law, is a quality possessed of little attractiveness, essential as it is to the stability and welfare whether of a state or of the universe.

But I pass over to the other side of the subject and remark, that *a character in which bare kindness or goodness throws all other qualities into the shade* secures no respect. And here we speak of *true* kindliness of nature, not of that semblance of it, which does kind acts on *calculation,* in order to get back the like from others. It is felt, when we observe a character where this ground color in its various shades is discernible, that it has some essential deficiency, that it is incapable of meeting any of the crises in any of the kinds of society which God has ordained, that it is unmanly and unheroic, if not often deserving of contempt. Illustrations offer themselves on every hand, from which we can pick out but one or two. The first which we notice is *indiscriminate alms-giving.* When the tendency to relieve distress appears in the character as an uncontrolled instinct; when a man scatters his money or good deeds without inquiring into the claims of the petitioners, who need only ask to come away full-handed; who pronounces such an unreasoning freeness of beneficence worthy of honor from mankind? Is it not rather felt to be an *amiable weakness*, an evil in the shape of good? Such a man may have a certain kind of love bestowed on him; he may be popular; he certainly will be popular in a community of beggars, though even they, doubtless, will discover his want of moral strength.

Another form of the same one-sidedness is seen in *reluctance to reprove others.* Many amiable persons can never rebuke for their faults those even whom they sincerely love, from an unwillingness to wound their feelings. To their minds reproof is a kind of judicial act, which ought to come from a superior sitting in a trial of conduct; they cannot nerve themselves to the discharge of such an office, much as they desire to see the fault corrected. Now, is it not evident, that when one intimate friend acts toward another on this principle, much of the respect which would otherwise grow up, and without which love itself cannot be deep, must fail to exist? May not even the stern, when the sting of reproof has passed away, and the benefit remains, occupy a higher place of regard.

So too, to give but one more illustration, the *indulgent*

person, when that quality is excessive, not only does a vast amount of evil, but is unable to take a high place in other hearts. Indiscriminate or unreasoning indulgence fails in the end to secure the love which it obtains at first, and comes to be despised. The child is delighted with it, but taxes it more and more until compliance is outrun, and then complains; the grown-up, reflecting person feels that by it his interests were sacrificed.

And if we look into several of the principal employments of life we shall see that a tendency to either extreme, of gentleness or of severity, is most hurtful to society. *In family government* the lax discipline of the father *hurts* the child, and the father's sternness *ruins* him. *The teacher by over indulgence fosters idleness* in the pupil, while by *harshness* he makes him hate study and rouses rebellion. The *military officer* by *slack discipline* corrupts and enervates an army, as well as makes it a pest to the region where it is quartered, and by *cruel rigor* destroys that pride in the service, and that attachment to the leader, without which an army cannot fight well. The *magistrate* who out of pity *pardons* every convict is a foe to the state's true interest; he who drives *law to the extreme,* causes law itself to lose its power. *The judge* must lean towards *equity,* or the strict letter of the statute will be an injury to society; a Draco whose laws are written in blood will arouse, by and by, such a feeling that the laws will not be enforced. In short through all the forms of life, when authority is given to some over others, the existence of either of these qualities without the other destroys all sound moral government.

On the contrary, where both qualities are found in due measure, they insure the best government which the circumstances allow. They do not check each other, as might be supposed, but add to each other's power. The indiscriminately kind man is felt to be weak; the harsh, rigorous nature may have intellect in abundance, but fails to warm the souls of men. When united they form *character, a character in which there is depth, the depth of intellect resting below temper and impulse on a foundation of wisdom and true excellence of heart.* There can be no moral government among men without wisdom, for he who makes men good must look not at immediate impressions but at results: he must take long stretches of time into view, and long series and interactions of causes shaping character. When did instinctive benevolence ever fail to thwart its own wishes and to corrupt its beneficiaries?

The union of these opposites, where alone wisdom can be found, ensures the best government, and as every one must be in some way a governor, of a family, or a workshop, if not of a town or state, the whole of the vast interests of mankind depend on this union.

II. If God is to be honored and loved by human beings He must present himself to our minds under the same twofold aspect. He must be seen in the light of those qualities which we may call by the name of justice, and of those to which we give the names of goodness, kindness, tenderness or mercy.

What would be the kind of manifestations of the divine character suited to the nature of unfallen human beings, it is, perhaps, not very important to inquire. But we see no reason to suppose that they would differ from the exhibitions of God given fully in the Scriptures, and less clearly in life and history, to man in his state of sin, except that the peculiar trait of mercy would not then be called forth. Human character as such, whether innocent or fallen, is made for moral government, for obedience to the law of a superior, and for the acknowledgment of the rights of equals, as well as for the reciprocation of benevolence; so that display of divine justice or righteousness and of divine goodness or kindness would be needed for the education of the race as much then as in our present fallen condition. It can hardly be supposed that the sense of justice would fade out of the minds of men in a perfectly pure society, or that righteousness and the consciousness of obligation would then find no place in the intercourse of men. There must be law so long as there are finite beings; only law would play a very subordinate part in a pure world. But, however this may be, *sin*, by the law of our moral nature, brings with it the sense of the displeasure of God, a sense which the heathen cannot destroy, even when they form gods to themselves with human passions and a human standard of morals. And thus in a state of sin divine justice, divine wrath, divine punishment must occupy such a foremost place that all eyes can see it. Now these principles of human nature have strong appeals made to them by feelings which lay dormant in a state of innocence,—fear of retribution, a feeling that our interests are separate from those of God and His universe, remorse for sin, the desire to hide our guilt from our own eyes and to keep out of sight of God as much as possible. These are either the wounds made by the sword of justice, or the human methods to cure those wounds without looking our condition and our character in the face.

Suppose now the revelations of God to man, all of them, to take this one form of severe justice or indignation against sin, of stern authority or vindication of injured law. Man, we will suppose, remains as he was, and nature contains all the sources of enjoyment which it had before he fell, but the heavens of God are covered with a black cloud, out of which issue lightnings and thunderings upon human souls. Sinai itself will now retain only the latter part of that matchless verse from which we take our text. We hear no longer of "the Lord, the Lord God, merciful and gracious, long-suffering and abundant in goodness and truth, keeping mercy for thousands, forgiving iniquity, transgression and sin;" but the words which follow—that "God will by no means clear the guilty," that He "visits the iniquity of the fathers upon the children unto the third and to the fourth generations"—these words are re-echoed and rebound continually from the angry skies. Now what is the influence of all this disclosure of unmingled justice upon temper and character? Is there any education in it towards a life of love and of trust, towards a life of virtue growing out of these sister affections? *Remorse* may be aroused by it. Is not remorse a paralysis of the soul, making it more helpless than before, unnerving resolution and killing hope? Or *pleasure* may be sought as a relief from the burden of gloomy care. Does that bring men to God, or is not its very aim to forget Him? Or the soul may swerve from just conceptions of its relations to God; it may abrogate for itself, so to speak, His law of righteousness and construct a laxer code. Is *such error* any fit education for the race in righteousness and goodness? And if man should compare this unmitigated justice of God with the gentleness of human law, which allows pardons and respites, would not the awful sternness of the divine character be made so much the gloomier by the contrast? Or if, what we must regard as the truer supposition, such manifestations of God were to make their impress upon human law, would that not become a law of inexorable cruelty and of bloody revenge, and would not law—if law there could be—deepen the traits in man's nature that are most fell and deadly, while the tender ones would find little room to expand? Let those savage tribes, whose characters are formed by and assimilated to the malignant beings they worship, answer.

On the other hand let us think for a moment what kind of a moral training the human race would have under the one-sided exhibition of the divine goodness. And here suppose first, as we have done before, the race to be *uncorrupt*, and that there is no positive need, in order to aid restoration to virtue, that a disclosure should be made of forgiveness. In this state of things would not man—knowing nothing of divine justice—remain a weakling in rectitude, unable to dare or resist? Could he have any strong points of character about him? Could he be a minister and interpreter of God in any high sense outside of the natural world, and would not the higher world of morals be to him an unexplored, unknown kingdom? We conceive of the angelic hosts as siding with God, when they see the majesty of His righteousness even in the punishment of sin. And in the Apocalypse Heaven is full of the cry, "Even so Lord God Almighty, for just and true are thy judgments." *They* have been educated—perhaps by the spectacle of sin in the universe—into indignation against sin, but *the race of man* in the case supposed would be little more than higher animals, undeveloped in those moral faculties which behold God in His entire character.

But let us turn to the existing state of things in a race of sinners. Let this race, which has swerved from righteousness, be educated under impressions of divine goodness and kindness, only excepting from these manifestations of God a revelation of forgiveness, for forgiveness implies antecedent justice which in the case supposed is set aside. Let then all that looks like forgiveness take the form of clemency or rather of indulgence. "You are conscious of sin," the divine government will say to mankind, "but you need not trouble yourselves about sin; God overlooks it; He has no censure or penalty or prison for it that you know of. So you may take your way through life with the less burden, because you can shake off the thought of divine wrath and retribution." But is this the true means of maintaining the rights of God, or of educating man for a life of virtue? Nay, rather, is not such an exhibition of God's feelings towards sin calculated to destroy all respect for His character, even in the very persons who may be supposed to draw benefit from His indulgence?

For how could a policy which would ruin a family and dissolve a state, which would make children and citizens feel that their interests had been neglected,—when emanating from a higher throne—be any safer or wiser? We can see also, that God, so manifested, could secure as little affection as respect; for *the good* could not put their trust in Him, *the bad* would be won from their sins by no evidence of love on His part; all would feel that the most essential character of a ruler was wanting. And the influence on civil order would be most disastrous; either human government copying after the divine, would abolish its punishments, open its houses of correction and let every one do as he chose, or would make a vain attempt to maintain righteousness and order, when the whole current of religion ran against it. We cannot conceive of a greater disaster than such a divine administration, the very belief in which, if it had no reality, would unsettle everything man holds dear.

But when *both sides* of God's character and government are revealed together, every point is gained. God *can be revered* and felt to be worthy of reverence, *can be loved* and be felt to be worthy of love. The righteous can feel safe under His shelter, and the wicked can dread His displeasure. The trembling sinner can look with hope toward the light which beams from His mingled justice and holiness. Man, in all the forms of society, can feel that God's known character and will is the cement which binds the *family, the State,* the *nations* of mankind together by a *twisted cord* of justice and good-will. Man can now be educated for the offices of the world and for eternal life, for all time and all places *on one plan,* because the policy of the family and of the State is seen to be the policy of Heaven and of the universe. Law reigns and pardon is offered to sinners without weakening the authority or venerableness of the law-giver. "There is forgiveness with thee that thou mayest be feared." Sinners are recovered and reclaimed first by a sense of sin, and then by a perception of divine love, and without the latter they would not think of their sins, or grow into *that filial fear, that holy worship* which the Psalmist intends. Only under this two-fold aspect of God is true religion, the religion of the soul, possible.

III. We add thirdly, that it involves a *very high degree of wisdom* to know when to be just or severe, and when to exercise goodness or grace. The mere impulse of benevolence would, as we have seen, destroy every government from the lowest to the highest, from the government of a family to the government of the universe. Nor can a *strong sense* of the evils of sin determine whether sin ought, in any particular case, to be dealt with in the way of forbearance or of punishment, of grace or of wrath. The *mere attribute* of justice would not be a safe guide for any administration, divine or human; only it is *safer* than the mere impulse of benevolence, for its object is to maintain law and right. But the presence of neither quality in the soul is any guide of conduct. If a magistrate, invested with the pardoning power, *pardons because he hates to see suffering*, why should he not, with as good reason, *punish because he hates to see crime?* And so the attribute of *justice* in God renders it *at least as certain* that He will *punish*, as His *goodness*, that *He will save.* What is there then that shall decide under any government, divine or human, whether law shall have its perfect course or shall be interrupted? Nay, more, if the law be good, must there not be a reason for its interruption, a *reason lying beyond the pity of the law-giver and the sufferings of transgressors?*

We come then *to this result, that only* wide-looking and far-looking *wisdom* can decide in the case of a particular offender whether such interruption of law by pardon is possible, without hazarding the permanent good of the society in question. *Feeling* cannot decide, mere *experi-*

ence cannot decide; only a wisdom confirmed by experience, acquainted with the play of motives, capable of judging how the moral education of society will be affected by different ways of administering law, only this high gift, granted in scanty measure to the best minds, is *fully equal to a problem* of setting law aside and yet maintaining its force.

How much more then, would it be a problem beyond man's power to solve whether God could pardon sin, if He had not disclosed Himself in His feelings and His measures? For *in* the case of *human law, equity* often demands exceptions, and *pettier offences* are beneath notice, and the *sentiments of the subjects* of law concerning the law are to be taken into account. But *there, in the universal law before the mind of God* there is no divergence between strict justice and equity; a little sin, if there be such a thing, is caught by the net of omniscient righteousness as surely as a great one; and the unerring truth of God is to govern, not to be governed by, the sentiment of the worlds. What man then, who but a *peer of God,* can rise to so high a seat of wisdom as to decide whether or not *He* can pardon sin? I marvel, when I hear men who could not decide a case aright in court, who in a chair of state might do vast mischief by unwise pardons, nay, who spoil their own children, perhaps, by indulgence or by harshness, I marvel, when I hear these men legislating for the universe, as if they were "gods and all of them children of the most High." I marvel, when I hear their theories on sin and on retribution, as if defection from the Maker and Father of the universe were a little thing, all the dimensions of which they could ascertain by their square and compass. What? Have not men been *legislating* for centuries and yet with all the lights of transmitted experience unable to reach the golden mean between severity and laxity, *complaining* of their fathers only to be found fault with themselves by the next age, *disputing* until now on the very principles of criminal law, and shall such a race that cannot govern itself sit in judgment on God? He who can comprehend the universe, and can fathom character and the bearings of His dealings on character, He and He alone can tell when to be forbearing and when to smite, when to forgive and how long to hold out offers of forgiveness, how to mingle and to proportion holiness with love in His dealings with sinners.

It is a *great* problem to govern a nation; it is a *greater* to govern a virtuous universe; but a *greater still* is presented when the element of evil is thrown into the question, and the interests of the many come into conflict with the happiness of the sinful few. Especially when we look on God as training His creatures up for a higher condition; enlarging their powers, helping the strong to grow stronger, pitying the weak and revealing Himself as their forgiving God; then above all does it appear that the balances of the moral universe are exceedingly delicate, and that there is need of a hand, firm and wise beyond our thought, to hold them.

No solution of the intricacies of things has been offered to man deserving of notice but that which Christ has made. The reconciliation of holiness and love in His work, its just, well-balanced training of the whole moral nature challenge our respect, our admiration, even if we will stand aloof from Christ. He is made of God unto us wisdom and righteousness and sanctification and redemption.

The training of our race depends more on the moral impressions that are made upon it than on anything else, and these moral impressions depend mainly on the recognized character of God. With a certain character of God, law and society, family life and state life, would have no foundation to rest upon, no defence of their integrity and their sacredness: with a certain other conception of God, severity, wrath, ferocity, all the harsher qualities would be cultivated, religion would wear a malign countenance, law would be a minister of death. How vastly important then is the religious conviction concerning God for the welfare of mankind. And may we not go farther and say that other worlds besides ours, that principalities and powers in heavenly places need a similar training? Is there anything strange in the hints thrown out by our sacred writers, that the scheme of God, as it culminates in Christ, should be used for the ennoblement and perfection of the heavenly host? I do not mean that sin is necessary to manifest God more fully and clearly to the higher intelligences, but that when once it exists, an incidental but a great good is drawn from it for those who have never offended. Conceive of them as spectators of the fall and the first measures of God for the restoration of man. Something yet remains in this world-history to satisfy their minds for which they wait in faith. At length the full solution comes in Christ incarnate and suffering; now they burst into rapturous joy and learn new wisdom, and become more faithful to righteousness, as they see the mystery of grace unfolded; now "unto the principalities and powers in heavenly places" is "made known by the church the manifold wisdom of God."

And now, having brought your minds to Christ, I close with the remark that *He united the two sides of character* which we have spoken of, *in their due mixture, in His one person.* There has been one man who has shown a perfect balance of character in this respect, and He is fitted for this reason to represent God and to be a moral legislator for mankind. This is remarkable in regard to our Lord, that a person who should have become acquainted only with His traits of love, as *forbearance, condescension, patience, mildness, pity,* and *forgiveness,* would be apt to suppose that he had seen the whole framework of His character; while another person who heard His awful rebukes of the Pharisees, and saw with what zeal He defended the rights of God, and observed what He thought of sin and what were his threatenings against it, would take Him for a man made out of iron justice alone. But He united in unrivalled harmony both these aspects of character. And it is well worthy of being remarked that their union proves their genuineness and their depth. He who could *love so* and *forgive so,* notwithstanding His deep sense of the sin, what *strength* of character must He have had, what a *depth and truth* of love, *what a power* of loving, *what an inexhaustible richness* of soul! And He who could *rebuke so* and show such strong displeasure against evil doing, how hard, humanly speaking, must it have been for Him to love objects so far from loveliness; and *if* He loved them as He did, must not His love have been *of another kind than ours,* one superior to personal slights and injuries, wholly unlike instinctive kindness of temper, partaking *of a quality of lofty wisdom!* You would think that each of these traits would check and neutralize the other, that the holy hater of sin could not bend into love, that the man 'compact' of love must be blind to justice, but it was not so. The strength of His holiness and justice proves the depth of His love, and His love was the stronger, because it rested on the fixed rock of justice and holiness.

This union of qualities, which, as in the case of the Saviour, leads *not to a dead-lock* of character, *but* to *active living perfection,* is allied to wisdom or rather is itself wisdom, for it implies moral judgment perfectly sound and rectitude unshaken. Christ then, with such a nature, would be *the loving Saviour, the friend of sinners,* but he would be also *the wise law-giver* and *the just Judge.* He is thus *like God* and fitted to represent God; *he embodies* that idea of God, *which, with the help of the noblest passages of the Old Testament,* our minds, in their best frames of thought and feeling, are able to form. And if, in a larger sphere, the Son of Man shall judge the world He came to save, it will be not in a new *character*, but only in a new *office*.

> Worthy His hand to hold the keys,
>   Guided by wisdom and by love;
> Worthy to rule o'er mortal life,
>   O'er worlds below and worlds above.

SERMON XI.

EARTHLY THINGS MUST BE BELIEVED BEFORE HEAVENLY CAN BE.

JOHN iii. 13. If I have told you earthly things and ye believed not, how shall ye believe, if I tell you of heavenly things?

THESE words contain an argument from the less to the greater. If you disbelieve what I say in cases where human experience and consciousness give their voice in favor of my testimony, how much more will you disbelieve, when I declare to you that which is far beyond the reach of human knowledge? And if the elementary knowledge within your attainment is rejected or denied, how can you receive that superior or divine knowledge, which has no force nor meaning for the mind, unless it is brought into connection with these very earthly elements?

I purpose to illustrate and unfold the words of our Lord, *first*, by attempting to find out what the earthly and what the heavenly things are of which He speaks, and *secondly*, by showing how unbelief in the heavenly things is necessarily involved in rejection of the earthly.

I. *First*, then, the earthly things are those which it did not require a teacher from Heaven to make known. A large portion of the truth which affects the interests of our spiritual and immortal nature is of this sort. Such truth is generally admitted in civilized communities with more or less distinctness, because it reposes on primary moral convictions which are common to all men. Even through Pagan and barbarous lands, it is involved in the feelings and confessions of all the people. The office of a religious teacher or of an inspired prophet is not to disclose these earthly things, as if they were the matter of a new revelation, but he takes them for granted, or else he reaffirms them because the minds of men, for some reason, discover them dimly and blindly. It may be, indeed, of the greatest importance that he should reaffirm them, for he needs to carry the minds of men with him when he advances to the higher and heavenly things, and doubt or disbelief at the earthly threshold would be a most serious impediment in his way. But we may say of Christ, at least, that He never would have come into the world to show men what their own reason could show them without His help, and that all His work about such earthly things was preparatory to a much higher work, to a revelation of that which lay beyond the eyes and ears of men, of that which He knew in His heavenly existence in the heavenly world.

An illustration or two will, I hope, make all this plain. Christ had told Nicodemus that a man must be born again, or born from above, in order to see the kingdom of God. Nicodemus, after receiving his instructions on this great subject, exclaimed, how can these things be? The Great Teacher, in reply, asks with surprise, how Nicodemus could be a master in Israel and not know these things—not be familiar with the necessity of regeneration before Christ had placed it within the view of his mind. The necessity of regeneration then, as the condition of entrance into the expected kingdom of God, was one of those earthly things which Nicodemus ought to have known before; it was a truth, discoverable without revelation, and needing no messenger from Heaven to unfold it, not to know which argued surprising blindness on the part of a master in Israel.

Now let us look at this truth, in order to see whether it be an earthly thing, or whether the great Teacher did not expect too much from the educated Jew who was sitting at His feet.

Was it then a new doctrine in the world,—so new, that a learned Jew might well stare when it was first propounded to him? Let the prayer of the penitent, "Create in me a clean heart O God, and renew within me a right spirit,"—answer. Or such a passage, again, as that in Ezekiel, "A new heart will I give you and a new spirit will I put within you! and I will take away the stony heart out of your flesh, and will give you an heart of flesh."

But perhaps, if not new, it was a heavenly truth, taught by inspiration first, and received on divine authority But how is this consistent with the fact that through the Old Testament, essentially if not in so many words, it is implied in every exhortation to repentance, every description of the state of men in their sins, every statement which makes of the godly or the holy a class distinct from the rest of mankind? We must admit then a natural foundation for it in the universal consciousness of sin. Was it strange that a Jew, whose sense of sin was kept alive by the moral and the ceremonial portions of the law, should feel his need of a spiritual renovation? Was it strange, when he struggled with himself and found his fleshly appetites too strong, that he fell back on God as a helper, and admitted the presence of God's life-giving Spirit to be his great want? To what other conclusion, in fact, could any one arrive, who started from the fact of sin and was earnestly bent on improving his own character? Surely such earthly teachers as consciousness and experience were enough to reveal this to an earnest Jewish soul. And may we not go farther, and say that every thoughtful mind among the Greeks and Romans who regarded the improvement of character to be of prime importance, came to the same result,—that the soul was in a state of disharmony, that life was in ruins, and that *he* would be man's greatest benefactor who could point out to man a better help than the discipline of philosophy. Nor is this to be argued more from individual confessions, than from the success of the Gospel when it went through the heathen world preaching its heavenly announcements. Men received these because they were prepared for them by a sense of want and a sense of sin which had been smouldering in their hearts. To them the necessity of a new birth seemed like an old doctrine of their own experience, with a more vivid light thrown upon it by the Gospel.

And so all those decisions which our moral nature pronounces, when the fact of sin is honestly admitted, are earthly things which Christ needed to preach, but did not first reveal. The ill desert of sin, the anger of God against sin, the judgment which will follow sin, the helplessness of him who is under the yoke of sin—these and such as these are the earthly things which conscience and life had impressed on many a Jew, yes, and on many a heathen all over the world, from the realms of Druid worship to those lands in the East where men have sought to purify the soul by the torture of the body.

Such, then, are the earthly things which our Saviour has in view: they are what man could discover for himself, or, if by reason of his blindness he could not do this, might realize to be true as soon as they were told him. What, on the other hand, were the heavenly things? Plainly, such as no skill of man could discover, no philosopher could reason out, no consciousness, or experience construct,—such as needed a Divine messenger from the skies to make them known. It may be that some intimations of these heavenly things were conveyed to God's people by the old prophets; it may be that God's dealings of forbearance and compassion suggested the possibility of them, or of something like them; it may even be that human nature in thoughtful heathen minds is never without hope of some light to come, some intervention or deliverance; but, granting all this, still, the heavenly things needed to be disclosed by the same hand that had fanned these embers of hope, and had forborne to punish sin, and had inspired the prophets to promise future good.

What these heavenly things were, our Lord lets us know in the verses following our text. They were such as the lifting up on the cross of the Son of man for the sins of the world, the love of God in sending His Son for man's salvation, and not for his condemnation. That a rescue of man in his sins was desirable—*this* might be freely admitted; that there was no other hope for him, *this*, too, experience might teach, but that God had resolved to interpose on man's behalf, in what way He would interpose, who was to be the deliverer, what He was to do for this end, what man would do to Him—*all this* was wrapped in impenetrable darkness, except so far as prophets had caught glimpses of heavenly realities, which they themselves imperfectly understood.

Those religious truths, then, which consciousness and experience reveal to a candid spirit, are called by our Lord earthly things; those truths, on the other hand, which lie beyond the knowledge of man, and which only a messenger from heaven can reveal, He calls heavenly things.

II. In illustration of these words of Christ, I remark, that belief in the earthly things is a necessary antecedent to belief in the heavenly. It is impossible for him who rejects the first class of truths to accept the other. No man can receive Christ, as a teacher come from God, and making known what no earthly teacher could discover, and yet deny or discard that which he assumes as the very reason for which His revelation is brought to man. Nay, further, no man can receive Christ without being made ready for Him by the teachings of conscience and of reason. The root of unbelief and of skepticism lies deeper down in the soul than many a man thinks: it is not merely rejection of the supernatural, or even the closing of the heart to God's infinite love, manifest in His dear Son, but it is shutting the ear to the very voice of nature crying within us, telling us of our immense needs, and thus bringing us to *a* Christ all ready for our reception. And thus unbelief takes its true place: it is not only sin against Christ, blindness to revealed glories, insensibility to love from heaven,—it is, also, sin against nature, sin against reason, sin against the soul's deepest, most universal convictions.

Observe, then, that without faith in the earthly things pointed out above, Christ's heavenly revelation can have no interest, is not a practical subject, and is altogether improbable.

God must have manifested Himself in Christ, for some good reason lying outside of the revelation itself? It was not in order to make a revelation for its own sake, that Christ was sent, but it was for some cause arising out of the nature and condition of man. It was to provide a remedy for some existing evil, and for some evil bearing a proportion in its magnitude to the grandeur of the intervention. But the evil, in order to be cured, must be felt and acknowledged, for there are no magical processes in God's government, there is no way of getting rid of evil in man's nature or in human society without the effective co-operation of man himself. Now such co-operation is prevented, not only by unbelief in the value of the remedy, but just as much by unbelief in the need of any remedy at all. How is man to discover his need of a remedy? Not from the revelation which places it within his reach,—although the uses of this may be very great in drawing his attention to moral maladies from which his eye was turned away before—but from his own moral sense, his consciousness of sin, his observation of the laws of character, his study of society, and of his fellow-men. Suppose now he will not admit his sinfulness, can the revelation do him any good? Can it even be received for true? Will he not reason that if sin is no evil, there is no need of any remedy for it, much less of a remedy so marvellous as the incarnation and death of the Son of God? And if his premises are true, will he not have a right so to reason? Suppose that among the multitudes preached to by the Apostle Paul, there had been one sinless man, one man utterly unconscious of having ever offended God, or suppose there had been one utterly devoid, by his nature, of a sense of good and evil. If the Apostle in his ignorance of human hearts had offered the salvation from heaven to either of these men, could either of them have received it? Would it have been a revelation intended for either of them? Was not the nature of both such that they would be obliged to reject a revelation pre-supposing sin? And so, too, all men who will not admit the great fact of their sinfulness, as discovered from their earthly experience, must reject, cannot fail to reject, a revelation from heaven which without that sinfulness can have no meaning.

I have spoken exclusively of sinfulness in this argument, because all the *earthly things*, all the religious doctrines which Christ's heavenly doctrine pre-supposes, revolve around this one fact of human sin. Our nature is such as sin makes it, our relations to God are determined by sin, our power of self-recovery is crippled by sin, the question whether God can pardon sin is an unsettled question before a positive offer is made, the future prospects of the soul are dark as long as there is sin past or present to be taken into account. Let me add too that sin itself, and sin alone makes us unwilling to admit those *earthly things* which furnish the reason why Christ came into the world, and thus prepares the way for all skepticism—that relating to our nature and obligations towards God, and that relating to the grand recoverer. Sin seeks to deny its own existence, it pretends to be dead, it succeeds in making the soul insensible to its own state, and thus incapable of receiving Christ.

One or two illustrations will, I trust, make it plain, that the unbelief which rejects Christ has its root in the denial of those very truths which need no revelation for their establishment.

The philosophy called Pantheistic denies the freedom of man, and holds that sin is a necessary stage in the progress of the development of a finite creature. Now between such a view of man's moral nature and wants, and the coming of Christ from heaven to save him, how can there be any harmony? If man is *unfrée,* why call on him to believe, or complain of him for not believing? If sin is necessary for the finite mind, if it is an unavoidable stage of being, why not let it alone, and what wisdom is there in a remedial system which assumes that it can be cured? And indeed how could a God who is Himself bound by necessity, who is in a process of evolution over which He has no control, out of His own free love send His Son on an errand of mercy into this world? Or if He came, since nature is subject to the same bondage, how could He work miracles, which by the theory are impossible? Thus, then, there is no need of a revelation, nor any possibility of one, nor can there be any evidence for one. Is the rejection of Christ's heavenly message, then, on the part of the Pantheist, due chiefly to its nature, or its difficulties—or, is not the conclusion in this school a foregone one, good against any possible or conceivable revelation, good against any opening of heaven to earth, and any way from earth to heaven,—good even against that fixed consciousness of sin, which cleaves to the race, and which must, on Pantheistic principles, be pronounced to be a fixed illusion?

For another illustration of a more practical nature let us look at the Pharisee. Here is a man who believes in the *earthly things,* as it seems, for he believes in God, even in the God of Israel. He believes that there is such a thing as sin, and it troubles him, as is evident by the trouble he takes to get rid of the sense of it. Now, why does he reject the Saviour's claims to be the Christ ot God? It is because his view of sin, of his relation to God, of his character, is shallow. He can, by external observance, by decorum, by morality, by almsgiving, by bigoted attachment to the faith of his ancestors,—he can in these ways satisfy himself, and keep religion from invading the inner provinces of his soul. But the sacred Teacher has a battery to play upon him: He says, except a man be born again, be born of water and of the Spirit, he cannot see the kingdom of God. Here Christ comes into border-land where the earthly and the heavenly meet; He opens the world of spiritual power, and shows him that all works without the work of the Spirit are works of the flesh. This is a step beyond where he is willing to follow the Teacher come from God. This, which he ought to have found out of himself, he is not willing to admit. "How can these things be?" But if not, how then can those other things be—those glorious announcements out of the heavens which Christ is all ready to tell him? He must shrivel up in his skepticism. And he does not see all the while that he is passing judgment on himself. For if, with all his Jewish lore, and his access to the books of God, and his ready faith in a portion of the truth there announced, he cannot receive the doctrine of a new spiritual birth, when it is taught by Scripture and by experience, do not his blindness and unbelief show that he needs to have his eyes and his heart opened before he can enter into the kingdom of God?

Not very unlike the state of the Pharisee is the state of that class of worldly men who live an easy, self-satisfied life, in entire unconcern for the future interests of their souls. If they had even the convictions of Plato in regard to the lapse of souls; or the convictions of Aristotle in regard to the importance of character; or the convictions of the Stoics in regard to the freedom and nobility of the virtuous soul, could they think so meanly as they do of their immortal part? If then, when Christ tells them these things, which the best heathen in substance admit, and they believe not, how can they believe, when He begins to tell them of the strength of a Divine love which drew Him down into this world? If He tells them about themselves, and holds the mirror before them that they may look into their souls, and they believe not, how can they believe when He tells them of Himself, of this unknown being beyond the skies? He can have no hold on their minds, He can be of no practical interest whatever, there is no good reason which they admit for His coming into the world. How then can they believe when He speaks of Himself as having come from God?

Thus it appears that when the earthly things of which Christ discourses are rejected, all that He says of heavenly truth will be rejected also. On the other hand, he who receives Christ's testimony concerning the former will believe what He says of the latter.

We have already seen that in the condition of human nature and its wrong relations to God,—truths within the reach of an earthly mind,—lie the reason for Christ's coming into this world. But these reasons, it is plain, must be perceived and acknowledged by each soul that hears the Gospel, otherwise the Gospel can be of no use to him whatever. And the faith which receives Christ is a faith which contemplates His coming to relieve some acknowledged want, to cure some felt evil, to readjust some controversy with God of which there is a painful consciousness. Suppose now, that an individual has reached this station of faith, that he believes in the sad reality of sin, that he believes in a discord between the soul and God, that he believes in the necessity of a new spiritual life, if men are to be holy or blessed; and suppose that Christ now manifests Himself to such a person, confirming first what He was but too conscious of before, and then adding a revelation of love and hope which offers through a crucified Saviour reconciliation to God and eternal life. What will be this man's treatment of the new heavenly things thus disclosed to him? The first effect will be to confirm and deepen his impressions in regard to all those soul-truths which he previously admitted. The next effect must be to receive Christ's new message, and to come into a state of harmony with God. For what is there to prevent this. He has no prejudice to surmount. When Christ tells him of his sin and his need of a spiritual life, it is what he has already felt. He finds no difficulty in the evidences of Christ's mission. It carries with it, taken in connection with the character of its author, its own evidence. He cannot regard God's new revelation as in itself incredible. Far from this, it is very credible. He could not, indeed, have solved the problem of what God would do, but in what God has done he sees a beauty, a glory, a divine perfection of love and holiness, a suitableness for man's wants and sins, which confirm and are confirmed by the character and works of the Messenger. Thus he cannot but believe the heavenly things, the new revelation, since he believes the earthly things, the religious truths discernible by man and already known before the heavenly things are made manifest.

We learn from these words of our Lord, as thus illustrated, that there is nothing strange in man's rejection of the Gospel. When we look at Christ's message from one point of view, when we take into account its offer of free grace, its promises and helps, the moral beauty of its founder, the new relations which it institutes between God and the soul, together with all the wants, the anxieties, the sorrows which it can be seen and be shown to relieve, we marvel that any one should stay away from this feast of love, and so we begin to think that there is some want of evidence for the Gospel; that difficulties in the Gospel, not to be explained, keep men with some show of reason in a state of skepticism. But, my friends, Christ and experience teach us something truer than this. Skepticism or disbelief is not the marvel, but faith is the marvel. It would be more of an evidence against the Gospel that it should be believed by men as they are, than it is an evidence against the Gospel that men as they are reject it. If a Gospel came offering peace and life without any mention of an inner process in the soul, if the Saviour, with the evidence of His mission which we have now, had distributed external gifts, and changed society by His benevolent agency, there would have been a crowding of all men to Him, He would not have left a few half fledged, doubting disciples in this world, when He left it for the Father. No! the Gospel is not disbelieved for what it is and for its want of evidence, but for what it pre-supposes. It is the under-pinning of the Gospel which is unsightly in the eyes of so many. Christ is beautiful enough to penetrate with a kind of joy into the hearts of unbelievers, but these dreadful postulates, these sad realities of man's nature and of his relation to God—these are the barrier and must be the barrier between Christ and souls in their sins. It is not miracles, again, or difficulties touching the matter of inspiration, which keep men in unbelief. Remove these and there is some other intrenchment behind them. But let a soul receive Christ's postulates, and miracles or no miracles, inspiration or no inspiration, it throws its gates open wide, and joyfully surrenders to Christ. This is shown by those instances, not uncommon, where men who had intrenched themselves for years in some scheme of thought opposing the foundations of the Gospel, suddenly, in affliction or adversity, or under the unusual influences of religion, abandon their scheme altogether and go over to Christ the redeemer. Christ is where He was before. But they denied the very reason why He came into the world. Therefore they could only disbelieve. Now they can only believe. The unbelief while it lasted was as natural, as inevitable as the faith was afterwards.

Such cases show also that unbelief in the earthly things of religion is weak, so that there is hope in some favored moment of driving it from its place. Christ, when He speaks, is sustained by the deepest, most fixed things in human nature, by its standard of character, by its ideal of perfection, by its sense of waut, by its sense of guilt, by its longing for the favor of God. These and such as these are the helpers of faith, the guides to Christ. These the objector overlooks when he thinks that the Gospel must fall under his blows. These the unbeliever covers up but cannot extinguish. And if, at some blest time, the Spirit calls the soul into the presence both of these things and of Christ, so that it sees itself and its deliverer face to face,—then it enters into the kingdom of God.

SERMON XII.

THE PLACE OF FEAR AS A MOTIVE IN RELIGION.

LUKE xii. 4–5. But I say unto you, my friends, be not afraid of them that kill the body, and after that have no more that they can do. But I will forewarn you whom ye shall fear; fear Him, which, after He hath killed hath power to cast into hell; yea, I say unto you, fear Him.

THESE words were spoken by one who perfectly understood both God and man, and who, having no fear but rather a perfect love of God in Himself, was under no personal inducement to over-estimate the fear of God, as a motive to be urged upon others. The quality of the fear spoken of is defined by the words applied to men—"them that kill the body," and by the words applied to God—"which, after He hath killed, hath power to cast into hell." It is, then, no filial fear or reverence of God, it is nothing else but a dread of wrath that our Lord had in His mind. The importance, again, of entertaining such a fear, is shown by the emphatic repetition "yea, I say unto you, fear Him." Nor can the words be softened in their meaning by saying that it is God, rather than man, who ought to be the object of fear, or at least, the object of some persons' fear, for they are positive, they point to an evil greater than death, which Christ treats, and must have regarded, if He was honest, as a fearful possibility. They are used, moreover, by the moral teacher of mankind, as bringing a motive to bear upon His hearers, which He held to be necessary for their good, and as counteracting another motive—the fear of man, which unduly swayed or might sway their conduct.

Fear, then, may sometimes, and in the case of some persons,—we have the authority of the author of the

Gospel for what we say—be used, under the Gospel, with propriety and with benefit, as a motive to counteract the force of sin. It is, and it ought to be known to be, a "fearful thing," for some descriptions of men, "to fall into the hands of the living God." And yet there are many who would discard this motive altogether, or at least are unwilling to have it urged. The essence of religion being confessedly love, and Christ Himself having made peace between God and man, they argue that love and peace alone should be preached; that no sinner should be alarmed or agitated at a view of his sins, but only drawn to God by His free offers of life; that it hurts the character and has marred the aspects of religious life in past ages, to act on the soul by presenting to its view its deserts and its risks; that the sinner is driven away from God and made desperate by appeals to His fears, and the Christian, if thus introduced into a religious life, is made a slave rather than a child. In short, they would let the motive of fear act where small earthly risks and evils are to be avoided, but where great perils lie before the soul, and a black cloud overhangs the future life, they would shut men's eyes, if possible, or turn them towards another quarter. And thus they seem to reverse the teaching of Christ; they tell us to fear man who at most can kill the body, and not to fear God who can cast into hell.

I admit all their premises, but it seems to me that their conclusion is false, foolish, and dangerous. And it is for the purpose of showing that fear has its place in a practical system of religion, and of settling the boundaries within which it is a wholesome motive, that I address you on the present occasion. It has appeared to me to be an important subject, because in the oscillation of religious sentiment men have become unduly ticklish in regard to the use of such a motive as fear. There was a time when terror was too much preached, or preached in too exciting a way, so as to overpower the soul and not even to secure the avoidance of danger. This was revolting to a sound Christian taste and a healthy Christian experience, and so there came a reaction. But it seems as if the world could never keep in mind the two halves of truth at once, but must shift from one side to another according to the last impression made by practical evil, and so the reaction went too far. Just as a severe father is apt to make a son indulgent, just as despotical authority is succeeded by licentious private judgment and unbridled will, so here the opposite of wrong is regarded as of course right, one truth is lost sight of while another engrosses the attention of all. It were well, too, if besides this reaction, we should not have to say that a false and weak doctrine of benevolence had not enfeebled the conviction of the righteousness of punishment, and so the dread of it, and if a pantheistic view of the world, stealing over men's minds without being acknowledged, were not taking away from sin its freedom and responsibility, and so its ill-desert and its peril.

I. I proceed then to remark in the first place that fear is implanted in the soul by divine benevolence, as a self-preserving impulse, and if there are dangers to the soul from sin it may have an important office in avoiding them. If there were no dangers, or if they could not be foreseen, or if, when foreseen, they could not be avoided, there could be no place for fear and no explanation of it in the plan of our nature. But what could man do without fear, surrounded as he is by enemies of his life, of his health, of his peace, of his prosperity? It is one of the earliest of emotions, as the life of man in its first stages manifests. It is one main condition of human improvement; we seek security because we apprehend evil, and the apprehension stimulates us to provide for our defence by stable governments, by military, naval, and police defences, by criminal law and courts of justice. What value would there be in life, or what stability in health, if fear of loss did not move us to guard ourselves at these points? or how could we hope and calculate for the future, if fear went not along with hope to provide against the dangers by which the hope might be frustrated? The prevention of risks is one of our principal activities, and men tried to insure themselves against dreaded evils thousands of years before insurance companies were thought of. Nor is it in regard to our material interests and life only that fear has a work to do. Our reputations and our characters are not placed beyond its action, and that a wholesome action. How many reputations have been saved by a dread of reproach, which thus brings the power of the moral judgments of the many to the support of the halting and tempted one? How many characters have been aided at weak moments by the fear of the consequences of sin, when reason and conscience were giving way? And this, too, we may notice, that fear is generally in the service of morality and rectitude, as much as it is in the service of the life and material welfare of men. There may indeed be false moral judgments afloat in the world, and a perverse public sentiment may frown on the righteous more than on the wrong-doers; but in general fear must be on the lookout for the conservation of society, and thus it will ally itself to that moral rectitude which is society's chief conservation.

These things being so, if there are dangers from sin, why should they not be feared when perceived, and be pointed out to the sinner if unperceived. If there are risks to character, how can a reasonable being fail to take them into account, or if he is not aware of them, how can a benevolent man fail to forewarn him? If God's favor is worth everything and we can forfeit or have forfeited it, what but fear can lead us in a world like this to avoid or repair the evil? If sin is eating into our life, blasting its blossoms and despoiling it of all solid fruit, and the time for amendment has not slipped by, how good a friend is that fear which can bring us to reflection, to resolution, to a new life? Why should we refuse to appeal to the motive of fear, when great interests, paramount interests are at stake, and yet appeal to it when the risk is small and the loss would be trivial?

II. Will it be said that fear is a base motive, and has no power to make any man better, inasmuch as a character formed under the sway of fear can never have any freeness or elevation? I accept the statement in part, but it does not tell the whole truth, and needs to be guarded and qualified in order to be capable of practical application. Fear is not a base motive if it aids us in securing our welfare. It may at times be the only motive within call. A character built on fear is a base character without doubt, but a character in the formation of which fear at the right time and in the right degree has had some share may be the best of all characters.

No active principle of our nature is base, which is necessary, as fear is, for our preservation. If there are objective dangers to body or soul, to the interests of time or of eternity, it is not base, it is rather wise to seek by a subjective impulse to avoid the danger. Some persons seem to admire unthinking brute courage, which makes no estimate of the assailing or of the resisting power, which flies by instinct in the face of danger instead of avoiding it with the resources of reason. But while such animal heroism is more admirable than unthinking, palsying fear, it has no moral quality whatever. True courage calculates danger, provides against danger, and thus has need of fear itself to obtain information of threatening evil. Moral courage, the highest form of the quality, does not consist in having no sensibility to public opinion but in standing up against it, whilst it fears and would gladly avoid it.

And again, fear is not base and debasing, for this reason, that a higher fear often counteracts and overcomes a lower. The fear of doing wrong may overcome the fear of death; the fear of God, the fear of man; the fear of hazarding our eternal interests, the fear of injuring our temporal. Does not fear thus in the eye of reason take the color and borrow some of the nobleness of the cause in which it is enlisted? It may, therefore, be appealed to rightfully by the noblest persons, by those who are agitated by no fears themselves, and are acting in the best of causes. "Be not afraid," says our Saviour, "of them that kill the body, and after that have no more that they can do; but I will forewarn you whom ye shall fear." "Who art thou," says the prophet, "that thou shouldst be afraid of a man that shall die and of the son of man which shall be made as grass, and forgettest the Lord thy Maker that hath stretched forth the heavens and laid the foundation of the earth?" Such is the language of those who were not afraid to face the world, while men, who tremble like an aspen at the thought of encountering a hostile public opinion, maintain that fear ought never to be appealed to in matters of religion.

And again, fear is sometimes the only force which can act on our character. To this I shall refer again, and will only say here, that thousands of times a sudden unforeseen temptation has been resisted by its aid, when reason was asleep, and desire was kindled into passion. If this has happened in the case of persons in a state of sin, when yielding might have ruined them, and if Christians in like circumstances have been saved from shipwrecking the soul and dishonoring God, who shall dare to exclude such a force from its proper play in the formation of character?

But, with all this, we freely admit, that a character formed under the predominant influence of fear, is a low and base one, incapable of anything generous or noble. This, which is true where the family government is severe, and the civil government a despotism, is eminently true in religion. Love is the brightest principle in a religious life, without which there can be no communion and no cheerful obedience. As perfect love casts out fear, so perfect fear casts out love. We hate, and we seek to avoid those whom we only fear. How then can a character have anything heavenly in it, when the controlling motive is one which excludes the sway of love and of duty? Fear *alone* would not only never make a man better, but would prevent him from ever becoming better. Just as the necessity of self-preservation, if constant and strong, would keep our eyes away from higher thoughts, and cultivate an ignoble love of life, so would dread of God withdraw us from those truths which are the true remedy for the moral disease of our nature.

There is another evil attendant on the predominant sway of fear, when it is less strong. The efforts to which it prompts may be directed not toward the avoidance of danger, but towards the prevention of fear itself. For this purpose all subterfuges may be used, all falsehoods welcomed, which can lessen the subjective estimates of danger. And that this is very common, and very fatal, all experience will testify. The world is full of falsehoods, that get their strength from this very source. We all know how unwilling we are to listen to a class of truths lest our anxieties should be aroused, and we may have discovered in ourselves a bias against truth, a desire to disbelieve it, for this very reason.

But all this may be admitted, and it may be true that the control of fear is neither elevating nor truly reformatory; while yet it is most true, that fear within its just limits may be both beneficial and necessary for creatures such as man. Why should not religion make use at the right time of every emotion that is not sinful in itself, of fear and shame, as well as of hope and gratitude and a sense of duty? These must all be applied in the moral education of the individual for an earthly life, and they are equally essential in the concerns of the soul with God.

III. Fear, when used as a motive in religion, must take counsel of the reason and not of the imagination. If it becomes too intense, if it amounts to terror its use is lost. The foresight of danger and the apprehension it must awaken do us no good, unless they turn us towards the means of escape and of safety. These means themselves lie within the reach of our reason alone, and in order that reason may take advantage of them, it must be collected, sound in its calculations, not wholly absorbed by the danger itself, able to bring all the considerations that bear on the case before the view of the will, and to direct the active powers. The emotions, when they become extreme, paralyze our powers: we feel only and are incapable of action. There is such a thing as being swallowed up in overmuch grief. Remorse or the sorrow of the world for sin worketh death. Shame, when excessive, prevents reform. Even hope, if unduly confident, destroys the power to attain to that which we hope for. But of all the emotions fear may become the most unmanning and paralyzing. It was given to us to avoid danger, but when it rises into *terror* it leads to despair. It destroys the presence of mind which is essential to effective action. Its connection with the imagination is very intimate, if not on account of its own nature, as anticipating a vague unknown evil, at least on account of man's sinful nature, which the more easily pictures a frowning future, because it knows that sin is linked to punishment. Of this the dark superstitions of the heathen world give most abundant proof.

Such being the case, it must follow that the office of a preacher of the truth is to appeal to fear only in that degree that the mind may fairly view the risks to which sin is exposed, and may be able to use all its energy to avoid them. He is unwise and hurts the souls of men who goes beyond this limit. He thinks, when he sees evidences of alarm produced by his startling pictures that there is power in his preaching; but generally—at least among persons accustomed to reflection—it is not so. He forgets that a high excitement of the soul for the most part ends in listlessness, and when repeated and habitual, passes into a dreadful hardening and deadening of the active powers. He forgets that lasting and useful impressions are those in which the truth has the predominating share. He does not seem to be aware that the most fearful things, the most truly to be feared, are those which will not fit into his shallow declamations. The fearful callousness of the soul which the Gospel has only hardened; the dreadful power of habits of sin to destroy as well the love of truth, as the honesty of purpose, and the energy of the will; the awful certainty of remorse, as the soul becomes alive, when it is too late, to its self-ruin and to the displeasure of God; the dreary isolation of an impenitent selfish soul, as it pursues its way through its existence—these considerations and such as these, growing out of the inevitable laws of man's nature and the unchanging government of God, rouse the soul to action when they are realized,—they are truly fearful and yet they allow the soul, while they are contemplated, the free use of all its powers. But terrors painted to the imagination, like a thunder-cloud, appal, pass away and are forgotten.

IV. The proper use of fear, then, is to aid the higher class of motives in conversion, and afterwards, through a Christian life, above all in the first stages of it, to spring to the rescue of the soul on a sudden assault of temptation.

The office of fear is analogous to that of miracles. It does not and cannot convert men from sin, as miracles alone cannot produce a rational faith. But fear will bring eternal things into the minds of those who would otherwise think nothing of them, as miracles bring the presence of divine power in confirmation of truth to the notice of mankind. Still more, fear adds the motive of a pressing interest to all the other appeals which the gospel makes to the world. Men may say what they please of the baseness of being made good by such means, they may feel it to be unworthy of a man to obey a lower motive, when there are so many higher to which the gospel and its preachers can appeal. But what if these higher considerations have been pressed for years without effect? What shall arouse a man in his sins who has resisted all the claims of duty, who has been deaf to the voice of love, whose conscience is dead and his heart hard? Is he growing better under these high appeals, so that by and by his whole nature will be open to the power of the gospel; or rather is not some uneasiness, some sense of danger at the right moment, some anxiety about his higher interests needed to lead him to give his attention to the old story of the gospel? Do you say this is a low point to start from in a religious life? Very true, but it is a still lower fall of an immortal soul, when it has not only cast off the sense of duty but the sense of fear also. And is it not compassionate in the gospel and in its author to place, by the side of the mercy which invites, the peril which is to be shunned? Moreover, what does experience say if not this—that few or no persons are led to break the chains of worldly habit, unless some sense of risk, some solicitude for their future welfare, lifts up its startling voice in company with the soft expostulations of the gospel. Suppose that the gospel had sounded no notes of alarm; would man in his sins, who, as it is, moves so sluggishly and tardily in the prospect of a remote evil, be ever led to move at all? Nay, might he not argue, if there were no danger threatened and no harm to be avoided, that sin must be an inconsiderable evil, since the divine law-giver has not thought it worth His while to call in the aid of a strong motive, to which all human forms of government find it necessary to appeal even in order to secure outward peace?

Or will you say that if unbelief is the grand obstacle in the way of the gospel, this unbelief will cast off fear as well as benumb conscience? But there is a ready answer to this, that a soul in its sins cannot help doing homage to the violated law of duty, so far as to retain some uneasiness at least, some suspicion, that all is not right, that its highest interests are at hazard, that law and God cannot be at peace with sin. And this is fear in some form, whether it gives forth a whisper or a loud proclamation of danger, whether it renders the soul restless only or summons it to an instant escape from the consequences of sin.

Thus fear is a most efficient and necessary auxiliary, before conversion, to those higher and nobler truths which bring on this happy change. But after conversion also, so long as the old habits of sin retain anything of their power, and the religious nature is as yet unripe, it is of the highest service. There are crises of temptation, as many of us can testify, when the ground was slipping under our feet, when some sophistry was taking the edge off from the right and from duty, when the desired evil seemed so good, and the enticement of sin was growing so irresistible, and the will was becoming so weak, that all was well nigh lost for us, and we had perhaps half given ourselves over. If at such a time fear—fear of divine wrath, or fear of loss of reputation, or fear of remorse, yes, or fear even of hell,—came to the rescue of the discouraged forces of Christian virtue, and we were enabled to refuse and to overcome, ashamed as we might well be of our surprise and of our all but defeat, we had in that experience a measure of the service that fear could render to our salvation at such a time of imminent peril. Verily we are sometimes saved by fear as well as by hope. Its office in the Christian life is only occasional, it may have long furloughs, and be off duty the greater part of our lives, but blessed be the author of our salvation, that in our extremity it does its work well, and we are safe. Such times may be turning points in character; and if permitted in the eternal life, to study ourselves and the dealings of a redeeming God with us, we may well adore the grace that saved us, "with fear, pulling us out of the fire" by an arm of strength.

V. Finally, when fear has done this its work of an occasional auxiliary to the higher motives of the Gospel, it is no longer needed. The last stage of a purified character is the perfect love which casteth out fear. This stage is within the attainment of every tempted, erring Christian. It is not, even on earth, wholly an ideal state; nay, it is so far within the reach of all, that all Christians ought to aim to reach it. There are, I doubt not, anxious, trembling Christians who are much better men than some who feel no fear and make no question of their salvation. There are some again, who are assured of Heaven with no good ground whatever. But there is a state such as the Apostle John speaks of in his epistle, such as he probably was conscious of, in which love has arrived at that perfection and strength, that the soul is in unwavering and complete harmony with God. What can now disturb its peace, what call forth its fear, conscious as it is of its own love, and strong in trust on Him? Can anything hurt it? "All things work together for good to them who love God." Can anything lead it into sin? But all its desires are in subjection to the reigning principle of love. Can anything separate it from the love of God? No, "neither things present nor things to come, nor height nor depth, nor any other creature." Can its salvation fail? But perfect love is both the assurance of salvation and is salvation itself.

Thus for the Christian who has reached this stage of the higher life fear is no longer wanted. In the soul's infancy, in the infancy of the renewed nature, it threw in its contribution to the upholding of the character, but now it may never cease to slumber, it may fade out of the soul for any need there is of its service. In the first part of the voyage there were sunken rocks, there was a call for anxiety, there were outcries of pressing danger, but the pacific seas are entered, and there are no alarms any more. Blessed is the man who has tasted of this peace within. And how does he contrast with the sinning man who is uneasy and yet will not forsake his sins; who practices on his own mind and conscience by false excuses, the shallowness of which he himself half discerns; who is dimly conscious of the wrath of God and yet will not secure the divine favor. Can he drown fear? No, it will never die; it may sleep for the present but must awake at length. For him the first part of the voyage seems quiet, but the alarms, the rocks, the shipwreck come at the end.

SERMON XIII.

PETER HELPED BY HIS FALL TO STRENGTHEN HIS BRETHREN.

LUKE xxii. 32. Second clause. And when thou art converted, strengthen thy brethren.

THE deplorable sin of Peter was not destined to cut him off from Christian hope or from the power of serving his Master. He was to be converted anew, and when so converted, he was to have the office as well as the faculty of strengthening his brethren.

These words of our Lord are not a little remarkable. On the first view of such a crime as Peter's, we should suppose that all his influence over his brethren, all his ability to do good, his capacity to impart strength to others, were lost, and that forever. At the most, he could only hope to be forgiven, and to live as an unnoticed believer, brooding in the shade over his ingratitude and content to take an obscure place during the remainder of his life.

For consider in what position he would now be placed.

First his own shame would naturally bring with it a sense of weakness, and would furnish a good reason for concentrating his efforts upon himself. The power of shame *who* does not know, who has acted unwisely or wickedly, when better things were expected of him, when he expected better things of himself, above all when he had made a profession which implied a high standard of conduct. The man himself is pierced and stung by a most painful consciousness of being unworthy. How can he have the courage to warn or comfort his brethren, when he has sunk lower than all the others! He reads his shame, also, in the countenances and the carriage of all who come in his way. They reflect back on him, like so many mirrors, the traits of his own fallen character. They reaffirm his verdict against himself. How then can he face them, how can he presume to aid them in their struggles against sin, when every admonition, every instruction given to them reminds him of his own lapse! He will be apt then to feel that the remainder of life will be fitliest spent in seeking to cure himself in penitential retirement. What more can he do than to save himself, and serve as a passive warning and example!

Again, his brethren in such a case would naturally lower their opinion of him. A sin, the recovery from which is like a second conversion, is a startling thing to a Christian Church. The Christian body is a holy brotherhood; holiness is the very essence of their renewed character: when, therefore, one of their number, above all one who, like Peter, has stood high in the affections and the confidence of his brethren, falls away, what can prevent a loss of confidence? Is it strange, that suspicion at times goes to an unjust, to a cruel extreme, and denies to such a man the possession of the Christian character? At all events, the opinion of him, which was so high before, is greatly lowered, and the power with which he acted on others before must be greatly lessened, if not wholly destroyed.

Moreover, thirdly, his brethren will naturally feel that a man of such glaring sins is not the man to be put foremost in their efforts to do good outside of the Church. "We want a man for our representative"—they will be apt to say—" who, when he goes out among men, will reflect no dishonor on us, who will not be met by taunts and jeers, as having deserted the cause which he advocates in its times of danger. Would not a general, convicted of cowardice, be likely to encourage the foe, would he be the best man to send against them, would he smite them with terror? Let the man of glaring sins retire into the ranks; let him take the humblest place, and not seek to convert others, after he has fallen so low as to need a new conversion himself."

Such reflections have reason and justice in them, but they are not the suggestions of the highest Christian feeling. Our Lord points us to higher wisdom, to a wisdom built on that glorious system of grace which makes use of our sins as so many warnings to us, so many helps in the future, so many arguments for the glory of Divine forgiveness.

Let us then turn our thoughts to the power which such a man as Peter acquires, from his very sins, of strengthening his brethren.

And here let no one suppose that sin, which is moral weakness, can of itself in any way or by any experience be a source of strength. Innocence, sinlessness alone is strength. Sin is feebleness, and that is the falsest of all doctrines, the most inconsistent of all with our experience, which affirms that sin is a necessary stage through which a finite being must pass towards moral perfection; that a time is coming in the future, when all blots and blemishes of character will wipe themselves out, when all falsehoods, all dishonors, all selfishness will blossom into perfect benevolence, nobility and truth. It is the best possible thing never to have sinned. It is the next best to be recovered from sin. He is the best Christian who leads the holiest life. And no sin in the Christian can bring him of itself into holiness. It rather destroys his peace, separates him from God, fills him with self-distrust.

But, notwithstanding all this, it may be true, under a system of grace, that the *manifestation of character which is made by a particular sin* may turn into a blessing to him who is allowed to fall into it. In this case *it is not sin, but* an *outward sin* that is the source of good, and this is accomplished, not in the ordinary course of things, but through the grace of the Gospel. Of two persons in the same moral condition before the eye of God one may be untempted and so far forth innocent, while the other yields to a temptation, before which the first also would have fallen, had it been allowed to assail him. Now I say in such a case as this the outward sin may under the Gospel be made a blessing to him who commits it; nay, more, the blessing may extend beyond himself to all around him. He may become a wiser, better, stronger Christian than he was before.

1. And this will be made apparent, if we consider *first* that in this way he arrives at a better knowledge of his own character and is impressively warned against his own faults.

A Christian believer may have defects of character such as pride, or self-confidence, or envy, or animosity, without being aware of them. In the even flow of his life there may be no conflicts with besetting sin, and therefore no revelation is made to himself of what he is and what he can do by his experience. Perhaps even he may be aware of his peculiar biases to evil, yet by mere self-examination he is incapable of measuring their strength. He contemplates only an imaginary trial, and gains an easy victory, because he cannot estimate the force of those real incitements to evil that attack him in the moment of temptation. He is thus profoundly ignorant of himself. He says with Peter, "Though all should betray thee, yet will not I." Now how is such a person to become a better and a wiser man, without some new discovery of himself, and how can he make this discovery except by being left to himself amid the assaults of temptation? We make no progress in any kind of excellence when we are self-ignorant, and our ignorance can be broken through only by a disclosure of our weakness to our own eyes—a disclosure so vivid as to make a permanent impression. In short, temptation is necessary for self-knowledge, and yielding to sin is necessary, because our state of mind involves it. The discovery we make is worth the sin, because we shall thus be enabled to triumph over future temptation and to avoid future sin.

And not only does the Christian thus arrive at a knowledge of himself, but at the same time he is put on his guard for the future. No lessons are so impressive as those which our mistakes teach us. In the province of mere knowledge what recollections are so lasting as those which our displays of ignorance before others fasten upon our memories. Or what incentives to better manners are so efficacious as the keen sense of mortification, when we have violated the laws of polite society. Many a man has become learned because he made ignominious mistakes; many a man has become polished, because his ill-breeding has become evident to himself. Can the same principle fail of acting in the spiritual sphere, if the hope of forgiveness be not cut off? Will not the sin, the attendant self-knowledge, the dread of future lapses and future shame be thus so many blessings? May not he who is converted, become stronger, more careful, wiser, and therefore, so far as his own character is concerned, better able to strengthen his brethren.

All this is illustrated by the case of Peter. His great fault was self-confidence and impetuous haste in feeling and acting,—qualities capable by discipline, such as Christ intended for him, of being softened down into manly self-reliance, and earnest, toilsome affection, and yet likely, before they assumed such shapes, to lead him into most serious errors. It is interesting to notice how he tried the feelings and exercised the forbearance of the Master beyond all the other disciples, and how Christ, with a full discernment of his faults, was educating him for a noble work in the world. The crisis in his character came at length, when with a courage which we cannot but admire, yet with a presumption which not even Christ's predictions could restrain, he threw himself into dangers to which he was unequal. He courted the trial; and woful sin, never to be forgotten sin, was the result. But when he went out and wept bitterly, a lesson was engraven on his memory as lasting as his existence. He now understood himself, he was on his guard against himself, he lost all of his presumption and self-confidence but none of his courage. His renewed, purified character, fitted him to encourage his brethren, and to take the lead in the great work of preaching Christ to the world. We must say, then, that Christ's declaration concerning him was strikingly fulfilled; and that he was better, not because he sinned, but because the sin that was in him was made to stand out before his eyes in its real deformity.

2. But secondly, a person who is thus recovered from his sins has the practical power derived from a renewed hope of forgiveness. The influences of this hope of pardon on the character can hardly be estimated too high, but they vary with the strength and the vividness of the hope, or in other words, with the impression which the divine grace displayed in pardon makes upon the soul. He who feels sin to be a very great evil, who feels that his own sins have been very great, will be prepared to magnify the grace of God in forgiveness; and in the same proportion gratitude, love, humility, the sense of dependence, the feeling of obligation will be increased. Such is the decision of our Saviour. "When they had nothing to pay, he frankly forgave them both. Tell me, therefore, which of them will love him most? Simon answered and said, I suppose that he to whom he forgave most? And He said unto him, thou hast rightly judged." But the process here, by which sin ends in love is really a *subjective* one. We do not love much because we have much forgiven, but because we *feel* that we have much forgiven. And this feeling that we have much forgiven, depends again for its depth on our estimate of our sins. Here we

reach the explanation why an open outward sin, when repented of and forgiven, may bind us more closely to divine grace, and strengthen within us the principles on which Christian activity depends to a greater degree, than if our sin had lurked only in the secret places of the heart. Coming out into open day it can be better measured by such finite minds as ours; it can be seen in its full strength, as overleaping restraint, as a wild, resistless force which will reach its object in spite of conscience and of shame. He who hateth his brother is a murderer, says the Apostle John, but it is only when we see the murderous dispositions of a malignant soul breaking out into slander or violence, that we can properly judge what a fearful power of sin had lain there before. So too it is only when we find sin within us bursting forth like a deluge of fire, that we can understand ourselves. Understanding ourselves, we measure divine grace better, and measuring divine grace, we go forth into our future lives with new impressions, with a renewed hope. We are better qualified to speak to others of what the grace of God can do. We are enabled to set a higher value on the Gospel of forgiveness, and to make known how we value it by the labors of consecrated lives. Grace is more of a reality to us, than it ever was before.

I would not be understood here as saying that Christian believers need to sin openly and grossly in order to magnify the grace of the gospel. Such a remark would be put to shame by the great multitudes of most saintly characters, who have been led in all innocence up to the very summit of Christian attainments, who, without temptation, without external outbreaking sin, have come to a most enviable acquaintance with the heights and depths of divine love. Oh, that there were more of such! But I mean to say that sometimes true, but self-ignorant Christians are led to know what they are and what Christ can do for them by being left to themselves and being suffered to fall before temptation. Then they know what grace means; then they can speak of it in all humility, and yet, with assurance to their brethren; then they can fortify others against temptation; then especially they can make earnest, mighty preachers of righteousness and of divine love. In their self-ignorance they were only capable of falling: now they rise into a strong Christian life which rests on divine grace, and can testify to others concerning the gospel of the grace of God.

And how was it with Peter? Can we doubt that when, at Pentecost, he preached repentance and baptism for the remission of sins, his own experience a few weeks before helped him as he spoke; that knowing full well what remission was, and what the marvellous compassion of Christ was, he brought, whenever he preached, the treasures of his unfading memory before a world in sin? Or, when we read his first epistle,—that epistle of hope as it has been called,—as, for instance, where he speaks of believers being begotten again to a lively hope through the resurrection of Christ from the dead,—can we doubt that indelibly associating his own denial of the Master with the Master's death and resurrection, he was thus rendered perpetually humble, grateful, and useful?

3. A person in Peter's condition appeals to the affections of the Church, and he has a closer hold upon them than if he had never become a kind of representative of Divine grace.

A principal means of doing good to our brethren is the confidence we inspire, and this confidence depends principally on the exhibition of a clear Christian character. Within the Christian Church the same spirit prevails which God has. As He views the penitent sinner with favor, although his sins may have been as scarlet, so unquestioned conversion from the depths of sin establishes a man in the regards of those who believe in divine grace. The Church pardons those whom God pardons, and loves those whom God loves. It was nothing against Paul, it abridged the affections of none towards him that he had persecuted the Church of God—nay rather, as he walked around, a monument of that mercy which he once contemned and hated, he awakened in all a livelier sense of the excellence of redemption, and was endeared to all as a monument of the grace of Christ. Thus he was enabled to win his way to a higher influence than he could otherwise have attained. And the same is true when a Christian man, like Peter, is recovered from a lapse, and gives evidence of sincere conversion. He may have disgraced the body to which he belongs, he may have caused many to mourn over him, he must have awakened doubts in regard to his own sincerity, he may even have disturbed some minds with the suspicion that there is no such thing as conversion or as a genuine Christian life. But when his character shines again as gold, all this is forgiven and forgotten. He returns to his home in the affections of Christ's people, with an experience of the bitterness of sin, with an experience of the power of the Gospel, which is fitted to keep others from falling, to excite their thanksgivings, to kindle their affection as for one saved from drowning or the flames. And why should not such a one be able to recover, and even more than recover, his old place, his old influence? What is to prevent this on their part? They believe in restoring grace. They know that the same nature is in them. They do not measure character, as Pharisees do, by external acts alone, but they know that important as external acts are, a Christian, whose faults are patent to all, may be, on the whole, a better man, a nobler character, than another Christian whose life runs along on an unbroken level, never falling below the standard of his brethren, never rising into marked excellence. And so they can trust him, they can be willing to learn from him. And he, strong in their confidence, can seek to repair whatever wrong he has done to

Christ and to His cause. He has a deeper experience, from which he can draw lessons of warning, new motives to be more earnest in the desire to recover the ground he has lost, more humility and dependence on Divine strength, fitting him to work for God with more caution in the future and with more success.

We conclude these meditations with the thought that no other system except the Christian system of grace could thus afford to honor penitence, because no other gives such testimony against sin. It is because Christianity is so holy, that it can take hold of the fallen to lift them out of the mire in which they have sunk, and can make use of those even who have dishonored Christ, as promoters of His cause before a censorious and Pharisaical world. In the early church there was a stricter party, who withdrew entirely the confidence of the communities where they had the control, from such as had lapsed in times of persecution. But while it was altogether right to insist on full proof of repentance, their rigor showed that they did not fully comprehend the Gospel. While they honored it on one side, they departed from its spirit on another. Paul felt not so. The man who had disgraced Christianity at Corinth, when he evinced thorough repentance, was taken back into a holy body, to be a blessing again, and to be blest in that sacred circle. But if the Gospel had been another kind of religion, if external purity of morals had been its highest aim, then doubtless every marked lapse would have been visited with hopeless exclusion, lest the white, or rather the whitewashed, robes of the pure should be soiled by the contact of the unclean. But Christ came to call sinners to repentance, and so His Church is a blessed sort of hospital, where the faulty and guilty can be cured; where bitter, ineffaceable memories, instead of overwhelming the soul in sorrow, can be the starting-point of a new life, can be a motive to new fidelity, a warning against return to sin; where the sym-thies aroused by a common experience can greet the penitent on his return; and where those whose sin-malady has been of a more hidden sort, knowing that they, too, belong to the class of the recovered, can welcome him as a fellow in suffering, a fellow in salvation.

And if we, my Christian friends, would draw all the use we can from this subject, we shall feel that the recollection of our sins ought to guide us not only into repentance, but into the purpose of leading a more useful life in the time to come. Most of us may have no occasion to reproach ourselves with open and disgraceful sin. Let us praise God that this is so. But who of us does not know that the same seeds of death are in us, which sprung up and showed themselves in Peter's denial of his Lord? Have we also learned from our past sins? Does the time seem more than sufficient, wherein we have been less faithful than we ought to have been? Oh, let the recollections of a life, sincere, it may be, but full of stagnation, full of apathy, stimulate us to devote the future to the service of God, to the benefit of man! Then may we draw some good from our past imperfections, and rise far above our present level of service and love.

SERMON XIV.

FORGETTING THOSE THINGS WHICH ARE BEHIND.

PHILIPPIANS iii. parts of verses 12, 13, 14. Not as though I had already attained, either were already perfect—but this one thing I do, forgetting those things which are behind and reaching forth unto those which are before, I press toward the mark.

IT is an exceedingly painful feeling, when we look back on life, and have to confess that a great object remains unaccomplished. Thus, suppose a philosopher to have begun his work in all earnestness with the aim to explore the recesses of truth. He thought all mysteries would unlock their doors to him. Nothing would be uncertain. A harmonious system would unite together all truth and reconcile all contradictions. But now in his old age, after the work of years is ended, he finds difficulties which no skill of his can penetrate, and mysteries which defy him; there is more darkness even than he thought there was, when he first began to speculate; and he comes to the mortifying conclusion, that either he is no philosopher, or philosophy has no instruments with which she can penetrate into the true essence of things. So, too, let a man start on a career of noble endeavor to aid the cause of liberty in an oppressed nation. He has devoted to it his best thoughts, his time, his money; he has written, has acted, has suffered; and now, as his life is in its wane, a tyrant fills the throne, the people are no wiser or sounder, or fitter for freedom, and he is going to die with the conviction that his toils have been spent upon the wind.

The feelings of the Christian, as he looks back on his path, are like these, only more painful. His great life work has been or ought to have been, to live for God and to become united to God. This end was not beyond the measure of his powers, when he considers the helps offered to him. The philosopher, perhaps, labors under a mistake in reaching after that which is unattainable, and if he fails, need not reproach himself. The advocate of freedom did what he could and is not responsible for anything else. But *he* is responsible for his distance from that perfect standard, which, ever since his initiation into the Christian life has shone like a star before him. "Oh, what an interval there is, he cries, between what I am and what I might have been. Oh! how many in fewer years have put on a heavenly purity, breathe a seraph's fire, do work for God which seems almost miraculous, while here I lie or creep, dragging these chains that fasten me to the earth, unable, save at long intervals to feel like a citizen of Heaven or to have heavenly aspirations."

This too, is to be observed of the Christian, that as he advances in the Christian course, his standard of perfection rises, whence what satisfied him once fails to satisfy him now. As he put on godliness perhaps the change was great, and therefore the attainment seemed to be great. Perfection to his unpractised eye, unused to the distances and magnitudes of spiritual things, seemed close by, as blind men, on recovering sight, think they can take hold of the moon. But he walks onward, making fresh discoveries all the while of two objects, of himself and of the majestic law of Christian duty. His life pleases him less, for he sees through outward actions more into his soul. His standard rises and rises until nothing but godlike perfection is worthy of his aims or hopes.

Thus when he runs on into mature Christian life, although he may find nothing exceptionable in his outer man and his conduct, he has a burden on his soul which gives sometimes intolerable pain. Oh how distressing it is, when men, as they look at him, call him perfect, to feel that he has, concealed beyond their eyes, within his soul, the germs of a multitude of sins, that no constitutional propensity is wholly overcome, but the fallen enemy rises for new fight as soon as a little sleepiness or self-satisfaction overtakes him. When thus over-estimated by others, he feels sometimes, that to have a reputation so much beyond his deserts is to be a hypocrite, and he wants in all honesty to unbosom himself to the world, that they may not extol him above his true level.

This feeling, too, of not having attained, of not being already perfect, is a *disheartening* one. Is the past to be the criterion of the future? Death is a little way on; shall any attainments of any account be made before that great door of exit from life be opened? If not perfect now, not masters over our own sinful propensities nor thoroughly united to God as yet, shall we ever be? Oh! must life close when that great life-work is but half done, but just begun rather?

And the impression of sadness, at not having attained is deepened, when he thinks *of what he has done* to reach perfection. He may have been unwatchful, forgetful, careless, without earnestness, but he cannot blame himself for entire *lack of endeavor*, or *lack of strong desire.* He has in some sort been fighting against sin for many years, and that habitually. But the trouble is that so many struggles have been so unprofitable. For the power of thought in meditation, the strength of effort in desire, and the use of means have been perhaps beyond any that he has given to any other subject in the world, perhaps beyond all other efforts put together. What has been accomplished? Oh! it is as if a man were climbing a steep mountain with a dead body tied to him; he stumbles, he falls backwards, he rises wounded and weary. There the same body of death is forcing him to the same lapses still; and the mountain top seemed as far off, if not farther off, than when he set out on the journey.

And soon he must meet the Great Judge, who, however merciful, commands him to be perfect as He is, and expects perfection from him. Here is one eye that knows all his lapses, all his heart sins, all that which a cloud covers from the eyes of men. We men make strange work of judging, we solve all sorts of hard scientific problems, but we misjudge character, misinterpret motives, praising and blaming almost as if we were throwing dice; but there is one, and from Him lies no appeal, who hears the silence of the thought, and measures us with infinitesimal precision, and admits no excuses; who cannot swerve one hair's breadth from truth. Oh! what will he say of *me?* Can I in His sight have made any *attainment* in Christian virtue? Could I but hear Him say that I have been faithful in a few things, what a divine joy would spring up in my soul. But what if He condemns me, does not my own partial, blear-eyed heart condemn me also?

But perhaps Paul, when he wrote, "Not as though I had attained neither were already perfect," did not feel thus. Perhaps as he led no life of compromises with the world as I have done, as "the world was crucified to him and he unto the world," there was a security in his face as he looked forward and as he looked backward; as he looked from a hill top on the valley he had passed and looked towards the bright afternoon sun. Could he sympathize with the struggling but often conquered *Christian?* Can I presume to place myself, if not on a level, yet in the same pathway with him? Was there any need of further exertion that he might reach the crown, or had he it not on his head? In short, can I claim a share in the feelings of such a man? Is it for me he has left the declaration that he had not yet attained, and the advice to forget the things that are behind and press forward to that which is before? I cannot doubt that it is for me he has written these words, when I read his confession that he had something yet to learn concerning Christ and the power of His resurrection; when I find that he urges on himself the necessity of earnest haste and zeal to apprehend and secure these blessings for which he was apprehended and enlisted by Christ in his service; and when I find him exhorting all to whom he wrote to be together followers of him. Let me then consider what he intended by forgetting that which is behind.

It will be plain, I think, that he did not mean *absolute* forgetfulness, an entire fading out of the mind of all remembrances of past life. How would this be possible, or to be desired, if it were possible? What would then become of experience, of the motives running over from the past to guard and purify the future, of the fountain of thankfulness which deep memories supply, or even of faith itself resting for its support on past deliverances? Or are *sins* in the past alone to be forgotten? How, then, are the blessed fruits of holiness to grow out of sorrow for them continually? Will that argument of the Apostle Peter ever lose its force: "for the time past of our lives is more than sufficient to have wrought the will of the flesh?" Or can the sorrow of having wasted life and lived away from God ever be wholly buried up and smothered by time? Nay, will not holiness itself draw sorrow from the remotest recollection of sin?

It is *comparative* forgetfulness then, that the Apostle means. It must not be our chief religious work to remember the past, but to press forward towards something better in the future. And here we may say,

I. *First, that it is not good or healthy for a soul to brood over past sin.* There is such a thing as disturbing the balance between the two parts of repentance, sorrow for sin and active obedience. Sorrow for sin is foundation work. Should a man be employed all his days in laying foundations, what could he do besides? It may be well to look down now and then to see that there are no flaws or cracks in the lower parts of the house, but we must be putting story upon story, and finishing the upper chambers or we shall accomplish nothing. "Therefore, leaving the principles of the doctrine of Christ let us go on unto perfection, not laying again the foundation of repentance from dead works."

Sorrow for sin too is *subordinate* work. It has no value in itself apart from its necessary action on character. Let a man stop there, what has he gained, what has God gained? Is not forgiveness, or as it is called in the Bible, God's having our sins no more in remembrance, intended to put them in a certain sense out of our remembrance, and to aid us in thinking of better things towards which forgiveness opens the prospect?

And this also deserves to be noticed that *brooding over past sins has a dangerous influence on character,* as might be inferred from the fact that it is not what God calls us to. In its extreme, when unattended with hope, it becomes *remorse.* Did ever good grow out of remorse, or is it not a paralysis of soul, where power over the will is lost? What can be more deadening and benumbing to character than a fixed state of inaction, a sorrow followed by no effort to relieve one's self from that which arouses the sorrow? "The sorrow of the world worketh death."

And when this sorrow is not remorse, but is attended with a slight hope of forgiveness, it may be excessive—I do not mean out of proportion to our sins, but too great for the proper play of the active powers; in short, as the Apostle Paul says, such a penitent is in danger of being "swallowed up with overmuch sorrow." The whole harmony of our nature is disturbed by a tendency to brood over the past. In a certain sense it is right to say,—"I cannot undo my sins; regret for them cannot wipe them out! Why then should I give the whole energy of my soul to the thought of them? If I am truly sorry for them that is enough. It is better that I should be doing my life-work of glorifying God, and serving my generation than that I should be increasing the sense of my unworthiness, and crowding my mind with poignant regrets. The natural course is from a right estimate of sin to sorrow for it, from sorrow to the purpose of new obedience. If I fail of this last, I fail of whatever is most important, and I surely shall fail, if all my religion gathers itself on this one point of looking back upon my past life. Suppose I felt my ignorance as keenly without one exertion to remedy it by acquisitions of knowledge; or brooded in despondency over my ill health without the use of diet and medicine; or over any deficiency or inaptitude until my mind became full of it to the exclusion of other things. Is this a hopeful state of mind? Is there any cure in such treatment of our maladies, whether of the mind or soul? No; better would it be, if possible, to forget all my past sin, than *thus* to remember it, *without remembering also* the Gospel provisions and the Gospel motives for sinners."

II. But secondly I must forget the things that are behind in this sense also,—that *I must not infer what my religious life for the future will be from the probabilities of the past.*

The doctrine of probabilities is a very good one to go upon in worldly matters, wherever a permanent law prevails, or wherever there are constant reasons in nature or in man for exceptions from general laws of God. Only ascertain what has happened in the past, and you will know what shall happen in the future. Here the rule is—*remembering* "the things that are behind I press forward." Only ascertain by careful record how many have died and at what age, in a given climate and with a given proficiency of medical science, how many houses burn up in the year, how many shipwrecks occur, how many persons kill themselves or kill others, and you know what to expect hereafter, until causes of variation change the probabilities of things. You can thus carry on your insurances of lives and against wrecks to a profit; you will be tolerably certain that the average temperature, mortality, amount of crime, increase of population will be the same next year, or for the next ten years, as for the last year or the last decade.

Now suppose that I should adopt this principle of judging in regard to the probabilities of my spiritual course for the future. I have maturely considered my past life, and find just about such an amount of attainment, little if any progress, the same constitutional sins vanquishing me again and again, the same obstructions to my spiritual progress rising up here and there all along my way, effort scarcely rewarded, and great effort succeeded by a natural weariness and unwatchfulness. In short, I analyze my character as a chemist would his compound. I find such a small percentage of the noble metal and so much of the worthless earth. Or I judge, as the underwriters of an insurance policy,—so many failures, so many sins. To-morrow shall be as to-day. That is the law of character. No essential improvement, at the best a slow, fixed advance. My rate is ascertained, and will not materially alter until the machine gives way and the wheels stop.

Now I want to ask, if the Apostle Paul had in his mind all the statistics of character and condition that the newest tables supply, whether he would have made this use of the past? You answer, almost in scorn, No! by no means. And why not? *Is* it because character is not true to itself, has no principles to rest upon, and rules to work by, but flashes out, rocket-like, in random, uncertain vagaries? Or is it because there are not sad, disheartening probabilities running over from the past into the present, and filling the soul with a feeling of exhaustion and of fear at the great work lying ahead in life? Or is it not rather because there are *factors in the spiritual life*, which can change the face of things to any extent, and which hide from all calculations of the probable. Suppose you were deliberately to say, that it is not probable that the *divine Spirit* would give you more strength hereafter than now, or that He would not lift you up to a holier life, or that you should never have any renewals or quickenings, any cheering impulses more than you have had in the dull desert of the past? Would you not feel that such an estimate of spiritual probabilities was all but impious—that it was false, because it reduced the agency of the freest of all beings to the working of a law; that it almost denied the reality of a spiritual world, whose movements, powers, and intentions are wholly aside from finite calculation?

Beware then, my brethren, how you remember your past life only to throw discouragement over your exertions and hopes for the future. Such a habit is destructive of faith and of hope; or rather springs from the want of them both. Forget the things that are behind, and firmly believe, that it is very possible, yes! very natural, for you to grow faster in goodness in a year, than you have grown in ten, or in all your life. Firmly believe that resources, you know not how great, are within your reach, that you have within yourselves, with God's help, a power of resistance to evil, and of growth in good, which has never yet been put forth,—believe this; and you can and may yet see days of brightness such as you have always thought improbable. To him who takes spiritual agencies into view, progress is natural, sloth and stagnation are unnatural. You have been despondent because you have been worldly. Keep God in sight, and all things are possible.

III. Akin to this last remark is another, which deserves notice by itself, that *we must not remember the past as our standard of action or character.* It would be better to forget our whole life, sins and all, than to look back with a sense of satisfaction. And here let me make a distinction. A man who is conscious of high purposes running as main threads through the web of life may be glad, as he takes his reviews of bygone days, that the grace of God has enabled him to live on the whole up to the level of Christian principles. He will thus say with Paul, "for our rejoicing is this, the testimony of our conscience, that in simplicity and godly sincerity, not with fleshly wisdom but by the grace of God we have had our conversation in this world." Was now the Apostle, when he wrote this, satisfied with himself, and content to run along as he had done without rising higher? This we cannot impute to him, for he would be inconsistent, if such were his feelings, in writing, "not as though I had already attained or were already made perfect." There must ever be a discontent with themselves in the minds of Christians. Until perfection is reached in all respects, until all the inner movements are of the right kind and in the right degree, the chasm between actual attainment and the standard will seem vast, and the vaster, the higher the aim of the Christian. And he may well suspect himself either of declension or of something worse, who is content to live as he has lived in the past. This discontent is nothing more than the soul's judgment against itself of having fallen below the life to which God has called it, of having made little of its spiritual advantages, of having feebly used its spiritual capacities; and with such a deep-seated sense of short-coming there will often be united a desire to be transplanted to a better sphere in the hope of escaping from sin.

Hence to forget the past, in the sense of the Apostle, and to remember it in order to avoid its evils are one and the same thing. If we can feel with Peter "that the time past of our lives is more than sufficient to have wrought the will of the flesh," if thus we lose sight of it as a *standard* and remember it only as a *warning*, we shall do what Paul says he did. Feeling that we have not attained, and carrying in our minds the causes and items of our past mistakes, we shall run forward the more diligently and earnestly. The farther we get from our past experience,—so far as it is one of sin,—the better. The higher we can rise above our past selves the nearer we shall come to God. If the world has had an undue hold on me heretofore—let each one say,—it shall have so much the less hold in the future. If I have been distrustful, or covetous, or have given way to any besetting sin, oh, how much I have clogged myself. What a different person I might have been in these years since I first set out on my journey heavenward! Oh! let me now throw the more zeal into my efforts to lead a holy life, the more cause I have to be dissatisfied with my surveys of the life I have spent. Let me feel that I have made really no attainments until I have reached my goal.

IV. And thus we come to what is the Apostle's principal thought, that the soul must be so occupied with the future, that the past shall be only subordinate and subsidiary. If I have been in wretchedness all my past existence, the fact and the remembrance are of no account, except so far as they help me to escape from my misery and heighten my enjoyment by contrast. If I have been poor, and now the door to wealth is opened, exertion to gain it is the main thing, and I may wholly forget my poverty, if motives enough from other sources stimulate me to action. So if I have been ignorant and am now advanced a little way in knowledge, my sense of ignorance may urge me on a little, but the boundless expanse of knowledge, opening before me, will incite me far more. It is better to have the mind filled with what can and ought to be done, than to be living in the past, and living over the past. "Reaching forth unto those things which are before," is the Apostle's motto. The future has in it possibilities almost infinite. Two Christians starting alike to-day, but pursuing different courses, the one running on with his face turned to the past, and the other *pressing*, and looking towards the mark,—will be next year, or at the end of life, at an immense distance from one another. Here is a man who is forever brooding over his sins. What strenuous exertions can he make, if he do not rather give up the hopes of the Christian life with its joys? Here is another, who thinks the future will be as the past, the same gloomy record of unexecuted resolutions and unfinished efforts. If faith in God and hope of success are necessary for success, what can such a man do except stagnate in his sins? Here is a third, who thinks that the past presents a pretty fair record on which he can dwell without dissatisfaction. What will he do more or better than he has done? These are the men that are looking backward. But here is one again who has, we will suppose, been sadly foiled and disappointed heretofore, who has done very little of what he purposed when he began to be a Christian. Broken vows, unfinished efforts lie strown all along his way. His life seems a failure. Can such a kind of Christian he says, enter heaven? But I will not despair, he adds, until two things *fail*,—until God who offers the help of His Spirit deludes me, and until the object I have to attain shall seem less momentous than it does now. And so he throws himself on the effort to be a better, holier man, with a kind of self-abandonment, as the sailor trusts himself to the deep. Farewell, land, says he. I must look out at the bow, not at the stern, spread all sail, and get across this interval between me and my port, or perish.

Oh, my Christian friends, let us forget all but God and Christ, and the great work before us. Let us, by an act of resolute, constant will, make all things else of such minor importance, that they shall not take up undue room in our souls, leaving no space for nobler things. Are we dissatisfied with ourselves? But with God's help we can become other men ; we can, I may say, cease to be ourselves, even as we profess not to be our own. Are we discouraged? But "the Lord, the Creator of heaven and earth, fainteth not, neither is weary. To them that have no might He increaseth strength." Is it too hard a work to be an earnest Christian? Why did we set out, and why do we not return at once to our sins? Is there not a fair prospect of success? And if we fail, shall we lose anything by resolute endeavor? Is there not a positive gain to character, in heroic, earnest effort, even if we were to grasp a shadow? But what we aim at is not a shadow. It is that for which we are apprehended of Christ Jesus. It is the prize of the high calling of God. Unless God calls, and Christ takes hold of our souls for *nothing*, we are running forward to secure the very thing for which we were made. Let us so run that we may obtain.

SERMON XV.

SOBRIETY OF MIND URGED ON YOUNG MEN.

TITUS ii. 6. Young men, likewise, exhort to be sober-minded.*

ALL Christian goodness is one in its essence, and the many forms of virtue, with which it beautifies the character, spring from the same root. It is one sovereign principle for all relations, temperaments, conditions and ages, while yet, through the imperfection of human nature, one off-shoot may need more tending and vigilance than another. The Christian moralist will take both these considerations into view; while he insists on radical Christian virtue, in its forms of faith, love or godliness, he will not neglect urging men to those derived and particular qualities of character, which imply the principle within, and of necessity flow from it.

One such quality, or department of godliness, the apostle has in view in the text, where he would have young men exhorted to be sober-minded. The quality is of equal obligation for all periods of life—it is a necessary outgrowth of the hidden life in all; and yet, if Godliness has sway over the character of the Christian in advanced life, sobriety of mind will have become deep-seated in him almost of course, while on the other hand, the youthful Christian is peculiarly exposed to danger just at this point, and a failure here, would obstruct his course through life, if not prove fatal to the existence of piety.

But the reasons for exhorting young men to this virtue will be made more apparent in the sequel: at present we

* A Baccalaureate sermon preached in 1858.

propose to ask what the sobriety of mind is which the Apostle Paul directs Titus to enforce upon Christian youth? What is it especially as a Christian virtue, growing out of the realities disclosed by the Gospel? How does it differ from native phlegm and caution? Is it akin to prudential abstinence from whatever will damage our earthly interests, or has it a solider foundation and a higher aim? How does it differ from the virtue of similar name cultivated by philosophic discipline? What are the leading motives by which it should be enforced? Such questions I shall attempt to answer, in the hope that distinct views of the nature of this quality may be of use, and especially that the class, which will assemble for the last time in this house of worship, may carry something away with them, which may help them in the scenes of an untried world.

The term *sobriety* of mind, according to its original import, denoted a *negation*—the absence of intoxication. From this more sensual starting point it proceeded to denote the removal of all such exciting influences as tend to blind and bewilder the mind, to weaken the power of judgment, to bring our nature under the dominion of passions which plead for immediate gratification. It was felt to be a small thing if a man could control the love for strong drink; the mind could become stupefied and deranged by the force of more spiritual causes—imaginations and desires above the senses—and could lose the mastery over itself as completely as if it had suffered an intoxication. Thus sobriety of mind came to mean moral soundness or health, the dominion of reason over desire.

The word in our text, strictly translated, means "sound-minded," or healthy-minded, and implies the conviction that there is a certain standard of character, or condition of the mind which bears an analogy to health of body, a condition in which all the functions of the mind are in their right state, in which sound or healthy views of things are taken, in which no part of human nature is either inoperative or unduly developed. In this large sense, soundness of mind may serve as a description of the harmony or regular action implied in virtue; but inasmuch as the passions and desires, excited by objects which have strong influence over us in our present state of being, more than anything else destroy sanity of mind, the term is usually confined to the control over worldly desires, and to views of life which commend themselves to right reason. Thus, soundness of mind includes self-restraint and temperance, the former of which is the power of governing the passions, and the other the habit of using all pleasures without going to excess. But soundness or sobriety of mind is more radical than either of these, for it includes those just views of life, that appreciation of the value of enjoyment and of the world compared with duty and the higher life of the soul, without the sway of which in the soul it can neither exercise continence nor self-control, nor temperance. Soundness or sobriety of mind, also, is far from stopping at the boundaries of the passions, especially the sensual; all the desires, even those which have little to do with the body, as the desire of fame, of power, of superiority, and the desire of wealth—the means of gratifying all other desires—are placed under its control.

1. *As thus understood, sobriety of mind is to be distinguished, we remark first, from a native sluggishness or cautiousness which may conspire with it to prevent excess.* It is not, in its true idea, of a physical nature. Some men are born with more of the animal, others with more of the spiritual about them. Some are constitutionally impetuous and unreflecting; others are cool and thoughtful. Some are unsuspicious, others descry danger afar off. Some, by the force of imagination, dress up enjoyment to themselves in gala robes, and have the power of kindling up desire by beautifying and magnifying the object out of

which it is drawn; others are matter of fact persons who have no skill to throw halos around things either good or bad. Some again learn quick from the experience of evil; others, either because they are hopeful or because they forget past impressions, yield to the solicitations of desire, until a habit of being overcome, and a sense of moral weakness root out the very thought of resistance.

The mind which possesses a constitutional sobriety, derived from sources such as we have named, may steer its way safely through many of the perils of life, and, perhaps, when exposed to particular temptations, may conquer by insensibility, where weak Christian principle, united with strong propensity, might be overcome. It may be well to have a nature in which there is no master passion, or if that cannot be, to have one where the calculation of consequences is a wakeful foe of excess. But this native temperament is, of course, not the sobriety of mind to which the Apostle exhorts, since it is not voluntarily assumed, nor easily shaken off. Nor can such a nature go far in the way of moral discipline; if it keeps out vice, it keeps out virtue. It cannot, therefore, by victories over faults, promote the great ends of a life of trial in this world. At the best, such a cold, cautious nature is the negation of evil; no interesting or lofty character ever grew upon such a stock. If a man, for instance, can never become angry, he may be saved from many foolish and sinful acts, but it is many times better to have a subdued power of anger, which you have acquired by exertions which have cost you something, than to be a stone.

Moreover, if such native sobriety of mind exists, it is rare. There is generally some weak spot, where passion can with success approach men who seem like icicles. What class of persons is more thoroughly worldly than many who are proof against the allurements of vice, but speculate with the gambler's intense excitement, or burn with a devouring lust for power. Perhaps the greatest insobriety of mind belongs to those who, in most respects, have an entire mastery over themselves,—who view the world on many of its sides as it is, but concentrate all their forces on one object, with an untiring restless fever of soul, which the votary of pleasure seldom knows.

2. *A second thought suggests itself here, that the Apostle's sober-mindedness is not to be confounded with that self-control which springs from worldly prudence and shrewd calculations of success in life.* There are men who live exclusively for earthly enjoyment, who yet have attained to a mastery over their own lusts. They know what the laws of health will allow, what the body will bear, how far they may go in pleasure consistently with prudence and economy, what degree of restraint is demanded to preserve their reputation. They will, therefore, keep themselves sober while their less discreet, and perhaps less corrupt, companions are intoxicated at their side; they live a long healthy life, while others die of the effects of vicious indulgence, and retain their good name while others ruin themselves in the opinion of society. Verily, they have their reward; but their sober-mindedness is certainly no such virtue that even a philosopher could commend it.

Another illustration to the same effect is afforded by the money-making spirit. Covetousness is a passion which puts on a grave aspect, subdues the soul into regularity, methodizes time, prevents extravagance, leaves no vacant room for sensuality, and, like the nobler aims of our nature, looks far beyond the present moment. You would call a man, therefore, who is domineered over by covetousness, a sober-minded man; and, indeed, many of his feelings and opinions are on the side of good order and the well-being of society. It is a vice into which sober Pharisees are apt to fall. An avaricious man is often quite religious; he goes to church; he pays for a pew; he believes in conversion—perhaps, he thinks himself converted. Is he now deserving of the name "sober-minded," or "sound-minded?" Look into his soul, which is full of excited hopes, of speculative projects, of feverish anxieties; look at his mercantile morality, which permits false commendations of what he has to sell, unfair advantages in a bargain, jealousies and misrepresentations of a competitor, and say whether such a man is sober, or even sane?

Another form still of insobriety of mind, under the garb of gravity and decorum, is exceedingly common in this country; it is found in the political aspirant. A little knowledge of men convinces such a person that in order to succeed in his chosen life, he must gain confidence by the appearance of honesty and morality, but cannot gain office without suppressing his feelings and sacrificing his principles, on occasions when his interests demand it. Accordingly he gives an external adherence to the laws of morality by which society is governed, and professes to hold Christianity in respect. He bridles his temper, because to yield to anger in the conflicts of party would place him at a disadvantage. He controls his appetites, if he finds that self-indulgence will take confidence away from him. In short, he is consummately prudent, but within he is full of hatred, anxieties, cravings, discontents, which, if they could be seen, would show how far he is from a sound mind.

These illustrations bring us to the conclusion that prudence, as it is generally understood, is a low principle of action. Being nothing more than enlightened selfishness, it does not deserve the name of a virtue. It may be the helmsman to steer the baldest and meanest worldliness to its destined point, just as it may assist weak virtue by its timely suggestions. It is often found in opposition to the noblest impulses which man can feel. It would have been, doubtless, very imprudent for the young man in the Gospel to sell all and follow Christ, very imprudent to declare one's self as Christian and be burnt at the stake for it, very imprudent to avow your honest convictions and lose the good will or custom of society. In these cases, as the servant of fear, it opposes conscience honor and religious principle; in other cases, as the servant of an earthly mind, it may oppose faith in eternal realities. Sobriety of mind, then, is not learned by habits of mere prudence, nor is the character in which it prevails of course open to right impressions, nor is it a very great gain, if we look at the highest interests of the soul, to exhort young men to be prudent and there to stop. The Pharisees were more prudent and calculating than the publicans, but they shut their ears to Christ. And at this day, we find the worldliest persons, however used to prudence and self-control, the least capable of anything lofty or noble.

3. Sobriety of mind, being something more than a temperament averse to excess, something more than self-control on selfish principles, may be looked at as a philosophical, or as a Christian virtue. In both cases, it is a subordination of the desires and passions to the higher principles of the soul; in both, it is a spontaneous self-government according to the rules of right living, not according to calculations of temporal advancement. All philosophy has assigned to this virtue of *sophrosune*, as the Greeks, or *temperantia* as the Latins called it, a very prominent place. It is one of Plato's four generic virtues, and sometimes he assigns to it so wide a range as to include his cardinal virtue of justice. Nay, in the matter of desire, philosophers have gone beyond this point of self-restraint, on the theory that desire in its own nature is evil, and the root of all evil. They have taught that perfection can be reached only by extinguishing desire, by waging war with every bodily appetite and every affection. Thus they have substituted abstinence for temperance, annihilation of desire for moderation, apathy for

self-control; but they have also made virtue impossible for the mass of men, and introduced into the world an asceticism which bore the fruit of moroseness or of spiritual pride.

But where philosophy has kept near to the *true* idea of sobriety of mind, it has wanted authority and motive. It has found its arguments for the virtue in the beauty of the virtue itself, apart from the will of God, and from the sobering influences of the doctrine of eternal life. By not teaching that man in himself is weak through sin, and that he can obtain help from on high, it has lost sight of the greatest encouragement to perseverance, and the surest preventive of despair. By treating the virtues as if they were separate plants, instead of growths from one common principle, it has scattered men's efforts to improve themselves, and directed their attention to the stream rather than the fountain. Finally, it had not truth enough in its hands to work any radical change in human character: God, a positive law, the great issues of conduct, were hid from its eyes, and only such truth remained, for the discipline of natures prone to excess, as might be picked up along the path of experience, or derived from the doctrine of the beautiful and the good.

When we speak of Christian sobriety of mind, we mean nothing generically different from the notion which philosophy had already formed. But we mean sobriety of mind sustained by Christian principles, enforced by Christian motives, and dwelling amid other manifestations of a Christian or purified character. Let us consider it when thus broadly understood, in some of its most prominent characteristics.

1. *First, it involves an estimate of earthly pleasure and good formed under the power of faith.*

The first feeling of a noble soul, after discovering the doctrine of immortal life, might be conceived to be an intense disgust with everything earthly. So small a sphere for such a being! Such prison walls for a freeman with godlike properties and duration! Such food of the pettiest earthly trifles instead of ambrosial meats! Why should I not enter the great temple at once, instead of wandering listlessly about the gates? Why not imitate the philosophic youth of old, who threw himself from the rock, in order to reach his soul's higher existence by a short road?

But no! says the Gospel. Life cannot be disgusting to the wise man, nor is it filled with trifles, for everything in it connects itself with eternity. It is the school for the formation of unalterable character, the starting point in a course of endless good or evil, the first act of a drama of the profoundest meaning. Its little duties and trials are contrived with a view to vast results: they look forward to the attainment of angelic excellence. These desires which stir within you, and bring you into necessary relations to this present life, give also to this life much of its deep import, for on your treatment of them depends your everlasting welfare. The question in regard to them is, whether they shall reign or serve; whether they shall dazzle the soul, or whether the light of God, giving every object and each word its due importance, shall be perceived; whether, in view of the great issues of conduct, you will quit yourself like a man, keeping body and soul in subjection to righteousness, or lose the thought that you have any eternal interests to secure. You ought then to feel your immortality in every limb and every faculty, to move about as a creature of the skies which has shed its wings for a season, to carry into every plan and action a consciousness of your destiny.

The doctrine of a future life does not tend to calm and subdue the desires *only* by the *fear* of the consequences of excess, and the *hope* of the rewards of virtue, but it serves also as a measure of the immense value of virtue and the immense evil of sin. If the soul capable of stretching its thoughts into eternity and of loving like God were to die with the body, of what great importance would virtue be? Would not God, if moral quality were the highest of things in his regard, give it a duration reaching beyond half a century? Do we not judge of the value of other things in part by their permanence? So men must reason; and, on the other hand, in the immortal life which God has assigned to the soul, they must find a proof how He reckons the value of character, and a motive to subjugate the desires. It now becomes a more serious question how I shall live: virtue and vice have put on new dimensions, and grown to a gigantic size. Let us eat and drink, for to-morrow we die, says the unbeliever. Let us cultivate our undying powers, and feed with heavenly food that which is to last forever, says the Christian. To the one, the gratification of worldly desire is the essence and end of life; to the view of the other, they who live in pleasure are dead while they live, and there is no true life which does not take hold of immortality.

And, again, faith in the God of revelation and in Christ produces sobriety of mind, by exalting the standard of excellence. In the Scriptures the mind is brought into intimacy with objects most remote from excited desire; spiritual things are so opposite to sensual, that even a feeble conception of God's holiness tends to allay anger, quench lust, and bring a momentary calm into the soul even of the worst of men. Were there no express code of morals, the soul familiar with God would dread and shrink from inordinate desire by a moral instinct, for his character speaks with the force of law. So, too, God in human flesh, living amid these same lusts which corrupt mankind, and overcoming them, has brought a new standard into this world. What an infinite distance between His calm look at both worlds, His superiority to desires even the most innocent, and the feverish thirst, the intense longings for momentary good of earthly minds.

With His advent into the world, a new idea of life began, and the victory of the spirit over the flesh is rendered possible.

2. But it is not enough to have a standard of character; the young man, if he would be sober-minded, must have rules of living calculated beforehand to resist the allurements of the world when they arise. In some branches of morality, it may be most advisable to act without definite rules, making the inner spirit the guide of conduct. Nor will rules in any department of ethics, without such a central regulator, even if observed, fail of being followed by undue self-confidence, and thus of preparing the way for their own violation. But rules are especially needed to keep the soul in due sobriety, because the excited desires sweep in sudden gusts over the soul, prostrating reason, conscience, and even prudence before them. If a liability to such bursts of desire is allowed, the habit must ensue of giving way to them; thus two evil habits, that of inordinate desire or passion, and that of giving up self-control, support one another, and grow together. The rule or maxim at such times may be that on which the mind may fall back. It is a kind of fortress reared by the wisdom and thoughtfulness of the past, to which the assaulted soul may retire until it has recruited its strength for the battle.

It is the part of Christian ethics to make known what rules are needed for our moral guidance, and to enforce them by the appropriate motives. In this place, no such thing can be attempted, and yet I cannot pass on without calling your attention to one or two parts of conduct, where it is peculiarly important to have well settled principles of action.

In regard to the bodily appetites, Christian sobriety begins to be lost as soon as they are made *ends* in themselves, without regard to something higher. Here, then, if any where, we must begin to put forth a self-denying will. An appetite within its sphere, subordinate to the great purpose for which it was implanted, as that of hunger for the support of the body, has no kind of evil influence on the spiritual nature. Out of that sphere it becomes a ferocious tyrant,—one that not only enslaves the soul, but destroys the power of recovery.

The question of abstinence, or moderate use, apart from its bearings on others, and where gratification is innocent, is a question to be determined by individual strength. To abstain from things innocent, is a confession of weakness. Yet such a confession is better than presumptuous self-trust and indulgence after you are overcome.

In regard to amusements and diversions, sobriety consists in keeping them in their place, as recreations after bodily and mental toil. They must not then usurp the rights of labor, unless we are resolved to destroy the earnestness and seriousness of character, which grows out of a conviction that life is full of meaning. The insane love of amusement is even more despicable than the insane gratification of the appetites. We see natures of very high capacity enthralled by sensuality, who have glimpses of a better life, and struggle hard at times to fulfill the ends for which an immortal soul was given them. But the thorough votary of amusement is a mere earth-worm, without aspirations, and without powers to rise into the air.

The sober Christian is taught by the precepts of the New Testament to beware especially *of covetousness.* The *love of gain* is one of the most dangerous of the desires, on account of its expressing itself in the soberest acts of an industrious life, and on account of its comprehensiveness. As money stands for every commodity, so covetousness steps in front of every desire, acting now as the representative of the love of pleasure, now of the necessary wants of life, and now even of real or counterfeit benevolence. A desire so wide-sweeping is as widely dangerous. The Christian, as he looks abroad over life, beholds here the cause of shipwrecks of character, of damaged fortunes, of ruined hopes. It defeats its own ends by running out into wild speculation. It is, as we have said before, a sad, staid, sober passion, and seems to those who admit it into their hearts to be allied to all the virtues of society, but it is, for all that, a fire that consumes the soul with burning cares, it magnifies the world, and absorbs all the thoughts. To no man is eternity so far off as to the covetous man. No worldling is more justly called an idolater.

The sober Christian, then, will not aim and bend the efforts of his life to be rich. He cannot do this, for the love of riches is a brief term for the love of earthly objects, it is worldly-mindedness condensed. If in the course of his honest industry, or by some other act of Divine Providence, riches come into his hands, they are his to use under a sense of his increased responsibility. The probability is that he will have *more* of them, the certainty is that he will use them *better* than if he had spent the energies of his soul on the desire of accumulation.

The love of political distinction and popular favor easily runs, in our country, into an absorbing passion, which in its course we see overflowing honesty, truthfulness and all moral principle. How can a serious man consent to hazard his character and his soul in such a pursuit? He cannot seek office for its own sake, nor expose himself to those temptations which he sees ruining so many men of aspiring minds throughout the country. His only question will be, whether he may hold it when it is offered to him without his seeking; whether the depraving influences of public life are not too great to expose himself to such a snare.

3. Need I add that rules must be followed by a settled purpose, by a resolution formed in the view of spiritual and divine truth to adopt such a course of life as sobriety of mind requires. The purpose must be rigorous, admit-

ting no compromises nor exceptions, nor giving way when a great opportunity offers, as when some vast speculation would gather treasures for a whole life. It must be thus a settled purpose, on which temporary excitements shall beat without effect. We see in this country of ours too many fitful Christians, who are burning a large part of the time with the intensest craving for wealth, and deny to their souls all food of heavenly meditation. From this fever they are recovered by a temporary religious awakening, only to relapse again after a few months. Whether they are Christians at all we may not judge, but certainly they are far from the sobriety of mind with which Christianity endows the soul.

Such are some of the requisites for maintaining sobriety of mind: that a standard of life and thought be formed under the influence of spiritual things, that rules of conduct be provided to assist the soul amid the assaults of tempestuous desire, and that an earnest purpose of living according to the law of the Gospel engage on the side of Christian sobriety all the effective force of the will.

4. And if this essentially Christian duty of sobriety of mind is binding on all, it needs *to be pressed with especial earnestness on young men,* who are apt to fail just at this point. Without the lessons of experience, impulsive and incautious, proverbially hopeful, often dazzled by the colors which their own imaginations throw around the objects of pursuit, who need so much as they a voice of counsel and of solemn warning, drawn from the eternal issues of conduct? Who need so much to be led away in thought from time, in which they are just beginning to be actors, and to be instructed to measure things by a divinely furnished rule of judgment? Their minds naturally, and by a divine appointment, take hold of life with a strong zest; and earthly desires are at their side, urging them, according to the design of their existence, to the fulfillment of earthly duties, and yet able to draw

them away into every excess. Feeling is exuberant, temper quick, passsion strong; the evil of indulgence is unknown, or lies afar off and may not be guarded against; restraint has not become habitual. Let all go on in an unchecked progress, let there be no light from the skies to reveal higher duties and a nobler life, and what preservative is there against the mad sweep of sensual passions, if the temperament lead that way, or against the insane thirst for gold or office?

How precious then, ought that fountain to be regarded from which sobering draughts may be continually drawn, which tells us of a *blessed life,* that is passed in calmness where no gusts of passion invade, and is to be measured, not by outbursts of wild joy, but by the depth of an inward peace; which tells us of a *holy life,* whose communings with an Infinite Father and a Divine Saviour curb, as by a wand of magic, every lust, and bring the soul into harmony; which tells us of a *noble life* full of great purposes, the least of which is worth more to the soul than all that pleasure ever promised; which tells us of a *life looking out beyond the grave,* and in its measurements finding all objects bounded by this world to be ineffably small, all lusts which make us earthly to be our chief enemies. Oh! my friends, come to that fountain; wait not for the experiences of the bitter, to teach you the sweet; wait not to be taught prudence by the necessity of choosing between two master passions, one of which burns and the other freezes the soul, but learn wisdom here and take it with you into life.

To exhort young men to be sober-minded is also a hopeful task, however much the levity and thoughtlessness of youth may seem to make it a difficult one. They have, unless some premature corruption has gathered its black cloud over them, a readiness to receive impressions from moral beauty and harmony; they have an unworldly character; their earthliness having as yet taken the form of particular acts of exuberant feeling or of boiling passion, rather than that of fixed, downward-looking purposes. A young man, when won over to habits of sober-minded piety, has it in his power to cultivate a rounded, harmonious, beautiful life, which grows serener and calmer to its end. When the hoary victim of passion, the worn-out slave of covetousness, or the profligate, false-hearted politician, seeks the consolations of religion in old age, after he has lost the relish and the benefit of his sins, religion welcomes him indeed, useless as he may be to her. But her discipline of him is that of the hospital, where his maimed and shattered character can be nursed through the remaining fragment of life. But in the man who has taken on him, when young, the habits of Christian sobriety, we see the heavenly life engrafted on the stock of fresh character, and so penetrating it, that all his conduct seems to be the easy flow of an uninjured nature.

And if such a young man reaches the boundaries of old age, what a blessed sight is he. The fire of anger, which he has controlled his life-long, plays only in a genial flame of indignation against sin. Those baser appetites, which cost him perhaps many a struggle to overcome, have died out of his character. Covetousness, as it never filled him with evil cravings in his manhood, so has no torment of miserly fears for his old age. His brow of peace tells of numberless triumphs over sin, followed by undisturbed repose. Such an old age of dignity and peace, when we see it among us, is a purifying power in society,—it is a protest against exaggerated feelings and excited desires, it is a forerunner of heavenly rest. Compare it, in its tranquility and noiseless movement, with the disappointment, the self-reproach, the weariness and emptiness of a worldling, who feels the bitter penal sobering of life in its dregs, and see in it the beauty of the gospel.

It deserves also to be noticed that from habits of Christian sobriety a young man finds *a moral taste* springing up within him, which is both a beautifier and a conservator of character. To him, accustomed to the quiet workings of a soul obedient to supreme order, all lawless movement, outbursts of passion, fitful displays of force, whatever in the soul "suffers the nature of an insurrection," is a mark of disease and weakness. Greatness he symbolizes not by the vexed sea-surface, but by the profound still depths of ocean, not by the volcano, but by the mountain resting on its everlasting base, not by the super-human force of the maniac, but by energy of will controlled by reason. With such a taste he passes judgment on character, on literature and art; he is offended by agitations, convulsive efforts, action or feeling beyond the occasion. He is attracted by quiet unobtrusive manners and by natures which hold in reserve a part of their power. In religion he looks for action without noise, and feeling, ever gushing forth, but ever under control. Thus does religion, by subduing the fever of worldly desire, refine his judgment, and raise his style of feeling. Without knowing it, he has gained an instinct of moral propriety, which is one of the fairest blossoms of a religious life.

Such are some of the reasons for exhorting young men to be sober-minded. But besides these general considerations, there is *one* to be *drawn from the opposite tendency of our times and country.* The spirit of the times shows a preponderance of the subjective in all departments of thinking and acting. Feeling has become more intense, action more hurried, whether in religion, politics, or ordinary life. But in our country, there are reasons why there should be more of this spirit than in the rest of the world. By our temperament we are rendered rapid and eager. In action we are unfettered, and desire finds objects to attract it on every side. Our great prosperity and success add force to courage and zeal; we are hopeful, incautious and speculative. Freedom of intercourse, and diffusion of knowledge, circulate feeling with electric speed; we move in masses, and intensify each other's feeling by sympathy. We spend heedlessly on pleasure, because we feel no great need of laying up for the future. Material comforts are greatly enlarged without a due advance of intellectual improvement. The great energies of the nation are directed to that which is present and outward; we are unreflecting, like children. Intensely anxious to obtain present results, we cannot wait and let the future ripen our labors. And so pleasure bursts forth into enormous excesses, covetousness runs into the wildest speculations; contentment, calmness, unambitiousness, are rare virtues. A spirit like this ends in the most intense worldliness, which would be our speedy ruin, did not disasters continually call us back to reflection, and did not religion interfere to save us. How peculiarly great the need of watchfulness and self-restraint within, where all is thus in a constant agitation without us. How can we stand our ground against the prevalent sin of exorbitant desire, with no unusual effort to keep our hearts near to God and eternal things? Does it not become us preeminently to cultivate each for himself, that true independence of character which follows God's judgment of things in opposition to man's, so that, when the flood of popular thinking rushes by us, we may stand upright and unshaken in our place?

BELOVED PUPILS, CANDIDATES FOR THE DEGREE OF BACHELOR OF ARTS:—

The lesson of this discourse, which I hope to leave on your memory, is, that there is a sobriety of mind, far unlike a dispassionate temperament and the self-discipline of worldly prudence, which is built on Christian faith in things invisible,—God and Christ, and a future life—and which consists in subjugating the passions and desires to the law of reason enlightened by religion. To such a sobriety—the mind's true health and peace—I invite you this day. I exhort you, as you leave these scenes for a world of excitements, to resolve before God, that you will carry the realities of spiritual life in your minds, wherever your pilgrimage through this world may lie,—into business, into study, into office, if that should be laid upon you; that you will not rush into the absorbing pursuits of the world as if they were your life, but with the eye of meditative faith will keep in view the higher life beyond. Nor do I alone, following the directions of the Scriptures, exhort you to sobriety of mind. The same lesson is urged on you from every quarter. There are voices of providence which urge to it. Within a few months you have witnessed one of the most wide-spread commercial disasters that have visited this country, the cause of which, in the main, was an eager, excited, insane desire of wealth, leading to over-trading, speculation, fraud, and the bankruptcy of multitudes, innocent as well as guilty. How empty after such a crisis does the soul appear that has staked all its happiness on the world, while the sober-minded man of moderate desires lives through the storm in blessed peace. Voices too from the dead enforce the same lesson. More than one classmate is crying to you from the world of spirits that a life of earthly desires ends in the dark, while a life of faith brightens into the perfect day of God. Within one short week a new voice has reached you from the waters, that overwhelmed one once belonging to your number. "So live each day," it cries, "that a sudden death shall not come upon you like a thief, and remember that death is ever sudden to him who has not shaken off his sins." Voices too of the Divine Spirit have added their persuasives to the calls of Providence. You have completed a year which is memorable in our collegiate history. At its beginning, several of you in calmness and thoughtfulness listened to the invitations of heavenly truth, and before it closed, numbers more, with many of your fellow-students, gave evidence of altered lives and new hopes. The same movement you have watched in its progress, generally without noise or agitation, through the land: great multitudes you have seen discovering that a treasure in heaven is better than wealth, and submitting their souls to the sobering, enlightening power of the Gospel.

With such voices urging you to a life of religious sobriety, you are going forth into a fascinating world. I do not overstate its dangers when I say, that no man, be he Christian or not, can go through the world safely unless he guards his heart against inordinate loves, and with firm purpose shuts his ear to the suggestions of evil. How will you stand in the day of hazard, and how will the dread balance be at last—for you, or against you? Oh! that grace may be given you to act wisely and thoughtfully. Then, as each one reaches his earthly goal, and launches away into the untrodden life of the Spirit, you may meet again in heavenly places, to keep up a virtuous fellowship forever. God grant that this may be so.—FAREWELL.

SERMON XVI.

REVERENCE AND ITS RELATION TO WORSHIP.

Exodus, iii. 5. And He said, Draw not nigh hither; put off thy shoes from off thy feet, for the place whereon thou standest is holy ground.

The command of our text was given when God appeared to Moses in the bush, under the symbol of an unconsuming flame. The place was holy by reason of God's special presence and of His intention to select it in the future as the spot for proclaiming His holy law. But the soles of Moses' sandals had come into contact with much that was polluted, and were too impure to tread upon consecrated ground. In thus commanding, God speaks not of a holiness belonging to the spot which lay in His own mind, but accommodates Himself to the apprehension of the finite mind. To a creature like man one spot might be more holy than another, because it suggested to his thoughts some special manifestation of the divine presence; and Moses, in order to show his sense of this holiness or his reverence for God, might with reason be called upon to perform a symbolical act which was suited to the genius of the age, was the natural language of the sentiment, and without which the sentiment would be chilled or stifled.

Since the unconsuming fire appeared to Moses at his initiation into his great office, there has been a two-fold change in the form of worship, or the expression of religious feeling. The first change has been that symbol, the sign presented to the eye or made by the human body, has given place to the language of the voice. In the earlier ages every symbol meant something and was intelligible. The language of bodily movement far surpassed in impressiveness the as yet imperfect dialect of religious intercourse. Men sought an utterance of the obscure feeling in the soul by a visible token of its presence, and there was a natural sign-language which was fitted for the ideas pertaining to divine worship. The complex ceremonial, which we now understand but in part, was full of life and meaning; it continued so until language reached its maturity, until spiritual ideas found a freer vent, and carried more force with them through words than through signs. It was no empty or arbitrary thing when men stretched their arms upward towards God in heaven in token of need of help; nor when they bowed or fell down before Him in token of unworthiness; nor when the priest in confessions of sin put his hand on the head of the goat, as if laying the burden of guilt on him; nor when incense fragrant to man's sense ascended in its wreaths of smoke to the sky, as a sign of the rising of accepted supplications.

The other great change since the time of Moses, is that worship is no longer *local.* Then an altar was built and consecrated, where in after times God might be sought, and where, more than elsewhere, men might hope to find Him propitious. *Then* there was a common centre of public worship, away from which no part of the public prescribed ritual could be accepted. *Israel* among the nations, *Jerusalem* in Israel, the *temple* at Jerusalem, the *most holy place* in the temple were so many sanctuaries, one within another, where religion shut herself up from the gaze of men, as yet unprepared to spread her light over the world. But in Christ all this was done away. "The hour cometh," says He, "when ye shall neither in this mountain, nor yet at Jerusalem worship the Father," that is, ye shall not resort to Mount Gerizim nor to Jerusalem to seek the common Father of believing souls; but all such shall have free access to Him, wherever scattered through the world. For to the spiritual Christian the world is God's temple; he turns not towards Mount Zion, because God is everywhere, nor does he look for a visible Christ reigning at the earthly Jerusalem, because *He* is with all His people always to the end of the world. In the believer's highest states of feeling, life, in all its work, is worship; every where he is a king and a priest unto God.

But in spite of these changes, the sentiment of reverence, which demanded the ancient symbols and clung to holy spots, remains and ever will remain in the human soul. It cannot be repressed without a disjointing of our moral and religious nature. It cannot be extinguished without embruting man, whose highest office, even according to Plato, was to hymn the Creator. It leads to an expression of religious feeling, vague it may be or irrational, if without the guidance of the divine word: yet without it there can be no religion; and profaneness or the loss of reverence is the foe equally of feeling and of faith, of the sentiment which gropes for God and of the worship in which we are helped to realize His presence.

Let us consider first the nature of *reverence.* Here we have to deal with something incapable of definition, which is seemingly a simple, uncompounded sentiment, and cannot be known without being felt. In these respects, however, it is on a level with the other sentiments or sensibilities, with shame, for instance, and with remorse, which could never be described, so that even an angel could fully get at their meaning. As we know that human nature is alike, we assume the existence of such principles in every human breast. They may not be as lively in one as in another, or one sensibility may be dull and another intense, but probably no human being ever existed without some trace of them. They may also be blunted by a course of known and wilful sin. Thus it is a common experience of man, that shame, which was without doubt intended to deter us from that which is shameful, when it is resisted, and as it were trampled under foot, becomes dead and arouses no pain in the soul, as the liar's brazen tongue, and the harlot's brazen face testify. So too, remorse may seem to be extinct for a course of years, and the bold sinner seems to have gotten the victory over his conscience. But the deadness of the sensibility is often only for a time, and this fact shows that it is a part of us, which can here or hereafter assert its rights in tones which must be heeded. Under a new view of truth, shame will make the ears tingle, and remorse will lash the soul with its scorpions. In the same way, when profaneness and fleshliness seem to have shut the door of the soul to the presence of the divine majesty, the sentiment of reverence may return again at the call of spiritual truths, and *he* may bow in adoration, who not long before braved divine wrath by his profaneness.

Reverence has some points of resemblance to other feelings which seem to be simple, and with which it ought not to be confounded. And there is the more need of distinguishing them, since they may exist together as mingled but independent emotions. It differs from *fear*, for it can exist in circumstances where we have no sense of personal danger. And yet so similar are the two emotions, that in some languages, the same word will more or less be used to express them both, as indeed *reverence* and *shame* sometimes claim a common right to the same term. But shame differs from reverence in this, that it contemplates a judgment formed concerning our conduct by another, or has reference to a standard of conduct adopted by others, while reverence seems to be irrespective of our conduct and to depend upon something else. It is widely different again from the feeling of *dependence*, with which, in religious feeling, it is often associated. We both revere and feel our dependence on God, but it is evident that we can feel our dependence on a being without revering Him, and can revere one who has no power over our condition.

And finally the sense of the *sublime*—or if that be a complex feeling—the feeling of *awe*, which is contained in it, seems to differ from reverence, which relates to persons and their *actions*, while the other sensibility is aroused by operations in the material world. It will not be said that we venerate the phenomena of nature, or the great earth itself; and when we speak of venerable moss-grown trees, the language is justified by the transfer of personal life to such objects, or by their resemblance to what is venerable in man.

Reverence then is awakened by *personal attributes*, and not by mere power, which by itself repels and strikes fear into our souls, nor by *great intellect* separate from character. Qualities of character are its especial field, and the moral traits which awaken it run along the scale from the inferior exhibitions of human excellence to the higher and vaster perfections which a Christian ascribes to God. Thus fortitude, generosity, magnanimity, self-sacrifice—above all when they are great of their sort, or appear in the company of a great mind—call forth our reverence as really as infinite benevolence, justice, and holiness. But there are certain relations between men also, which call forth this feeling. They are of such a kind as to remove persons from an equality and to excite a sense of inferiority in the mind of one of the parties. Of this description are the relations of the child and subject to the parent and ruler, and of youth to old age, in which latter case perhaps the wisdom and experience usually ascribed to old age aid the feeling. In general it may be said that reverence will not be felt, unless we observe something which lifts a person above us, prevents entire equality and free familiarity, and impresses us with a belief of his moral greatness. We can scarcely be said to revere our equals; we may admire them, but they would not be our equals if we revered them. Under institutions which encourage the spirit of equality therefore reverence will be checked.

It is a common remark among Europeans, that such is the case in this country; that viewed from their point of view democratic America has less reverence for God, less respect for old age, less veneration for parents, than the lands where the principle of equality does not run so entirely through the institutions. And the religious sentiment seems to need a continual protection against these political influences, lest the decencies and the solemnities of worship become quite unable to stand their ground against disrespect of the simplest forms of religion.

As we revere man, so we can revere his laws and institutions, which are personal acts emanating from minds in times past, calculated to call forth our moral feelings, and by their authority impressing us with a sense of our subjection. In the same manner the law of God, the word of God, all that presents to us His character calls upon us to exercise the feeling of reverence. God is associated with all His institutions, with whatever is divine: His divine personality shines through them all.

II. This attempt to define the nature of reverence is important only as helping us to understand the uses and the abuses of the sensibility. Here we make two remarks, *the first that it is one of the pillars which support religion,* one of those fundamental feelings without which there could in the proper sense be no such thing as religious worship, and the *second* that *in itself it has no virtue and is no guide,* but may fasten upon the wrong as well as upon the right object.

Reverence is one of the chief pillars of religion. As soon as we feel that we are dependent on a Divine Being, as soon as we learn from observation of our finite nature, or are taught by our very instinct, that an infinite arm is reached forth for our support, so soon the sentiment of reverence prompts us to worship; and, following its voice, we try to lay down for ourselves the proper way of worship. Man has very often been called a religious animal, and is, without doubt, such. Wherever he dwells on the earth, in all ages and races, he has had some kind of religion, so that Atheism is really fighting against nature. If it succeeded in destroying the faith that binds earth to heaven, its triumph would be short-lived. Human nature would cry out again "for God, the living God." The sense of dependence, the tendency towards reverence and worship are indestructible. And if pantheism could overthrow the established faith, it could not prevent some kind of religion from rising up in the world. Probably polytheism—with a veneration of the personified forces or objects of nature, would be the result.

This office of reverence is similar to the offices performed by the moral sensibilities and by shame. If there were no moral sense there could be no obligation. The feeling of self-approval and disapprobation call for a moral code or standard, and would be unmeaning otherwise. Shame and love of esteem contain in themselves a reference to society and its judgments. If man were a solitary being, having no intercourse with his fellows, such sentiments would be unmeaning. Hence, we may say, that as shame supposes that we are to live in society, and remorse that we are to be under moral law; so reverence supposes both that we are made for worship, and that there is some object out of ourselves calling for our worship. Otherwise our nature would be a riddle, containing traces of a plan, but leaving the plan unfinished. God being acknowledged, we can explain reverence and the feeling of dependence. These, being parts of our essential nature, point forward to God. Then the plan appears to be complete. God and the feelings which His existence and nature awaken thus explain one another.

But, secondly, *reverence is no guide by itself, and has in itself no virtue.* The mere sentiment is blind, just as shame and remorse are blind. If shame were a perfect guide, we should always be ashamed of things shameful, and never of anything else. But it is not so. The opinions of a sinful society make men ashamed to do what they know to be right, and ashamed not to do wrong, so that no small amount of manliness and of religious principle is needed to follow a guide acknowledged to be better than the public voice. In the same way self-approval and remorse are no infallible guides. They recognize the everlasting distinction of right and wrong, they require us to admit, that some things must be right and some things wrong, but they do not enlighten us as to the contents of a law of righteousness. If they did, the history of morals would not be a series of mistakes and perversions, a calling of good evil and evil good, a putting of darkness for light and light for darkness, of bitter for sweet and of sweet for bitter. The same holds good in respect to reverence. Neither this sentiment nor the feeling of dependence reveals to man the nature of the object which he is prompted to worship, and on which he depends. Otherwise it would not be true, that nearly all the religions of the world have had objects of worship which a cultivated moral sense could not honor or venerate. Something *beyond* the feeling, *for which* the feeling is *preparatory,* is wanted to guide us into the knowledge of the real and living object of worship.

The feeling of reverence in outward religious worship is neither good nor evil. It must exist in some degree of strength; it may aid the mind in the worship of the true God; but worship in itself is not virtuous, nay, *religion,* taken in its general sense of a bond of union between man and a divine being, is not necessarily virtuous. There are many very religious persons, in that acceptation of the word, who are very wicked, and the religion itself may encourage malice, impurity and falsehood. I refer to this because it is beginning to be the fashion among a certain class of writers to speak of several of the emotions as if they had something holy about them, as if reverence, for instance, and the sense of dependence were virtuous sentiments and acceptable to God, whatever their objects might be, whatever the rites of the religion which call them forth. Thus the acceptableness of the worshiper's oblations would not lie in the state of his will or disposition, or in the fitness of the object worshiped, but merely in the existence of the sentiments upon which the act of worship is built. A very easy kind of doctrine this which overlooks the moral element of religion. But I trust no one who hears me will imagine that the worship of a Malay pirate to his tutelary god is virtuous because it is worship, or that the obscene dances and songs of many heathen nations are to be put on a level with the choral songs that ascend on high from Christian temples—"Holy, holy, holy is the Lord God of hosts, the whole earth is full of Thy glory," or "Blessing, and glory, and honor, and power be unto Him that sitteth on the throne, and to the Lamb forever."

And thus we reach the point that revelation is needful in order that man may know what he ought to revere with religious adoration. If our race had continued innocent, perhaps, a faith in God would have spread over the world, rivalling in its purity and elevation the conceptions of God drawn from the Bible. But a sinful race cannot originate a pure doctrine concerning God. The immoral, unholy feelings of man will color his conceptions of the divinity, unless there is a standard of truth to which he bows. He will worship, but into his worship the taint of lust, revenge, and falsehood will enter. He will make a mythology, but the mythology though full of beauty, it may be, will be full also of all rottenness.

III. But thirdly, what will be the office of reverence in connection with the religion of Christ, and what the duties to which it prompts and summons us? Here by way of illustration notice the effect on life and manners of some other sentiments and principles. *Regard for public opinion*—how inevitably this mingles its influence with all our life, so that we follow the fashions and judgments of society, receive its faith blindly, are afraid to depart from its law, which haunts us when there are no spectators, and brings into our solitudes the presence of invisible human witnesses. And so the *notion of equality*—how it moulds our manners, sets us on the watch for our rights, makes us coarse, disrespectful, arrogant, as if society were advancing claims all the while which it was necessary for us to oppose. It is the same with *reverence.* This sentiment may be traced in all the religions of man's devising as well as in the revealed religion of the Scriptures. In the former it casts aside from worship whatever is supposed to be offensive to the divinity; it leads to a posture, to forms and to rites of worship such as set forth the veneration and devotion of the worshiper; it leads with other sentiments to places of worship where acts of homage can be rendered, and to such accessories of worship as will help the spirit of reverence to rise up free from all impediments. In the true religion it is no longer blind but an enlightened handmaid of true spiritual feeling. Here the problem is not simply to excite reverence together with the other feelings that rise towards God, not merely in worship to place before the soul the high and holy One who inhabiteth eternity, but to do this as an intelligent service built on the truth, and drawing its supplies of emotion from the truth of positive revelation.

The worship which the Scriptures encourage is made up of the form and the spirit. Let us look at each of these by itself.

There has ever been a difference in regard to *the form of worship.* Some minds, some states of enlightenment, some stages of religious knowledge crave more of form than others. Yet if the question, what the forms shall be, were left to the sentiment of *reverence* alone, the decision how much form we should have in Christendom, would be comparatively easy. But as soon as a *form* expresses the natural language of reverence or adoration, or of gratitude and love mingled with reverence, art takes hold of it. The *sacred house* of God, where the style ought to partake of that severe simplicity and majesty which kindle the purest feelings, is overloaded with elaborate ornament, telling the worshiper nothing but the builder's art and the costliness of the structure. That is false art which drowns other thoughts in admiration of the finish, which injures worship by that which draws the mind away from worship. So of *music.* It is one of the noblest sensibilities of man that he can pour forth his soul to God in song; but here, again, while true art favors simplicity and grandeur, false art favors that style of church music which exhibits best the skill of the singers, as if man ought to be thought of in an act of worship, which is unmeaning and useless if it do not move and then compose the soul. And there is, again, a natural *form* of reverence for the worshiper. His posture, his attire, his decorum in all respects must be such that worship can be in harmony with the place and with the great being who is worshiped. There is a reverential feeling which, as an accompaniment of spiritual ideas, will regulate all this. As at a festival among his fellow-men, a man will be polite and friendly, as his garb, his words, his manner will suit the occasion, so it should be when he meets God. Our respectful treatment of our fellow-men is dictated by the thought that they have rights which we cannot violate without selfish rudeness; but God has His rights, which to violate is to sin, and reverence in the heart will show us how to worship Him aright, and the question in all the forms of worship will be how the soul can be aided in communing with God.

The *spiritual side of worship,* then, is the great thing. It is better to worship on the lonely heath, or under the stars than in the most gorgeous cathedral, if Christian feeling is called forth amid God's works and not amid the lavish adornments of human art. The forms, simple or more elaborate, prepare for the spiritual service; they help the soul upward, but they are not spiritual themselves. Here truth comes in. The recognition of God in all His relations to us, of Christ in His work, of our sin and want,—realities of this magnitude entering the soul with the sentiment of reverence, dispose us to adoration, confession, praise, to sympathy with sacred song if we cannot join in it ourselves.

And here we notice briefly two offences against the true spirit of worship, formality and profaneness. *Formality* is the form without the spirit. It is found most generally where an elaborate ritual is in use, and the worshiper by a decent or reverent observance of the outward rites satisfies his conscience, or purchases for himself, as he thinks, exemption from higher obligation, since he has satisfied, as he imagines, the claims of God. But formality may exist also in modes of worship, where there is the least of a ritual. A decorous posture and manner, conduct due to the place, is all the worshiper of this kind has to offer to God. But he ought not to imagine that this is enough, or that a heart-searching God can accept of this, or that he is fitting himself for the worship on high, where they sing "Holy, Holy, Holy, Lord God Almighty, which is and was, and is to come! Blessing and honor and glory and power be unto Him that sitteth on the throne and to the Lamb, for ever and ever!"

But *irreverence*, which in its extreme is *profanity* and blasphemy, is a sin of deeper dye than formality. The demands of reverence are satisfied by the decorum and seriousness of formality, while the higher claims of a spiritual religion are overlooked or forgotten. But *profanity* has overcome the natural restraints of a sentiment to which even pagans pay regard. It is a contempt of God, as if He were not worthy of being treated with the respect due even a man like ourselves. The religious sentiments in the habits of a Christian believer are associated with the time and place of worship. His spirit is subdued into a devout, solemn awe of God; he can in his best frames realize that the church is the house of God and the gate of heaven. But the profane worshiper has formed no such tie in his mind between God and His house, between God and the prayers and praises that go up to His throne. His thoughts are profane. His words are mingled with curses. Nothing sacred has any hold on his mind. How can he have any fellowship with God or God with him? And if there is a heaven, a place of God's special manifestation of His glories, how could he enter it without dismay and despair?

What has been said suggests the thought that Atheism and Pantheism lead to idolatry of the creature. The remark has been made already that reverence involves a personal object, and as the sentiment is universal in man's nature it seeks for a personal object above nature; man cannot be satisfied with worshiping his fellow-man unless his standard of greatness and goodness is miserably low, or unless he has by his dogmas ruled all persons higher than man out of the universe. When now this happens, when the great object above nature is denied to exist or to exist as a person, the source from which the reverential mind can supply its wants is *gone;* the heavens and earth are now an empty temple. But man, after this denial of God, remains as he was before; he still needs something to admire, something to revere, something to take the place of the lost divinity. What has he now to construct his object of adoration, his idol out of? Is it the heavens, or the earth, or the sun, that almost living symbol of the infinite, ever present Lord? But by his science he finds these to be dead matter, under law, acting by mechanical necessity. What is there venerable in a mighty machine more than in a small one on the same plan; in an engine of a thousand horse-power more than in one of ten? He must look for his idol beyond the material world. But the only *mind* remaining after God is cast away is man's. To this, then, in its highest forms of power he looks as his make-shift for the living God; this he invests in the course of time with an unreal superiority drawn from his imagination; it becomes his hero or demigod, and he strives to fill with its presence his soul, emptied of God and which only God can fill. When Atheism reigned in France the church of St. Geneviéve became the Pantheon, was dedicated to the great men of France by their grateful country, and received the bones of persons like Rousseau, Voltaire, Mirabeau and Marat. How near an approach to those pagan times, when the Roman emperor obtained divine honors after his death, and his genius was sacrificed to in his life-time.

Our subject, again, helps us to see how man is prepared for religion in his nature, and how the revealed religion carries on that preparation. The native sentiments fit him for communion with a God, and among them reverence especially controls the manner and form of his approach to his Deity in acts of worship. If this were all, if he had no light from heaven, religion would be ignorant worship of the unknown God, or impure worship of a false and foul Divinity. But Christianity now appears to disclose to him what sin had hidden before, and the new way of reconciliation to God, which sin had rendered necessary. But if the Gospel, while thus throwing light and hope into his soul, had not provided free play for all the original sensibilities which take hold on God, it might have been charged with imperfection, with not developing the whole of our nature in harmony. It has, however, food in its glorious realities for them all; its majestic representation of the infinitely holy One give full scope to reverence; gratitude is excited to the full by the doctrine of God's providential care and gracious presence; trust and hope by His promises and offers of mercy—in short, all our nature is taken into account by the author of the Gospel; a skill and a provision for the human soul appears in it; it aims to round off the human character, and to bring man to his highest earthly perfection.

And so, also, the Gospel cultivates the sensibilities, reverence, among the rest, for the heavenly state. Prayer here, such as God can accept, adoration and praise here are qualifying souls for the deeper and nobler emotions which will accompany the grander revelations of that world. Whether any of these sensibilities will be superseded there, I will not venture to inquire. But it is not probable that reverence will ever cease, since the disclosures of the glories of God there, natural and moral, will make the distance between the finite man and the infinite God greater and greater, so that there will be the more need of reverence, and the more room for its exercise.

Prepare, then, my hearers, by worship here for worship there. Wherever else light-minded, be devout in God's house and in worship. If you have been profane, shake off the habit; learn to see God everywhere and to adore Him. If you have been formal and yet decent, think that God cannot accept such services. Give your mind to the grand thoughts of the Gospel, and enter on the worship of God in spirit and in truth. Then you will have joy when you unite with all the good ones of earth and heaven in the cry, "Holy, Holy, Holy Lord God Almighty, which is and was and is to come!" "Blessing and honor and glory and power be unto Him that sitteth on the throne and unto the Lamb forever and ever!"

SERMON XVII.

THE VIRTUES WHICH HAVE TRUTHFULNESS FOR THEIR BASIS.

EPHES. iv. 25. Wherefore putting away lying, speak every man truth with his neighbor; for we are members one of another.

THE quality of truthfulness, or of allegiance to truth, in the character, extends far beyond the point of scrupulously avoiding untrue statements. A person may never tell what would usually be called a falsehood, and yet may have a thoroughly insincere, hypocritical, or artificial character. It needs but a coarse, dull-sense of right and wrong to abstain from telling lies, while it belongs to a very sensitive, delicate conscience to shun the numberless by-paths of false appearances and false pretences which meet one on all sides and are very pleasant to walk in. The finish of the character, in regard to truthfulness, is one of the noblest attainments of Christian manhood, and it is as difficult as perfection is in any other department. To make any progress in this direction we must have a clear view of the field; we must form an idea of what it is to be an Israelite indeed without guile; we must perceive how insinuating in some of its forms untruthfulness is, and how blessed the height—if we can reach it—where our whole soul shall breathe the air of truth, and of nothing but truth.

Give me then your attention, dear brethren, while I lay before you in a miscellaneous way some of those faults of character partaking of the quality of the false, which, as men and as Christians, we ought to avoid, and some of those forms of truthfulness which we ought to admire and must possess if we are followers of Christ.

And may I not mention first, as worthy of being in general avoided, the quality of dissimulation, or the concealment of our real opinions, which has been contrasted with simulation, or the pretending to be, or to think, something other than the reality. Here I do not refer to those native differences which must always be observable between frank or demonstrative and reserved or undemonstrative characters. Nor do I at all say that we are always bound to *express* what we think, or that we may not put ourselves on our guard by concealment against *designing enemies.* But I refer to studious concealment of principles and feelings in order that others may have a false impression of us from our silence. The kind of frankness which consists in avowing our true sentiments, or at least the readiness to do this, on the right occasion, is what all men admire; and when the moving cause to dissimulation is fear, the opposite quality may be a very manly and even a highly Christian one. So, for instance, he who confesses Christ amid a company of scoffers, instead of holding his peace and covering up the convictions of his soul, has the spirit of a martyr. And he will have this good fruit of his openness, that besides feeling conscious of doing a noble act, he strengthens his convictions themselves. It has been laid to the charge of Cromwell that he was a dissembler, who allowed others to interpret his silence as they would, and then surprised them by acting otherwise than they expected. His most favorable biographers have defended him on the ground that he told no lies, and that being in the midst of dangerous plotters, he was unable to save himself or his cause in any other way. I will not dispute the justice of the defence, but I notice the instance as showing how men confound dissembling with falsehood, and therefore how these must border on one another; and as showing also that a high religionist like Cromwell, by his dissembling, gave color to the charge that his religion was insincere. It is obvious that the practice, carried out to any great length, is wrong and fraught with danger. It is *wrong*, for what right have I to live on terms of confidence with others, hear their indiscreet utterances of honest opinion, give them impressions by my constant silence that I think with them, and yet all the while differ from them entirely? Would they admit me to their communion, if they knew what *I* know of my sentiments? And is it not an obligation of honor and justice that in a free interchange of feelings I shall not be an insidious spectator, on the watch while others are opening their breasts? Nay, rather, does not a certain freedom of intercourse imply that continued silence means assent or at least no disapprobation? We may appeal to instinctive feeling also, and ask whom men will respect—him who hides his true self in important respects from others out of fear or that he may have the benefit of their companionship, or him who is resolved to put on no disguise, but to let himself pass among his fellows for what he is? Such a man loses nothing, for all see that he has a love of truth superior to fear or interest.

And again, dissimulation is fraught with danger, for it leads into falsehood. The habit of making false impressions or suffering them to be made by silence lies next door to direct untruth. You feel that you have deceived by concealment, and that you may just as well reach the same point by a lie. Suppose the case of an early Christian, who shut up his faith in himself, heard Christians traduced and heathenism advocated, and kept his peace until the heathen around him thought him lukewarm or one of themselves—would he, when trial came, be as likely to say, "I too am a believer in Christ," and suffer for his Lord, as he would have been, if in all modest ways he had let his faith be known? He kept still because he was afraid, and he nursed his fear? Would not the same fear be the more likely to make him recreant to Christ?

Dissimulation, then, if dictated by fear or policy, is

dangerous as fostering a cowardly, unmanly temper, and as leading across the line which separates disingenuous concealment from positive untruth.

Next to dissimulation I mention *pretence*, which implies an intentional concealment of the reality by something false or feigned offered to the inspection of others. A man is conscious of something pertaining to him which he would gladly hide from view, and so he endeavors to make a false impression of himself before his fellow-men by some specious show or unfounded claim. Or he desires the reputation of that which he is not or does not possess, and endeavors by his conduct to lead others into error. Thus a merchant who has no capital makes a false impression on others in regard to his pecuniary ability, that he may obtain a loan of money; or a sciolist pretends to have learning, when he is ignorant; or a libertine to be moral when he is immoral; or a hypocrite in religion to be a believer or a good man when he is neither. We call by the name of hypocrisy the worst kind of pretence, false assumption of the religious character for selfish purposes. All men, good and bad, concur in condemning and abhorring this class of persons; and truly he is among the worst of mankind who lives directly under the truths and motives of a gospel which loathes hypocrisy, and yet for selfish purposes puts on a cloak of religion. He is so bad that many who are no hypocrites think quite well of themselves, because they are better than he. But, in fact, all pretence is one; and all pretenders are players of a part; they put on a mask to hide their true characters. There are pretenders to wealth, who, by dexterous shows get the reputation of riches, when they cannot pay their debts. There are pretenders to skill in a learned profession, who impose on the ignorant by making the little they know seem great. There are pretenders to familiarity with great people, who want to seem important in other men's eyes. There are pretenders in all the departments of business—such for instance as sell a few articles cheap in order to make the more upon their principal goods. In fact all competition as the world goes, encourages pretence, for men will not wait until their character brings customers, but will seek custom by pretence, before they can establish a reputation. There are, again, pretenders in the fashionable world, who impose on the judgment of others, or creep into good company by audacious assumption. These and all other pretenders—pretenders to *morality*, who talk smoothly and eloquently of virtue, while they practice vice in secret; pretenders to *sentiment*, who borrow the language of others to cover dead and worn-out hearts; pretenders to *taste*, who ape the judgment of critics or connoisseurs with no sensibility of eye or ear or soul; pretenders to *religion*, who dishonor and disgrace religion, and yet all the more show the value and the need of it in the world—all these need only to be mentioned, for the moral sense of mankind is against them and awards them scoffs or indignation, according to a milder or harsher rule for measuring their characters. And without doubt, the feeling of man reflects herein the moral estimates of God, and of our Lord, who has said things of hypocrisy as fearful as any words that were ever uttered. For let us think of the great God watching every kind of hypocrite as he tries to deceive his fellows by empty shows; as he glories in his success; as he thinks the secret is known only to himself. Can He, the infinitely pure and true, fall below man in His abhorrence of such a character? And if the blind man could once open his eye on God, seeing Him in all the glory of His truth, and seeing that there is one immortal witness against him, who knows all and remembers all, could he help being withered and loathing himself?

But enough of these: there is a less obvious kind of pretence into which we are all apt to fall, which, however, cannot stand on its defence, when tried by the laws of truth. It is what is called *cant;* a word which denotes the aping of others in expressions of feeling and opinion, by the use of set, stereotyped words which pass current in a certain circle of religion, fashion, or taste. Take religious *cant* as the most signal example. I refer not now to the words peculiar to a certain sect to denote their views concerning doctrine and a religious life, for there must be such words, and they contain more or less of truth. Nor can the term *cant* be applied with any propriety to the terms for conversion or repentance, or an exercise of our religious nature in view of truth. He whose taste would be offended by these words, when used on the proper occasion, would most probably dislike the thing denoted by them, and the Gospel itself.

But, there are many senses of words peculiar to certain classes of religious people, and many phrases, also, coined by them in the fervency of their feeling,—expressions of a genuine Christian spirit in their mouth, which others without their earnestness borrow from them: perhaps in the next age, when piety no longer burns with a bright flame, they remain on the lips, as marks that religion has become a mere lip-service. Now the use of such words may offend a nice taste, but *cant* is something beyond want of taste; it is deadness using the language of life; it is insincerity clothed in the garb of sincerity, and it is, therefore, a sin against truth. In the most marked cases, *cant* is the dialect of hypocrisy, using on calculation terms to which it attaches no living sense drawn from experience. In the least marked cases it is catching up from others and saying over by rote that which proceeds not from the heart. But there are other kinds of *cant*, as that of sentiment, when a person adopts language of feeling or of fancy, which is not the utterance of the soul within, but a lesson taught by society; or as the *cant* of taste, where an instructed person apes the language of critics and seems to have lively sensibility, when he is incapable of perceiving the beauty or the majesty, whether of nature or of art. Such pretension, which passes from one to another, like a contagion, a truthful mind will instinctively shrink from. He cannot say what he does not truly feel. He cannot profess to judge where he knows he has no power of passing a judgment. It gives him pain to be thought better or more knowing than he is, or to be rated higher than the truth will warrant. And this without doubt accords with the judgment of the God of truth. Avoid then all pretence. Act out not a borrowed character, but that which belongs to you. It is better to bear our own fruit than to have foreign blossoms hanging on us. Develop your own life into Christian perfection, rather than ape another's words and put on his likeness. There is none of us, the most crabbed, the most ungainly, the most inflexible, that cannot be built up with God's help, into a living temple beautified by holiness; there is none of us, however promising and apt, that will cover his true self up in a borrowed robe, who will not readily be detected by sharp observers, and at last be laid bare at the great trial of character.

We mention next, as closely bordering on the vice of character already named, *insincerity*, especially *in professions of regard and in the bestowment of praise.* When a person puts on the semblance of friendship for another, expressing it in warm terms to his face, while he laughs at him behind his back, we call this hypocrisy of a black dye. But some insincere ways of making another believe that you are his friend are not so obviously wicked as this. You have a kindly feeling towards him and exaggerate it in your words or shows, so that he mistakes by your fault his true place in your esteem. Or you are indifferent to him and yet abuse the signs of politeness, so that he puts a false construction on your words and shows. You thus present yourself to others as ready to do for them what is beyond your intention, and when the test comes and you fail, they are wounded and feel that they have been falsely dealt with. Most of such insincere professions are the refuges of selfishness ashamed to come to the light and putting on the forms of good will. They are produced by a high standard of character around us,—we are ashamed to be thought to fail in kindness or friendliness, and so assume its garb. Here we see how love in the heart would prevent all such false shows. Having the feeling within us we should not be anxious to exhibit it. It would manifest itself freely. Our civility would not be well-bred but heart-felt; not a manner put on but an expression of the hidden man within.

The same insincerity appears in the form of flattery. This *may* be no sin of falsehood; one may tell the *truth* to another merely to please him and secure his esteem; the evil here lying in the motive and the disregard for his character, which is injured by having only its best side placed before his eyes. But there is another flattery more insidious and full of the spirit of falsehood, as where one shows a deference to another in his manner which he does not feel, or where he exaggerates his excellencies or glosses over his failings, or where he imputes to him motives which could not have existed. There are then two evils in this bad practice, the motive for it and the false representation. Love would prevent both. It would praise where praise would do good; it would insinuate nothing which was not strictly true. It would not rejoice in iniquity, but rejoice in the truth.

We pass on next to the faults of character *opposed to simplicity*. This word denoted at first the quality of being unfolded, as contrasted to that which was folded together, and so simplicity in a moral sense and duplicity are moral opposites. But the word has a wide application; when used in reference to taste it denotes the avoidance of the artificial, the overwrought, the overloaded with ornament, the pretentious. When used in reference to our purposes it denotes that two motives, as self-interest and good-will, are not mixed in producing the same act, or that we aim at truth rather than at impression. As a moral quality it denotes the absence from guile, a character without artifice. Everywhere we perceive that it implies the true as against the false, the real and natural as against the artificial, and we feel that a general simplicity of character, if native, is a most valuable characteristic, and if a fruit of Christian principle, is a following of Him in whose mouth was no guile. On the other hand the want of this quality is a serious defect. Even a taste which rejects it, a taste for excess of ornament, for instance, is a sure result of an *immoral* civilization, so that here we have another sign that truth as a trait of society is necessary for all healthy judgments as well as sound morals, and that as soon as falsehood creeps in, it brings a blight upon art as well as on character.

It is noticeable that simplicity of character or freedom from artifice and guile is often connected with openness or transparency of character. Now a man whose guilelessness is apparent seems to other men, in a community where falsehood prevails, to be destitute of a power which it is often desirable to use. He has an aversion native or from principle to falsehood, and, therefore, appears to be unable to defeat the designs of falsehood. Hence simplicity and kindred words come in a number of languages to mean want of penetration, want of common sense, and the more depraved the community, the more easy and natural will such a transition of sense be. Trickery, the power to circumvent and to deceive, will pass for talent, and the simple-hearted will be despised. But in truth there is no necessary connection between simplicity and folly, between knavery and shrewdness. And no characteristic is more successful in life, or more widely esteemed than simplicity. The man who gains his objects in a round-about way, who covers himself up in a mist, who resorts to indirect means to gain his end, becomes suspected and feared; he in turn suspects and fears others; and thus his character causes an alienation or even an opposition between him and his fellow-men, which interferes with his success by destroying confidence, and, it may be, lands him at last in positive dishonesty. The simple-hearted again not only are loved and trusted, but have their souls open to all truth which rests on evidence. They *may be as wise as serpents* while they are as harmless as doves; they may see the stratagem and chicanery of others, while they would shrink from using the same weapons themselves. They often defeat artifice by simplicity, because a trickish, artful mind cannot understand a quality so unlike its own. They come with the best preparation to the truths and obligations of religion, for they are apt to be not far from the kingdom of God, as having a love for simple truth and a sincerity of purpose.

Simplicity in statements, again, is a form which the truthful spirit assumes, and the fault most opposite to it is careless or reckless exaggeration. There are causes for exaggeration which are not strictly criminal. Such are excitement of feeling and a lively conception. The orator or the preacher with all due love of truth may run into overstatements, may enhance the relative importance of that which arouses his soul for the time—this is pardonable, it may be not easily avoidable; but even here, the desire to conform to the strict truth, going along with all the movements of the mind, will give rise to a certain sobriety of statement, and especially will prevent a conscientious man from aiming to produce an effect by intentional exaggeration. This is a sin against the law of truth. The impression must be heightened beyond what the reality will warrant—the person thinks—in order that any effect may be produced. He confounds overstrained expression with force, and adherence to the reality with weakness. Thus he betrays a want of confidence in the power of truth, and this fault of his brings his own reward. For men will easily discover his exaggerations and will make excessive deduction from them. If he gives statements of events, men will distrust his reports; if he argues, they will be unconvinced, because this quality of his injures all his arguments; and so it turns out, that *he* is weak, and simple truth in all its forms of bare statement, of eloquent but honest representation, of honest feeling not put on for effect,—simple truth, I say, is ever *strong*.

Another and a kindred fault opposed to a spirit of truthfulness is *inaccuracy in representation and reports*. It may be in this case that an imperfect memory of particulars prevents a person from retaining exact outlines of events in his mind, or that the power of observation is impaired by physical defects. In such a case a person ought to be aware of his liability to error, and the love of truth will supply him with caution, or lead him to qualify his statements. But there are cases where inaccuracy is more culpable, as where it proceeds from *undue haste* which cannot stop to sift evidence or collect materials for judgment, or—what is far worse—where the inaccuracy is due to partiality or prejudice. In the first case loyalty to truth demands that a man should not sacrifice it to impatience or indolence, which is a common sin. How many books are rendered worthless and pass away because they are unreliable through the hurry of their authors. How many reports have to be recalled, the circulation of which might have been stopped by a little care, but the injurious effects of which nothing can heal. In the other case the sin is equally against truth and love, and approaches to the nature of slander,—a sin so unsocial and malignant that all men unite in detesting it.

Another of the truthful virtues is *candor*, which partakes of the nature also of justice. It admits the weight of what makes against ourselves and confesses this with readiness. It acknowledges mistakes out of a spirit of fairness. In argument it gives an impartial view of the reasons urged by the opposite side. In stating the arguments of another it has no bias but gives them just as they are, mingling with them no conclusions of our own. In repeating facts which concern ourselves it puts no color on them and conceals nothing, but is willing to concede what may be injurious to our own cause. It prevents us from using false reasoning, from arguing for victory and not for truth. It is, in short, an unselfish, equitable love of the right as well as the true, and as such places the man who manifests it on a vantage ground against unfair, trickish, unscrupulous opposers. The want of candor, whether passion, or prejudice, or selfish desire of success leads to it, is a trait which every lover of truth will avoid.

I only add the mention of a sin somewhat akin to pretence and hypocrisy—the assigning of *pretexts and motives for our conduct which do not exist.* This is a very common fault of our sinful nature, and it springs from the consciousness that the real motive is not good enough to be displayed, but must be put in the back-ground while some other is thrust forward. This is often not very deliberate—in which case there would be a condemnation of the act at the instant as of something false—but is half self-deception and half deception of others, like those polite expressions of regard which mean little or nothing. It takes place often in regard to actions of trifling importance. Little acts of selfishness are whitened into something better; excuses are plead which are unreal; by a series of petty deceptions unpleasant impressions concerning ourselves are brushed away from the minds of others.

And the little hypocrisies pave the way for great. They blind us to ourselves. The pretexts we use to impose on others we half put faith in, and thus we weave a web of falsehood in which we ourselves are entangled.

Such, presented in a miscellaneous way, are some of the forms of a character which departs from truth and from the God of truth. And now, when we look at the law of truth and the virtue of truthfulness in their details, does there not appear to be a great breadth in them? Do they not form a bulwark for the whole life and character? Let us think, my dear brethren, of the great beauty of a life built on truth, which avoids falsehood not in its grosser forms only, nor in those shapes which all condemn, but in those aspects of it which many fail to perceive. It is the noblest attainment, next after being in love with God and man, to have a truthful spirit. As falsehood supports all sin, so does truth all virtue. But it is not an easy thing for man in his state of sin to live a life of unsullied truthfulness. Temptations to vain shows, to insincerity, to double-dealing meet him on every side. He loves esteem, and this principle leads him to wear false colors, to practice hypocrisy that he may seem to be good when he is not. He falls into sin, and to save himself from its consequences he resorts to falsehoods. He colors facts or suppresses them; he misrepresents his motives for the better, that some faint traits of that worth which he will not possess may seem to belong to him. Then, too, he is exposed to corrupt examples; multitudes around him are false and hollow, and to save themselves from the gnawings of conscience they invent false arguments for falsehood—thus adding an assault on truth itself to falsehood in practice. And in this career of pretence, the whole moral nature wilts; their souls feel a general blight, for he who has lost his veneration for truth has a mortal wound in his soul.

And how is it among us, my dear brethren? We are

gathered from the great world into a little community to study truth, to become exact, to enter into the reality of things; our intellects are trained to detect fallacies, to draw nice lines round the borders of truth, to construct systems of truth rising up to the throne of God. In such a community ought not veracity, honor, sincerity to reign? Where, in any gathering of young persons, should a high standard of general uprightness so easily be formed, and be maintained by so strong a sentiment? But what is the actual state of things? Do not facts, every now and then coming to light, do not your own charges made against one another, authorize us to believe, that not a few live here in a course of deliberate deception from year to year, that false excuses are invented, as if it were a small thing to sin against God and your own souls for a trifling purpose? You are under very mild law, you assent to it by placing yourself here, and yet you avoid its operation by the most unworthy of all expedients. But if the evil stopped here, it would be trifling compared with what it is. Think of the general distrust concerning character, which it brings in its train, instructors necessarily distrusting students, and students distrusting each other. Think how falsehood, as I showed in my last Sunday's discourse, helps on every other evil habit, so that you open the door wide to the enticements of all other sins, when you consent to commit this sin. Think, that if you do not lower your standard and justify lying, you cannot help despising yourself, nor help knowing that others must feel the same towards you; or if you have built up a wall of sophistries, in order to stifle the calls of conscience, so much the worse, for a callous conscience is the beginning of the soul's death. Think, if you should be aroused into repentance, what self-reproach you must pass through—self-reproach often bursting out into confession, and not content until it has made known the worst even to man. And all this is the preparation of intelligent, educated persons, taught to take large views of life and of the issues of human conduct—this is their preparation for the throne of the Judge, for the future life, where shame shall be exposed, and truth shall penetrate every dark recess. Oh, my dear friends, I beseech you to think of these things with that sobriety and that candor which they deserve! If you have yielded to a false sentiment, resist it henceforth. If you have helped to make it, help to unmake it. If you have come to believe that all are dishonest, become honest yourselves and you will confide in others. If you have sinned, turn from sin. Blessed be God, that while there must be an entire alienation on His part from the untruthful, His compassions are always awake for those who forsake evil. Enter into fellowship with Him by ingenuous confession and by avoiding "every false way." Pass over to the side of a Saviour, who never deceived men, and will be true to the end. Take the part of all honor and uprightness. Let each one, in all earnestness, say, "Give me Thy help, O God, that I may live a life of strict, unchangeable truthfulness."

SERMON XVIII.

THE DEBT OWED BY EVERY GENERATION TO THE PAST.

GOSPEL OF JOHN iv. 38. Other men labored, and ye have entered into their labors.

I WILL not stop to ask who were the *other men* here spoken of by our Lord; whether He refers in the plural only to Himself, or points back also to others—to the prophets, or even to Moses, as the forerunners of the Apostles and the pioneers in the work of the kingdom of Heaven. In any case, a principle of the widest application is brought before us—that no individual, in the strictest sense, begins his own work; that all enter into and carry out the labors of others; and so, too, that all the generations of the world reap the fields their forefathers sowed; that there is a dependence, a succession, in all the labors of men, a running account kept up by each present age to the credit of the whole past, and especially to the credit of its immediate predecessors

This is indeed a characteristic of man in which he differs almost wholly from the best endowed animals. They, in their successive generations, reach the same point of maturity, act out the characters of their races to about the same degree of perfection, and die without advancing their kind or leaving any new store of power or enjoyment to their posterity. If man, by taming and training them, can in a degree improve their breeds, even *his* action has the least effect upon their races as wholes. The individuals may be more graceful, or strong, or useful; but no quality of self-improvement has entered into the species. Man, on the other hand, the feeblest of creatures at his birth and the most dependent, is able to retain, transmit, record, and plan; by his social and moral instincts he forms commonwealths and makes laws; he learns from others; he communicates to others; he trains the young members of the community up to the measure of its knowledge and wisdom; he invents and spreads inventions—he thus builds a tower of one platform upon another, reaching toward the skies, from which, as its stories ascend, he holds nearer converse with Heaven and casts his eye over ampler spaces of earth.

Now for all this the labor of one generation will not suffice; but there must be constant, world-wide work and transmission. Human progress consists in this: that men have labored with body, with mind, and each next age has entered into their labors. It is possible indeed for a generation to send nothing of value down the stream of time; nay, it may obliterate or corrupt, and so put its successors into a worse position than if it had not existed. Such retrograde movements show that the law of progress is not a fatal one, nor dependent solely on the stores of knowledge that have been laid up; but on the other hand there is no other law of progress aside from this which we have before us: that each generation, by the help of its predecessors' toil handed down and retained, adds something to the general stock for the benefit of coming ages. Nor does God, when He intervenes in human history by supernatural revelations, disturb this law, for forthwith the truth, the power, the moral advancement, are leaven thrown into an age or a people, or possibly into a single mind, to leaven the whole world afterward by the same process by which human improvements produce their effect. And we ought not to separate progress from God, as some do, for He is in it all, whether it springs directly from something done by man, or from *His* own revelation. He is in all invention; in all learning and science the plan is throughout His. Bezaleel, the ingenious artificer of the tabernacle, was animated by His spirit; and so all genius, all power, that starts the world forward, is as truly a part of His world-plan as is the Christian scheme of redemption.

I. Let us consider, in some of its particulars, this plan of God for the human race,—that each generation enters into the labors of its predecessors, reaping what they have sown, while at the same time, if it is true to its appointed work, it hands over something more to posterity than it had received. Reflect then first *on the labors which the teachers of mankind have undergone,* in order that the world might reach its present state of advancement. The class of teachers may be divided into two portions, into such as *transmit* only and such as also *originate.* The first act directly on those who are just following them in the order of time; the others have a much wider field of direct action; they are the teachers of all time, the "masters of all who know." To few is it given, out of the whole human race, thus to act over many ages and through many lands. The greatest portion either move the thought of their own times in new channels, or, in a more humble office still, simply make known to others what they themselves have learned. Yet all these teachers have labored and men are entered into their labors. They have labored hard and long. Men, as they enjoy a work of art or give themselves to the study of a work of philosophy, must not suppose that everything flowed smoothly while the composition was going on, or that there were no difficulties in the preparation. "He that goeth forth *weeping,* bearing precious seed," is the fit motto for all who have employed their minds for the benefit of mankind. What agony of mind have inventors endured; what anxiety and heart-sickness; what unfruitful experiments, reaching through long years, have they tried, before success crowned their efforts. The same is true of any work of art which has long kept its place in the heart of a nation or of the world. A work of genius is the essence, it may be, of a whole life, the condensed knowledge, judgment, skill, that make up the man. So, too, in all the sciences, as in the philosophy of thought or of morals, what perplexities has a mind contended with, what hope and patience has it spent, what weighings of evidence, what reflection, what consultation have been needed before the painful work of composition began. It must not be supposed, that glimpses of truth are vouchsafed to those that skim over the surface of things in the spirit of curiosity or amusement; nor that inventions enter vacant minds unsought and in full perfection; nor that to the great poet or painter even the labor of composition or of correction, severe as it is, at all compares with that preparatory thought and work on which the whole achievement depended.

So, also, the other class of teachers whose office it is to put knowledge derived from others into form, and to train the minds of their generations—they too have labored long and earnestly in order to fit themselves for their work. The conscientious instructor has gone through three series of toils; he has labored hard to learn as he would have his scholars labor, he has qualified himself by still severer toil for his special duty, and then comes the new office of imparting and guiding from day to day—the hardest labor of all, because the fruits of it do not at once appear.

Now into the labors of these classes of teachers and trainers each new generation of the educated enters. You my friends are debtors to the past and indeed to the remote past. For you Aristotle thought his best thoughts, though they may have taken new shapes before they reached your minds; for you the Greek poets and the English of high renown have sung their strains; for you, art has brought to light its treasures; for you discoverers have ventured into untrodden seas—a thousand forgotten names have lived and wrought for your benefit, without whom, it may be, society would have been far behind its present point of advancement. For you, too, the teacher of the present has spent the best hours of his life, has thought his best thought, has patiently drilled and inculcated, that you may enter into his labors and may, if you will, go beyond him in cultivation and in wisdom. Small perhaps is the proficiency which you may have seemed to yourselves to have made under his training, for the natural and one of the best fruits of a true education is to reveal to us how little we know, and how far we are from the heights of perfect science. But perhaps in the years to come, even although the knowledge and power gained here may be indistinguishable from that which other masters or yourselves have procured for you, you will gratefully attribute something of your culture and something of your success to those who have labored for you here. They will then, perhaps, be beyond the reach of your acknowledgments; they may be little conscious of what they have done for you; they can see but little fruit, of course from the toils of each faithfully spent day; but if it should appear that some good thought of theirs was fruitful in your minds, some ideal of patient, finished scholarship was awakened within you, some solid preparation was given you for the work of a true life, then will they deserve to be remembered, and you will be called by such remembrances to hand down what they have imparted and whatever else you shall have gained by your own labor to the next generation.

II. Other men have labored *in the practical spheres of life*, and we are entered into their labors. Here there arise before us all who have labored for the social, political, moral, religious, welfare of man, from the mother, into whose hands all the tender beginnings of practical life are committed, through every faithful teacher and faithful example up to the founders of states, and the founders of religion, up, even, to the Lord Jesus Christ Himself.

It is to be observed in regard to these laborers both that their work is of all importance, and that it is necessary for the success of those other laborers who work in the fields of science. For life is more than thought, and without a well-ordered life there can be little progress in thought. Such is the action of the moral nature on the mind that a bad soul is unfitted for all the science that is directly concerned with life; it is warped and blinded by selfish interests, it often falls into doubt, and is wanting in those higher impulses which are of such aid in intellectual pursuits. Nor is the sway of society over the individual less marked. A corrupt society, a vicious government are uncivilizing agents of the greatest power, not merely by their neglect or repression of what is good, but by their sympathy with positive evil. And above all the other influences rises religion in its power to ennoble or to degrade the soul, to fill it with fear and falsehood, or to raise it to a communion with God and with His thoughts.

It is to be observed, further, in regard to *these* laborers in the vineyard of life, that their work never ends. The results of knowledge stay in the world, but society and government are ever changing; religion at one time reigns, at another is conquered by doubt or vice, so that there is an endless struggle here between the powers of corruption and the powers of progress,—a struggle in which the interests of science also are involved. Had the race been good enough to have retained the faint primeval knowledge and faith of God; had it been able, by reason of its moral strength, to have instituted everywhere just societies and governments, in sympathy with all truth and goodness; centuries ago, without question, the point of advancement which we have now reached would have been left out of sight, and a state of mankind have been begun of which we only dream almost without hope. The path of the reformers, civilizers, purifiers has been up-hill against reigning corruptions, against the hankering of man for a slothful, unthinking life; in short, against that lapse of souls from God for which Christ furnishes the only all-sufficient remedy.

The labors, therefore, of these classes of practical laborers have been greater than of such as encounter the difficulties and the mysteries of thought. No philosopher ever so toiled to find out or to spread truth, as reformers and preachers of righteousness to make the world and the soul better. They have begun their work in a sense of loneliness and insufficiency; they have held out against fear, scorn, and uncertainty; in the tragic language of the Apostle John, they have come to their own and their own received them not. Take the example of any of the pioneers of righteousness. Before them lies a life-work, which, to be fulfilled, must cross a thousand prejudices, a thousand interests; governments fear them, and are arrayed against them; priesthoods hate them; they are maligned; men fear to join them;—who so hated and so despised as the best patriots, the best philanthropists, the best friends of God and of man. Listen to the complaint of the tender-hearted Jeremiah, who preached wrath against wicked prophets and wicked politicians: "Woe is me, my mother, that thou hast borne me a man of strife and a man of contention to the whole earth! I have neither lent on usury, nor have men lent to me on usury, yet every one of them doth curse me." Or, mark the language of the Apostle Paul, in the same strain, only nobler and purer from the taint of discontent—"In all things approving ourselves as the ministers of God, in much patience, in afflictions, in necessities, in distresses, in stripes, in imprisonments, in tumults, in labors"—or where he says, "We are made the filth of the world and are the offscouring of all things unto this day." Or, let a greater and a holier one teach us what immediate reward awaits all who begin the great movement of the world: "If the world hate you, ye know that it hated Me before it hated you." And although religion, as coming most athwart the prejudices and the fears of men encounters the greatest opposition, the same fate has been tolerably sure for every true reformer of mankind,—first reproach, calumny, persecution, then death, for the patriot by the sword, for the martyr by the flames.

Is it nothing now to have endured this or the like of this? Nothing to have labored against hope and against fear, and then to die with the thought that the work is just begun? No one persecutes the philosopher who speculates on final causes, or constructs a theory of the parabola, or experiments on a new gas; their labors may be long and trying, but the souls of these other laborers, besides all their toil, are harrowed and lacerated, so that martyrdom itself may be a positive relief.

And we are entered into their labors. Your studies of history, my young friends, will have taught you what thanks you owe to the struggles and contests of good men in the past, nor need you go back beyond the few last years for one of the most striking illustrations. In order that a reign of justice in our land should be secured, that we should no longer be the reproach of the civilized world, as a nation of freemen holding four millions of slaves in perpetual bondage and justifying our curse as an institution of God, how many hundred thousands have given up their lives and how many cries of mourners have resounded through the land. We have gained a precious inheritance, precious at its beginning, to be more precious as years roll on, but at what a cost. So also the whole history of our land speaks of labor; of labor the fruits of which we are now enjoying. The toil and agony of mind which the first pilgrims endured in their separation from their homes, in their contests with the wild men and the wilderness, in their want and uncertainty; the struggles and sacrifices of the revolution,—easily read on a few pages of history, but hard enough to bear—these have sent down to us an inheritance more precious than has fallen to any other people. Or if you go farther back and read the record of each important addition to English history, of every new charter or petition or declaration of right, of every resistance against tyranny and every bulwark of freedom; remember that each of these had its contest, its patience, and that your acknowledged rights of speech, of worship, of secure possession, of a share in the commonwealth have cost many lives of men who have left no name, many sorrows of the unnoticed, and that thousands have been preparing the way for your era of light and freedom. Nor are the labors of reformers of less moment. You are in a better state of society than fell to the lot of your fathers, because divinely gifted men saw what were the evils that obstructed human progress, and had courage and patience enough to oppose them. Some one voice perhaps was lifted up amid derision and persecution, some one worked on hoping against hope, and died committing his cause to the few select ones who were as fearless and as loving as he. Then by slow degrees the stream widened and became a resistless flood to change the face of society. The fruits of all this belong to you. But you could not have these fruits, gathered by the patriot and the reformer, at your command, unless also a higher class of laborers in the spiritual field had co-operated with them and prepared the way for them. The preacher of righteousness and the martyr were the forerunners of freedom and of all improvement in society. The martyr did not think, perhaps, when he expressed his devotion to Christ by a painful death that any thing great was to grow out of it—he only acted out what he felt. But these religious laborers have changed the face of the world. They have brought into literature and art, new ideas of purity and spirituality, into life another standard of character, by which all truthfulness, honor, justice and benevolence are duly valued. And from them we go back to Him in whose cause they taught by word or by life—to the great laborer who came not to be ministered unto but to minister, and to give His life a ransom for many. It were easy to show that without Him the labor of all others would have served only to prop up decaying civilizations, and to supply short enjoyment to unsatisfied souls, but that from Him has proceeded the power that helps every laborer for man's welfare: all thinkers have better thoughts because He came into the world, all workers have better ground to stand upon, and better hopes. He penetrates beyond the religious, or the moral, or the social sphere into all art, science, invention: even the science of wealth, the lowest in one respect of the sciences, is not below His influence. Such a thing it is to have had the Son of God in the world, and to have entered into His labors.

What we have said thus far, has served to show the dependence of the successive portions of our race upon foregoing ages for their means of improvement and the relations of the benefactors of mankind among themselves, the thinkers being most indebted to those who have moulded life by their works, and of these the Founder of our religion with His successors taking the lead.

1. *An important reflection* occurs here, which is indeed involved in what has preceded, that a very great work, often the chief work of the best spirits of an age, must be to oppose, to seek to destroy the tendencies of the preceding one. Sin is ignorance, ungodliness and one-sidedness: therefore in our race there are perpetual obstacles to true progress. These obstacles the age itself may be most wedded to, and the spirit of the age can be met only by noble, self-sacrificing minds, who shed a new light on

the world. There are multitudes of these, at whose head stands Christ; and his service to mankind is to be weighed not only by what He positively taught but by His sublime courage in standing up against the existing forms of evil.

And so we, if we would have other men enter into our labors, must declare against whatever is outward, voluptuous, unbelieving and godless in our civilization. An educated young man in Christendom is bound not to follow blindly the lead of the spirit of the time. If there is a tendency among us to sink knowledge into a minister of pleasure, a caterer to wealth, he must in his practice preach the meanness of such a spirit, and the danger of putting the lower uses of this life above the higher. If there is a tendency to swift, unthinking action without meditation enough on principle, he must counteract it by the calmness of his soul, by his unshaken fidelity to his convictions. If there is a tendency in our thinking to exalt law above divine will, and to turn away from whatever claims to be supernatural, he must make up his mind on this immense subject, and being persuaded that there is divine truth among men, must defend it before the world, preaching to men that a civilization without God in Christ is a civilization without lofty motives and most earthly, hollow and decaying, corrupting to art, morals and society. This he must proclaim that others after him may enter into the labors of Christ, and of the true ones in all ages.

2. Another reflection which forces itself upon us, is that all this labor of successive generations does not pay its cost, unless man is an immortal. There are those who do not believe this, and who, in a kind of despair, look about for something great in lieu of the immortal individual whose light they put out; accordingly we hear much of the *immortality of the race* and of *collective humanity.* But who told them that the race is immortal? If it has lasted through all the æons and has made such

small advances until now, the prospect is rather dark for the future laborer. If it began to exist some few thousand years ago, it may cease to exist ere long. Who knows, unless he has access to some revelation, that a geological catastrophe may not sweep this race off, like so many others before it, or some conflagration, like that of which the Stoics taught, may not consume all things; or, if the race is to be immortal, what is its value and the value of laboring for it, or yet the likelihood of raising it up to a state of perfection, when all the motives drawn from endless life and from God are gone? Can a man conscious of high capacities, and proud of spirit, condescend to spend his strength to the advantage of these bubbles that float awhile and then vanish as they burst? To us, it seems that the means of improving the race depend on the question of the immortality of the person, and that the motive to undertake this work shrinks almost to nothing when this immortality is even soberly doubted. And above all, after the exalted conceptions of redemption and of communion with God had faded out, after the grand theatre of immortal life had dwindled into a little booth of twigs, would not a paralysis seize on every earnest mind? Is not the conclusion a most natural one—"let us eat and drink, for to-morrow we die"?

3. There is *another reflection* of immediate practical bearing for each one of us—that we have no reason to boast of our knowledge or refinement, for we have entered into the labors of *others*. What we have, we have acquired by extraneous help. Why then should we be elated, and not rather humbled, because we have made so little use of the help afforded us? Only he can on good grounds feel exaltation of mind who is indebted neither to man nor to God for his attainments. But where is there such a person? The day laborer is nearest to this state of perfect independence, but the hoe and the rake which extend his arms, the spade, by which he applies

the motions of his foot, are the inventions of distant ages; for the preparation of their materials, for the perfecting of their forms, hundreds of men have thought their best thoughts and done their best work. And so it is with all applications of mechanical power, so it is with all discoveries of principles and their reduction to practice. We make our labor profitable by means of the labor of others; their failures save us from failure, their successes are our inheritance. Who, in the widest reach of inventions, in the boldest triumphs of man over nature, has added a tithe to what men accomplished in the same time before him? "Other men have labored, and he is entered into their labors"

In the lower regions of work then no one can boast that he took his own path; is it otherwise in the highest? Must not he who has enlarged science, he who has blessed the world by his benevolent deeds, he who has refined his own mind or character, acknowledge the same dependence? For the thoughts which have disciplined such a one for his work are the undying thoughts of former sages and philanthropists. The examples that animated him were set by the wise and good of all ages, and "were recorded for his admonition upon whom the ends of the world are come." The drama of the world has been played for him. Martyrs have bled for him. And more than this, if he has been able to consecrate himself to the service of God, he knows that he would have remained a worldling, but for the divine grace which came to him in his sins and rendered him a man of faith, self-denial and execution, which raised his standard of attainment, gave him courage and patience, and helped him to do great things through a busy life.

There are two ways in which we can nurse our intellectual pride and self-conceit; we can compare ourselves with others, who are below us, and can imagine that we have reached our fancied height alone. The best cure for the first is to compare ourselves with something higher, above all with the infinitude of God; but we may also compare ourselves with the truly great of past ages, and we cannot fail to be humbled when we think how much more they have done than we with slenderer preparation, and how little the noblest spirits of the world have accomplished after all. But another cure ought to be the discovery of our dependence. Let us feel that the little we know has for the most part come to us at second-hand. We have dressed ourselves by the help of the wardrobes of the past. We should have been as naked as savages had not the poets and sages, the reformers and men of God met us on our way to clothe us in the garments of a Christian civilization. Not one of them, not one true man ever felt a conceit of knowledge. Hear Agassiz' noble words: "I have devoted my whole life to the study of nature and yet a single sentence expresses all that I have done. I have shown that there is a correspondence between the succession of fishes in geological times and the different stages of their growth in the egg, this is all." * Such is the humility of a comprehensive mind that knows what others have done and knows what remains undone. Such a mind cares very little what he may have wrought out, or who may have deserved the honor of this or that discovery. He grasps, rather, the whole of the truth within his reach, and seeks to make the most of it for mankind.

4. And thus we are led to our *last reflection*, that the law of our race, which we have been considering, our dependence on the past, and the hope of progress for the future, ought to carry us out of ourselves, to unite us to our species and to beget within us sympathy with man. "Freely ye have received, freely give," says the Master—words which may be applied to all our blessings as well as to that most necessary one proceeding directly from Him. Men have lived in the past for us. In a world of igno-

* Methods of Study in Natural History, p. 23.

rance, thousands have searched for knowledge as for hid treasures, and their labors have blessed us. In a world of sin, multitudes have lived and died to lay the foundations of order and justice, to reform evils, and to show the path to God. Unknown benefactors and teachers, as well as known, have handed down to us all that enriches and purifies the soul. Is it nothing that we are compassed about with so great a cloud of witnesses? Or is it nothing that the destinies of the world are in no small degree dependent on each new generation? Or that the success of all efforts beyond the field of pure science grows, in a great degree, out of the motive with which they were begun? Let us come, then, into sympathy with the wise and good of the past; let us pay over to others, in a grateful spirit and with interest, what we have received; let our aims in life respect the welfare of all.

And this deserves to be considered for our encouragement, that every advance makes a new advance easier; every conquest over matter puts it more completely at our feet; every correction of social abuses renders thinking well and acting well less difficult; every government, where justice and freedom go hand in hand, spreads its light over the world; every widening of the influence of religion makes it seem more like a natural thing that a nation can be born in a day. And if the world has made great advances in these latter days, and is making them, is there not something inspiriting to the laborer in the hope of greater and more rapid success, in the hope of success in the highest of all causes,—that cause of Christ which includes all temporal, as well as spiritual welfare? "Let us" then "not be weary in well doing, for in due season we shall reap, if we faint not."

SERMON XIX.

THE NEED OF THE MEDITATIVE SPIRIT IN MODERN CHRISTIANITY.

PSALM cxix. 97. O how love I Thy law! It is my meditation all the day.

[AN ORDINATION SERMON.]

THIS is one of many passages which show the thoughtful character of religious men under the old dispensation. The religions of the heathen were almost entirely an external service, with no obvious groundwork of doctrine or food for thought; but the religion of the Jews, with all its complex ceremonial, had a basis of thought, which supplied pious minds, trained within its pale, with the materials for life-long reflection. The pious Jew was not only religious, in so far as he saw the agency of God everywhere in the world, but he was meditative also, in so far as the constant object of his thinking was God in the works of His hand, in the history of His people, and in the law which proceeded from His mouth. His habit of meditation was encouraged and increased, we may believe, as from age to age the writings of inspired men increased the stock of religious thoughts; but from the first there seems to have been a tendency to thoughtfulness in the Jewish character, going hand in hand with conceptions of the character of God which called for profound reflection.

Religion thus among the Jews took the place which both religion and philosophy occupied among the heathen. Through the lands of idolatrous worship the great mass of men were ignorant and brutish, mere creatures of the senses, unused to reflection on any subject. But here and there a man would arise of deeper thoughts and higher aims, one who longed to solve the problems of the universe which crowded about him, and had for his only help in this work the powers of his own reason. By the efforts of such minds philosophy was built into a system embracing the doctrine of God, the doctrine of nature, and the doctrine of man. It took a scientific shape, and contained within itself all those means of moral and intellectual improvement, by the help of which the philosopher fondly hoped to escape from that thick ignorance and that subjection to sensuality which he saw all around him. Thus with him contemplation of truth was the way to become liberated from the dominion of the senses, to allow reason her full control, and to be united with God. Now what he attempted with such imperfect means, the Jewish religion had accomplished already in a number of pious minds by its sublime doctrine concerning Jehovah, as well as by its code of moral precepts; while at the same time by its ritual it ministered to the feeling of the worshiper and formed a bond of national union. And as the philosopher looked to contemplation to lead him to the perfection for which he aspired, so the pious Jew meditated on the word of God, as the means of his religious enjoyment and improvement.

It is my aim in this discourse to inculcate the importance of religious meditation, which the sages and the saints of old alike both practiced and recommended. My method will be,—after looking for a moment at the religious life of former ages of Christianity in this respect,—to notice the great preponderance of religious activity over meditation in the present age; to inquire into the causes of this characteristic, and to show that the symmetry and efficiency of religion are secured only by combining contemplation with action.

I. If now, in pursuance of this plan, we turn our eyes to the first or Apostolic age of Christianity, we find the religious life moving onward in a harmonious development.

Active zeal and thoughtful meditation were united in the characters first formed by Christian truth. The Apostles were daily familiar with the greatest of thoughts: the truths of the Gospel dwelt continually in their minds and souls: they found high delight in meditating upon these things. And yet, so far were they from living within themselves, from surrendering themselves to delicious contemplation, that the truth on which they fed spurred them to untiring activity in the service of mankind. Their minds were with Christ and upon Christ, as if they had no time for action, and they were as earnestly active as if they had no room for meditation.

Descending now a few ages from the days of the Apostles, we find that a change has fallen upon the Christian Church. Many of the most religious minds have fled from the world of men, as if perfection of character could be attained only in solitude by ascetic discipline and by the power of contemplation. There are now two kinds of religion: that of the multitude engaged in the commerce and sustaining the relations of life, who received on trust the scanty truth which was doled out to them; and that of the few who, escaping from the business of the external world, from family cares, and, as they hoped, from temptations, gave themselves up to a higher kind of piety,—to that which is concerned in religious worship and religious thinking. Thus the mass of Christian people have fallen into the profoundest ignorance, with scarcely an effort for their enlightenment, while here and there a secluded company are devoted to sacred studies, themselves in danger all the while, from want of motive and from doing violence to nature, of sinking into as deep ignorance and deeper vice than that which they sought to escape.

At length, in God's mercy, Protestantism dawned on the world. It is the glory of Protestantism that it has opened the Bible and trained up a thoughtful religious laity. By sending men to the Scriptures as the fountain-head of truth, by increasing the efficiency of the pulpit, by making use of the new engine of the press, it supplied rich food to multitudes of hungry minds. At the same time it was averse to a life of mere contemplation and seclusion; it appealed to the sympathies on which social religion depends, and it awakened a consciousness of power and a sense of responsibility in the individual which drove him forward on a path of active usefulness. Those nations, which have been the truest representatives of the Protestant spirit, have produced the largest number of men, not professionally addicted to the study of the Scriptures, who have meditated most profoundly upon their contents; and those ages have carried out its principles most faithfully in which a thoughtful interest in doctrine and in the preaching of the word has pervaded society.

The churches of New England were long characterized by containing a large number of laymen who made Scriptural truth their daily study amid the cares of business or of professional life. The means of studying the Scriptures were less accessible than now; a knowledge of much which forms the externals of divine truth, such as sacred geography and antiquities, was far less diffused; but the amount of acquaintance with the essence of the Scriptures was greater. Perhaps I may say also that thought moved in too doctrinal a channel, being controlled too much by the Westminster Catechism or by New England Theology, and not enough by the pure word of God; but find what fault you will with our fathers, the fact remains, that they were a meditative generation, that religious truth was the principal training of their minds, the principal subject about which the thinking of pious men in every kind of life was occupied. To familiarity with the Scriptures they united deep convictions of its truth, firm principles and unerring instincts in matters of practical life.

Has the present age of Christians retained these qualities of the past? I think not. And here may I be permitted to say that it is not my province at the present time to praise or blame, but only to discriminate. The age may be greatly in advance, for anything which concerns us now, of preceding ones. It may in regard to activity, compass of knowledge, and a catholic spirit, be superior to any since the landing of the pilgrims, and may give many promises of a still nobler future. With all this I have nothing to do. I only ask whether it is characterized by thoughtfulness to the same degree with the foregoing ages. And the answer must be that religion has to a considerable extent altered its type. It appears now under the forms of activity, of sensibility occasionally aroused, of interest in religious events, rather than in the form of meditation on the word and truth of God. This I think may be gathered from various indications. The manner in which men begin a religious life will be apt to leave its impress on their whole subsequent career. Now it is a common remark among ministers that formerly very many passed through what was called a law-work, that is, a time when they explored themselves, and thought seriously on the great problems of their sinful nature and of grace. At this work they were kept by their spiritual advisers, very injudiciously, it might be, as if there were but one and the same beaten path, by which all had to attain to hope and comfort. But no doubt the result of the process was to acquire a greater knowledge of the evil in their hearts and a higher value for the deliverance found in the Gospel. And no doubt also habits of self-reflection and a reflective, thoughtful habit of mind generally were built up the more easily on such a foundation.

Again a difference may be traced between the present and the foregoing age in regard to the importance which doctrine assumes in the minds of Christians. The old angular Calvinism of our Fathers' days has gone out of date, and even those ministers, who stickle for it most, use it less to build up their people with than to try their brethren by. Perhaps it is well that a milder type of theology has come into vogue, but surely it is not well, if congregations very generally, as I believe is the case, attach but little weight to doctrines, bestow but little thought upon them, do not love to hear them preached, and fail to see the beauty of the system of divine truth. One cannot help suspecting amid all these signs that the verities of the Bible have a weaker hold upon the faith of Christians among us than formerly; that it would be comparatively easy now for a set of heretical or half-orthodox teachers to sap the foundation of belief in a multitude of minds. Where are now those stern, perhaps, but firm and strong laymen, whose deep religious convictions and well settled theological opinions fit them to be pillars in the churches? Are they not few in number, and pointed out as relics of the olden times?

Another indication of the state of mind is the subjects which occupy the attention, and the conversation of Christian people. Perhaps I am not qualified to form a judgment here from not having been called to the practical duties of a parish: I will, therefore, rather hint the opinion than stoutly maintain, that the conversation of religious people, when they meet, is more on subjects external to the inner life than formerly; they will talk about revivals perhaps, or prayer-meetings, or preaching, or the work of missions, or some of the moral reforms in progress, but less than of old, about that which constitutes the essence of the Gospel, sin and redemption, the promises and the heavenly inheritance, the trials and the encouragements of our pilgrimage through this world.

II. Such are some of the indications of a change of tone in religious character. I proceed to assign several of the causes to which this change may be ascribed.

1. And here the first cause which offers itself to our consideration, is the wide field opened to religious activity in the present age. In the time of Edwards, a century ago, the Church and the instructions of the pulpit were the hinge on which everything turned. The relations of the parish and of the individual Christian with the great Christian world, were few and remote. Religious news, traveling from land to land, was a very small element in the training of the Christian mind. People found the centre of a religious life in the Bible, and its circumference in the religious affairs of their own little community. What was there to divert thought from the life-giving truths of the Gospel? Why should not texts of Scripture be the aliment of the mind, as godly men followed the plough, or sat at the last, or wielded the hammer, or journeyed along the way? If such an event as the great revival of 1740 broke in upon this stillness, this isolation of mind, it was transitory in its effects: communities, after being electrified by the news of the mighty work, fell back again nearly to their old state of quiet thoughtfulness.

Turn your eyes now to the present century and mark the change. No age has been so full of religious events, which draw to themselves the attention, awaken the sensibilities, demand the energies of Christians. The boundless freedom which our institutions give to movements, individual or associated, is rivalled by the boundless enterprise with which the religious spirit presses onward to the conquest of the world. The effort of the Church is now to do good. The old idea, that the first work of the Christian is to aim at perfection in holiness, has given way before the new idea, that his first work is to bring all whom he can reach into the kingdom of Christ. The enterprises of benevolence multiply and subdivide themselves daily. To those which are exclusively religious, such as missions, the circulation of the Scriptures and the Sunday-school, succeed after awhile others in which religious zeal commences the movement, but which immediately touch the moral and not the spiritual interests of society. Each of these movements has a history. Some of them have a great history. Some so link themselves to the destinies of our country or even of mankind, as by their grandeur to absorb the reflections of benevolent minds. Some enlist together all the strongest feelings of the citizen, of the man who believes in human rights, and of the Christian, to such a degree that they can easily disturb the just equilibrium of the soul, and kindle it into a dangerous intensity. In this system of religious activity there must be numerous agents, some of whom, in another state of things, would be foremost in inculcating doctrine and supplying fuel for thought, but who now are wholly occupied with the theory and the practice of active benevolence. There must be intelligence, too, of what is in movement. Religious newspapers must circulate, deriving their support from the news they give, or from their zeal in defending or opposing certain practical measures, and not from the generally unread article intended for edification, which occupies one of their columns. It is impossible, also, that the pulpit should not insist much on the claims of benevolence, should not stimulate to action, should not dwell far more on the external relations of religion than on its internal state and deep foundations.

Such now is the cause. I mean not to complain of it, but, as one who looks on both sides of him, to ask whether it is not adequate to produce the effect alleged; whether that effect will not inevitably follow if the cause operates with unmixed power? Must it not tend to educate minds which commune with history and with human progress rather than with themselves? Where, as long as it is all-controlling, can we find the inward-looking man, or rather, the upward-looking man, whose eye ranges beyond the rim of these bright earthly scenes, and sweeps through eternity? Where is the man of calmness, who daily converses not only with human wretchedness but with infinite purity; not only with God's kingdom but with God Himself; who asks not only what is to be the effect of a revolution in China, or of a war of the great European powers, or of crimes committed against freedom in Kansas, upon the kingdom of heaven, but whose mind rises to that heaven itself which lies in calm brightness above the storms of revolutions and the shakings of worlds?*

2. I mention next another cause for the change in respect to religious thoughtfulness,—a cause of more questionable character, and of great power. Not only does religion run into activity, but the age in all its secular aspects is eminently an active one, and draws away thought from the concerns of the soul and of religion to entirely another sphere. The danger from this cause is not merely that men will lose their interest in religious truth, but that they will lose their interest in religion altogether. Need I spend a moment in attempting to show that this must be and is a cause of immense efficiency? Let any one consider the vast amount of knowledge in science and history with which the mind may be absorbed; the daily news which is brought to every man's door; the career open to all in politics or business; the stimulus of endless competition; the great success and rapidity in the acquisition of wealth; the constant excitements which our free institutions bring with them; let him look at the spirit of speculation, the hot haste, the anxiety for the future with which so many minds are filled; and he will wonder that there can be any gaps of time which reflection can seize upon, any corner of the soul left for it; he will not wonder that men cannot spend much deep thought on religion, but rather that it is not banished from its old seat in the mind.

* Written in 1857.

3. I will only add as a third cause of the altered state of things, that the human mind now seems to crave an excitement of its sensibilities, which habit is inconsistent with calm reflection. The indications of this quality of our age are wide-spread and obvious; what its origin is it may be difficult to say. It characterizes our literature; the great poets of the older times are cold in comparison with the reigning poets and novelists. The eloquence of the present day must be fervid and impassioned, vehement and even violent, in order to suit the minds of men and to carry them along with it. Where-ever we turn our eyes we find questions of great moment touching social and political life arousing the highest intensity of feeling, so that calmness of mind is becoming a rare qualification. In religion we notice the same tendency, counteracted in a measure by the excitements of the world and by general familiarity with religious truth, but still manifesting itself by clear signs. The preaching of doctrine fails to interest the minds of many, and those doctrines which do not immediately affect the soul in conversion seem to be regarded as of small importance. I cannot account for this but on the supposition that men weigh truth by its effect on their feelings and not by an objective standard.

If now I have not deceived myself in regard to this characteristic of our times, is it not evident that a habit of mind ought to be engendered by it, which is the opposite of patience, calmness and tranquility? How little leisure or inclination can there be in men for studying those truths which immediately affect their souls,—how much less for pondering on those which have more remote relations to their interests! And even as to the feelings themselves, must we not suppose that the calmer ones, such as reverence, submission, contentment, will have but little room to spring up, since the truths in which they are rooted are but rare subjects of contemplation?

III. If now such are the tendencies and the characteristics of the present era, it is of great practical importance to urge the benefits of a habit of meditation as an antidote to present evils. It seems, indeed, at first view, a hopeless task to oppose or attempt to modify the spirit of the time, which draws its life from causes far beyond the control even of the whole church, and which cannot be counteracted all at once, even if all should unite in the endeavor. Add to this that many will fail to perceive any occasion for complaining of the existing state of things;—it is the best possible, they will contentedly or conceitedly affirm. Others will urge that the great ship of benevolence is flying forward with every sail set, and that it is unwise to do any thing by which its velocity can be obstructed, or its course altered. God will take care of His church, if it "goes ahead." Praisers of the past, and prophets of ill to come are birds of evil augury, whom every one with a modern spirit and in the midst of action speaks against. There must be, as there always have been, such persons, but the less they are heeded the better.

Now in reply to such feelings, which spring from a vulgar and trivial type of over-practical minds, I have only time to suggest in passing two thoughts. The first is somewhat personal and confined to the subject of this discourse. I am not advocating a return to the standard of religious life which any past age has adopted, for I am perfectly aware that attempts to reproduce the past are both idle and undesirable. The past had its faults as great, or perhaps, greater than those of the present. But it is roundness and entireness of Christian excellence at which I would aim; this, so far as I can see, is what God desires, what the Apostle Paul had in view, what every mind not blinded with conceit must see to be supremely desirable. I would have the characteristic excellences of the old times and those of the present united together, so "that we henceforth be no more children tossed to and fro, but may grow up into Him *in all things*, which is the head, even Christ."

But again I make the more general reply, that if the history of the Church teaches anything, it teaches that God does not intervene to counteract all the false and pernicious tendencies which grow up from age to age; that He expects much from the thoughtful foresight of the Church itself; and that this foresight properly heeded, may prevent great disaster. Take a single instance. The tendency to asceticism in the ancient Church, will be admitted to have been the parent of vast evil; to have crippled the energies and retarded the growth of good; to have given a wrong direction to the religious life. It does not seem impossible that Christian men should have discovered beforehand the falsehood which lay at the bottom of this movement; or, that being aware of it, they should have aroused the Church to its danger; or, that the danger being avoided, the progress of the Gospel might have been accelerated by many ages.

Believing that the active practical spirit has gained an ascendency in modern Christianity, we look to the cultivation of the contemplative tendency as its cure, not that the latter may prevail and seize the place of the former, (which would be a most undesirable result,) but that the two, by their blending, may form a symmetrical and a strong character;—a character in which every practical endeavor will have more success than now, because solid principle and firm conviction will be at the foundation.

1. In setting forth the benefits of such a spirit, we remark in the first place, that the man of meditation makes the Scriptures his own, draws from them their treasures, and incorporates them into his religious life. It is obvious that we must distinguish such a man from one who has a system of theology by rote, and from one who has a great amount of knowledge about the Scriptures without penetrating into their depths. He may be

nothing of a theologian, he need be a man of no learning, but he may be far superior in his habits of thought to both. Divine truth has a lodgment in his soul. It is looked at with serious attention. From long acquaintance he has become familiar with it, but it has not on that account, lost its importance in his eyes; on the contrary, it reveals to him new beauties, new treasures from day to day. It is linked in with his strains of thought, as he sits, or works, or walks. It fills him with thoughts while other men are filled with projects and restless desires. It supplies the wants both of his intellectual and his practical powers, and connects itself through his hopes and fears, desires and conscience, with all the conduct of life. The nature of divine truth is such, that its fullness of meaning and of bearing upon life, only reveals itself by degrees to a mind open for its reception. The thoughtful mind discovers this richness of the word; text after text opens and gathers power before the eye; truth after truth puts on new glory.

2. Such being the general effect of meditation, *it must* plainly *tend to keep the believer closer to the doctrines of the Scriptures.* The truth of the word does not take its proper shape or gain full assent by being *seen to be* in the Scriptures, any more than by being systematically arranged and proved. The best kind of orthodoxy I apprehend to be this: when a believer studies the word with thoughtfulness, he becomes imbued with its spirit, its parts and truths assume their true relations to one another in his mind, and thus, without his being aware, there has a system of Biblical doctrine grown up within him. Such a believer, it may be, is unable to explain or to defend the truth, but in the main it is with him, and he is shielded against the plausibilities of error.

Contrast with him a man of active executive mind, who is a true Christian but has given very little reflection to the word of God. What is there in the religious training of such a man to keep him from errors,—if not from fundamental ones which Christian consciousness will reject, yet from such as may greatly obstruct his progress? Can it be expected that the truth has taken a consistent shape in his mind, or that he has attained to a firm persuasion concerning it, when his thoughts are rarely turned in that direction? Will he not have derived his opinions from others and not from the original source of truth? Will not his opinions then be easily shaken if others around him fall away from the doctrine of Christ?

3. Again, the Christian who mingles meditation with action will be *a man of strong convictions and of firm principles.* He has formed his opinions, we have seen, not from a hasty examination of the word, not from leaning upon the faith of other men, not even from the letter of the Scriptures, but because by long thought their spirit has been wrought into him. If he believes at all, must he not believe with a strength of conviction which is unknown to other men? Will not his conviction answer to the faith described in the Epistle to the Hebrews, which is a confidence concerning things hoped for, a persuasion of things not seen? Is there any other entrance into such faith save by making invisible things the matter of daily and deep contemplation? Do we not find in our experience that we cannot make real to ourselves a proposition concerning an object not within the reach of the senses except by turning it around in our minds in all directions, by bringing it into connection with other truths and with our interests, and by assigning to it that place among our subjects of thought which its importance demands?

But the *principles* of the meditative man, for the same reason, will be firm. He has found in the Scriptures a guide of duty, and is supplied with the great rules of conduct. As he has thought over the word of God it has come into connection with his own life. He has not to decide upon the rule of action at the moment when action is necessary; he has not to find out what the law is and fulfill it at the same time; but the truth long ago established itself in his mind, both as a guide of his thinking, and as a platform for the government of his life.

If I am not deceived, what is especially wanting at the present time is that firm conviction concerning an invisible world, which can be promoted only by means of meditation. The world is in many respects a very different place from what it was in past ages. The arts which subserve the comfort of men, the knowledge which fascinates and ennobles, the manifold improvement in the social system, make it hard for us to conceive that we are on a pilgrimage through a strange country. Our homes—as we fondly call them—contain all that can cheer and charm, all that can make us happy at a distance from God. How difficult it is to be heavenly-minded amid such comforts in an age of refinement, plenty and peace! How much to be envied were our pilgrim fathers, if the hazards and hardships of emigration into these wilds almost forced them to commune with the better country! Can this feeling of distance from spiritual realities of infinite importance be shaken off? Can Christians live amid the attractions of the world, with the eye fixed, like the pilot's, on the port? I see not how they can but by means of such an outpouring of the Spirit as will make meditation on these things both easy and delightful.

4. The Christian who is given to meditation *will be steady in his feelings.* The man in whom the active spirit predominates and who is for the most part unused to reflection is liable to be impressed with views of religious truth, which are agitating by reason of their *novelty.* Their *importance* also, which calls for calmness of soul, rather adds to the agitation. And it may be that the *various* feelings to which religion appeals, rising in his soul together, will so crowd on his notice that he cannot take

correct views of duty or even feel aright. If indeed this were all, great upheavings might be, as they sometimes are, great blessings to the soul, the beginnings of a more constant state of the sensibilities. But by an inevitable law of nature a reaction comes on. The man becomes weary of this unnatural condition; feeling stagnates, and something like insensibility follows. Thus the religious life is fitful, spasmodic, and too often without result. There are no good religious habits formed. The soul has fallen down to its old level, and the same process must be renewed with the greater difficulty.

The Christian who has formed habits of meditation avoids this fluctuation of the spiritual life and the numberless evils which follow in its train. It is true that new views of divine truth will enter his mind continually, and a deeper significance will attach itself to the divine word. But there is at no time such a great alteration of his state of mind, there are no truths so new, that his soul will be agitated and disturbed by their entrance. As he has lived in the conscious presence of truth and of God all his Christian life, what is there to surprise or excite him, when he discovers a little more meaning in the word, or feels that God has drawn nearer to his soul? Will he not at such times, like a man accustomed to receive his prince, rise and greet the divine presence in all self-possession with reverent thankfulness?

> "He waits in secret on his God
> His God in secret sees,
> Should earth be all in arms abroad,
> His soul within has peace."

Is not this, brethren, that type of Christian character which more than any other is needed, and which more than any other exhibits the Christian in his beauty? I know not a grander quality of the soul than that quiet calmness which, while it feels deeply, yet remains sovereign over the feelings, and in which lordly reason sits upon the throne. Superior to this in usefulness and not below it as a source of power, is that steady, unwearied progress which is the result of permanent convictions, which is attended not with violent feelings, rising like gusts to-day and dying down to-morrow, but with an undercurrent of soul which "runs, and as it runs, forever will run on." Such characters are like the mountains for majestic repose; they are like perennial deep streams for constancy. Such characters we may have, if we mingle meditation on divine truth with activity in works of usefulness.

5. I only add that the man of meditation will, even *in the practical matters of religion, be most judicious and most efficient.*

He will be most *judicious*, for his policy will be guided by the great truths on which he has profoundly thought. As he understands what religion is better than others, he will be better able to judge of plans by the Scriptural standard. He will not aim at immediate or striking results but at enduring ones. He will eschew all devices to act upon the public mind, as one whose own mind is under the sway of holy truth. He will have no undue respect nor undue fear of public opinion, for his own opinion has been formed in silent thoughtfulness by something far higher than the judgment of mankind. He will be likely to know best both what can be done and what is unattainable. There is indeed a shrewdness of natural judgment which may not have fallen to his portion, and an almost intuitive knowledge of men in which he may not excel. But of what avail is such natural sharpness by its skilful use of means, when the end is a questionable one? And how often are *they* betrayed into grievous errors and frustrated of their hopes who rely on their shrewdness, and overlook something which proves an obstacle in their way, because it lies too deep down for their superficial thinking? The truly practical man in the end will be found to be one who has meditated long on truths and principles. There are men called practical, who have a shallow knowledge of both, and whose excellence consists in readiness, power of persuasion, fertility of resource, knowledge of men, and the like. But such qualities will go but little way, or rather they will disgrace their possessor, if his measures secure present success at the expense of ultimate evil. Those plans alone will stand the test of time which are built on principles outlasting time — governing past, present, and future alike.

And here, if I may be pardoned for the slight digression, I wish to speak of the contrast between the meditative man and that type of character of which the world is full, the man of noise and of platforms, and of influence by great effort and great display of power. There are men in our land, a great multitude of them, who seem not to believe in heat but in flame, not in a breeze but in a gale, who would scarcely recognize the still small voice heard by Elijah as the chosen manifestation of God. They believe in great impressions, in carrying everything by a storm of words and arguments, in wielding power over the public, especially over the people. They say, as Christ's brethren said, "If Thou do these things show Thyself to the world." And they are obnoxious to the censure which the Apostle John passes on those brethren of his Master: "For neither did His brethren believe on Him." For neither do these modern men more than half believe in quiet goodness, in the power of a life, in the strength of a silent character, in the use of unseen means to do good, in the retired scholar, in the still Christian. To them a force of the soul, to be really such, must be acknowledged by the masses: they have not enough of true taste and self-reliance to admire and honor what is not popular. Now is such a type of character the most Christian one? Nay, rather, is it not, as far as it goes, unchristian, being built upon a view of what forms character, and of the sources of true influence, which is wholly unsound? It is easy to see how habits of meditative piety would correct this fault, how they would put God's estimates of power in the place of man's; how, by fostering simplicity, they would make all unnecessary display, or power exerted beyond the due proportion and not reserved until it is needed, distasteful; how they would lead to a greater reliance on the truth, than on the form of expressing truth, and on impressions working their way silently, by the help of reflection, rather than on all the power of that oratory which aims at immediate effects.

The man who meditates deeply, will, also, be *most efficient.* It is thought by some, that *he* can accomplish nothing who is not bustling and in a hurry. It is hard, at the present age, to wait for fruits: we must see them springing up before our eyes. We want to sow not for posterity, but for ourselves. Activity in doing good is thought to consist in working fast, in doing a great deal in a little time. Undoubtedly, if the trains are well laid, the quicker the explosion the better. But we believe, that true efficiency does not consist in speed, nor in the momentary effect. He may be the most efficient who lodges one truth in an ungodly mind, and leaves it to work slowly on the soul, and not he who forces a multitude of considerations upon it until it is distracted and wearied. He may accomplish most whose useful results no man sees, who makes no noise, who resembles the silent forces of nature, and not he who will have every thing finished up by a certain time or else consider nothing to be effected. The calmness and patience, the calculation on the distant future, the noiselessness, the unweariedness, which contribute largely to the success of some men's labors, are qualities in which contemplation schools the mind. The thoughtful Christian, will, as far as in him lies, construct a solid, durable, substantial edifice, or nothing at all.

Thus I have endeavored to show that the man given to religious meditation, being familiar with the truths and principles of the Scriptures, will keep close to them, will be a man of strong convictions and of firm principles, and will be steady in his feelings, while in the practical matters of religion he will be judicious and efficient.

That preaching, then, let me add in conclusion, will supply a want of the times and do great good, which aids the meditative spirit by dwelling on the truths and principles of religion. We hear many apprehensions expressed in different quarters lest the pulpit has lost its power. Doubtless there is justice in these apprehensions, and the great cause of this want of power is the worldliness which prevails on every hand. Or, in other words, a want of faith, a spirit of unbelief in regard to spiritual realities, marks the times, both in the church and out of it; and this unbelief is the effect of intense pursuit of worldly objects. The pulpit can have no great increase of power except the Divine Spirit lends His help in overcoming this earthly-mindedness. But still, among different styles of preaching, some will more naturally produce this effect than others.

Can the pulpit increase its influence by fascinations of style, by eloquence, or by passing over from the written to the oral method of delivery? No doubt a change of form or mode in preaching may be of use; but I should be slow to expect much from a cause which has nothing to do with the spiritualities of truth. There may be an entire change in the style of preaching in the next age; but if any change comes, it ought to be suggested by the spirit then animating the body of Christians rather than to be adopted for the purpose of recovering lost power.

Can the old system of doctrinal preaching, which still lingers in a few pulpits, be restored to advantage—that, I mean, which draws its staple materials from the sharply defined tenets of systematic theology? It would seem that this has had its day. Even those who think most highly of it, preach what is distinctively and formally doctrinal far less than the last generation of ministers were wont to do; nor can congregations now be made to listen to those logical exhibitions of the truth on which our fathers fed. This is in some respects an unhappy change in public taste, for that old theological preaching trained many minds into great clearness and acuteness, as well as supplied them with great conceptions of the Divine Government. But the change is not wholly unhappy, for the preaching was not biblical, but theological; it was not an exposition of God's word, but of a human system, and that put together, where Scripture failed, by rational arguments. But whether happy or unhappy, the change has come about; both preachers and hearers confess its influence. It will be well, as we have said once before, if men do not become indifferent to doctrine—not to the human modes of stating it merely, but to the doctrine of God itself.

Or can the pulpit maintain its power by that preaching which calls to action, especially to immediate action in the great business of conversion? Doubtless, there must always be, as there always has been such preaching, and no system is of any value which discards it. But I fail to see that preaching became successful in proportion as it demanded a choice at the very instant, and enhanced the agency of the sinner in the work of grace. And I suspect that the preaching, which inculcated action somewhat exclusively,—the sinner's activity in his conversion, the exertions of others for the same end, and benevolent effort as the sum total of Christian duty—was one-sided and imperfect in several respects. It did not sufficiently take into account, that the upbuilding of the individual in holiness was of supreme importance, and that benevolence could not be kept up by presenting to the mind something to be done, without purifying and strengthening the inner life by the glorious truths of the Gospel.

We are brought then, to the preaching which is most

to be desired: it is that in which the great objects of religion shall stand forth with greater prominence, while the interests and duties of man shall force themselves on the attention, as following of course. It is that which occupies itself more with invisible realities, and which trusts to the spiritual power of truth and of God rather than to the power by which man can move the feelings and the will. It is preaching which comes from a mind profoundly penetrated with divine truth, and used to long reflection upon it, rather than from a mind which has mastered and can retail a theological system. It is that which lodges weighty thoughts and wide-sweeping principles in the hearer's soul, rather than that which awakens sensibilities that die down again, because they are not rooted in deep truth. Preaching, even of the best kind, has now too *subjective* a tendency. Those parts of the truth which are the most telling and exciting; those parts which relate most immediately to the operations of the soul, take a front rank, while others have sunk in their importance. It results from the same tendency that the sentiments which lie deepest in the soul, such as a sense of dependence, reverence and acquiescence, are but little trained and cherished; while the more violent sensibilities, which are connected with human interests and doings, are appealed to and trusted in, as the regulators of the life. The preacher of meditative spirit, will avoid the extremes of this tendency. God and eternal truth being near and real to himself, how can he fail to try to bring them near to his hearers? He will thus be a serious preacher, being penetrated by faith in invisible things. He will be a preacher fitted to build up the Church of God, to make it intelligent, thoughtful and constant. He will carry his influence far down into the lives of men. Let him die young in his field, still he has not ceased to live or to preach. The best and ripest portion of his flock will associate him with principles which sway their conduct, with thoughts which have borne fruit through their lives, with their whole progress in Christian excellence. And he will lodge such convictions in the minds of the irreligious, as will sink into their souls below the reach of worldly desires, such as will be the means of bringing them to the cordial love of the Gospel.

SERMON XX.

THE HELP WHICH THE MINISTER GETS FROM HIS EXPERIENCE.

ACTS iv. 20. For we cannot but speak the things which we have seen and heard.

[AN ORDINATION SERMON.]

SUCH are the words with which the Apostles Peter and John declared their determination to preach Christ in spite of the orders of the Jewish Council. They had seen and heard such things of and from Christ, they had received such a commission to proclaim Him to the world, that it was morally impossible for them to obey the commands of the Sadducees. The courage to obey God rather than man proceeded from what had come under their own experience, from Christ's words, from His works, His life, His resurrection. But this outward experience could have inspired them with no such boldness, if it had not aroused an inward experience; if it had not attached them to Christ as a friend, a Master, a Saviour and a King. The influences of things seen and heard within their souls and in their lives, created their strength to endure, to resist, to hope on amid discouragements, to believe in the efficacy and the triumph of the Gospel.

Unlike the Apostles, preachers in all the following ages have heard and seen nothing marvellous; no form of a divine Saviour, no miracles of grace, no words never to be forgotten, no resurrection and ascension of the Lord have been repeated before their eyes and ears. But through that which the Apostles said and heard, they have entered into fellowship with the first preachers of the word; and so their fellowship with the Father and with His Son Jesus Christ took its beginning. Thus, through the outward facts of the Gospel they have reached its spirit, have had an inward experience of its power, a conviction of its reality, a confidence in its success, which is able to lift them up above discouragements and fears, which can nerve them with courage amid obstacles and dangers, which can assure them that nothing is strong enough to contend on equal terms with Christ.

It will not, then, be thought a very violent transition, if we apply these words of Peter and John to preachers of Christ now, in their somewhat altered position; if we put in the place of what the Apostles saw and heard the inward experience of their successors in the ministry; and draw the inference, that this can sustain the soul of the modern preacher, just as the personal knowledge of Christ sustained the first ministers of the Gospel.

It is then the personal experience of the Christian minister, as exciting within him the spirit of faith, hope and courage, which will be the subject of our discourse. A simple theme, but one, as it seems to me, which can never grow old or become unprofitable, for it deals with the life of the individual Christian; it starts from his deepest convictions, and says to him you must go forth into your ministry from the facts of your inward consciousness as a Christian; those phenomena within you, which came to your notice in consequence of some divine power acting on your soul, are to be repeated and can be repeated in other souls whom your ministry reaches. Unless you are unlike the rest of mankind and for that reason unfit to preach to them, there have been transactions between you and God in the region of your spiritual nature, in which they can partake just as well as you. Your faith is an experience. Why should not their's be? As you have a like nature with them, the same disease of sin, the same capacity of being united to God, common offers of salvation, a common Saviour, so they must be affected by the Gospel, if affected at all, in a way substantially the same as you have been, and the power of the Gospel is as capable of affecting them as it has been of affecting you. True, there are infinite differences among men and no experience can be exactly repeated. No experience of one, therefore, can be made the standard for others. But it is true also that man as a sinner is cast in one mould, and obligation is one, and holiness is one; Christ too, His promises and His spiritual power are one and the same, yesterday, to-day and forever. Deeper down, then, than these varieties of individual experience lies a generic experience common to all. While, therefore, we should violate charity by asserting that all the aspects of Christian life must conform to our pattern, we do not violate truth by asserting that the generic results of the Gospel on character are every where and in all men the same, and that the influences treasured up in the Gospel are about equally adapted for delivering all men from their sins and for making them the children of God; so that he who has become such may in all hope assume that what has been the power of God for salvation to himself may be the same for the people of his care, for all the dwellers in Christian lands, yea, for all mankind.

I. From these general remarks we proceed to particular illustrations, and, in the first place, the experience of the Christian preacher, assures him that the Gospel is able to awaken a sense of sin by means of his preaching. That which brought him to reflection, which opened his eyes to his guilt and danger, which aroused within him a new sense of want, unfelt before or stronger and deeper than any felt before,—that same truth of that same Gospel, can, in the same manner, sway and heave the souls of others. The Gospel has not changed, and human nature has not changed since he entered into the kingdom of Heaven. The powers of the kingdom of Heaven, are not exhausted or dead. If they were, why should he preach at all? So, then, his convictions awakened by the Gospel, which he has not lost, but which are the rather deeper than they were at first, tell him that the truth which aroused his sense of sin is equally fitted to arouse the same feeling in the hearts of others. And in the midst of discouragement, this deep sense of the power of the Gospel, of its adaptation to the soul of man, will inspire him with courage and hope.

Here let me give two cautions before proceeding further. The first, to which I have already adverted, is this: that the minister of Christ must not expect just the same sense of sin, with the same strength or the same liveliness, to appear in all the varying forms of human life and character. Formerly in New England, the law work was expected to go in all cases, through the same stages. This was narrow *in theory,* as confining the same Spirit and the same truth within one channel, as if there should be any the less variety in conversion than in other spheres of God's agency; it was also narrow *in its tendencies,* in making good people look with suspicion on those gentle, lovely souls, who, without struggle, and without any observable depth of emotion, began the Christian life. We have outgrown this narrowness happily, but our convictions are weaker in general than were those of our fathers, and we need sometimes for that reason, after the Christian life begins, to have a deepening of our impressions, if we are to become men of power. Let us then value a pungent sense of sin while we accept the openings of a Christian life under all their aspects.

The other caution is this: that the minister himself should guard against discouragement on the ground that his entrance into a religious life was attended by no marked upheaval of his soul. Perhaps he might be a better instrument for awakening the convictions of others, if this had been the case. But let him remember *first* that the value of convictions consists in the general sense of the reality of spiritual things which arises in the soul where they are present; and, *secondly*, that we cannot measure the strength or depth of our convictions or our emotions, for we have no accurate standard of comparison for them. Violent, outbreaking emotions may be shallow; unexpressed ones, may be deep. We forget the strength of past emotions, and cannot use them in our comparisons. One man will exaggerate, another will extenuate his feelings in description. A deep sense of spiritual reality makes every feeling seem inadequate. We wonder at our coldness because our souls are moved to their depths. This, then, is no ground for discouragement. The man who came to Christ without a marked struggle or a marked intensity of feeling may be the deepest in his convictions of us all.

Let us see then how the experience of the minister helps him in preaching to men in their sins, whatever may have been the peculiar type of his own initiation into the gospel. We will suppose an extreme case. He enters into his work in the parish at a time when everything in the spiritual regions is dead. There is no life in the church. There have been no conversions for months or years. There is all around him that feverish pursuit after money, that intense worldliness, that sense of the reality of the world which is so characteristic of this American people. All are indifferent, professing to believe, but in truth never thinking of the gospel. Oh! if some would only oppose the truth, thinks he, that would be a sign of awakening life, but there is not even opposition. And so perhaps in his discouragement he thinks, and it may be some of the less dead in his parish think, that the blame lies at his door. He ought, he suspects, to preach in a different style, or on different subjects. Perhaps, he thinks, he has mistaken his calling. He has, he says, no electric power over minds, or he has not piety enough, or he has faults of manner or of character which spoil his influence.

We can easily see that in a condition of things like this, an earnest Christian man must lose very much of his working power. His natural gifts seem to wither. His religious sensibilities are benumbed. He lacks the sympathy which should cheer him, as he goes among his people. In his despondency he overrates his ill success; he thinks the seed is dead because it is slow in germinating. And so at a time when heroic effort is more than ever wanted, when a man is needed with a voice lifted up like a trumpet to show unto God's "people their transgressions, and unto the house of Jacob their sins," his hands hang lifeless at his side, he can scarcely open his mouth, he is like one in despair.

If now at such a time a wise physician of souls were called upon for counsel, he might send him back to the facts of his own experience. Were you not once in your sins, he would say, deaf to the voice of the Gospel, blind to your true interests, living for this present world? Can you bring any charge against this people of your's for their impenitence and insensibility, which could not have been brought against you? But a time came when in your case all was altered. And why was it? What brought a change about? You did not begin to see your sins and feel your wants because you were given to reflection more than others, or because sin had hardened you less, or because you had a better emotional nature, or because something in your case counteracted the obstacles which lie in the way of your hearers. No! as one who owes allegiance to a life-giving Spirit, you can say nothing like this. You must place the cause of your conversion outside of yourself, in no superior, more impressible nature of yours, but in some power of the Gospel itself which is as well calculated to impress others, and in some divine control over hearts which can as readily move your hearers' hearts as it moved yours. And with this conviction, which your experience forces upon you, it is a shame for you to doubt the power of the Gospel or to fail to see in the world a divine energy which can at any time bring large fruits from your preaching, which even now, in all silence, beyond the reach of your eyes and ears, may be preparing souls under your care for the kingdom of heaven. Plant, then, in hope. Be not weary in well doing, for in due season you shall reap, if you faint not.

II. In the second place the experience of the Christian preacher ought to supply him with encouragement and hope in his efforts to promote religious life within the church. The bearing which his experience has in this case is not altogether the same as in the case of which we have just spoken. Here it is a long experience, easily recalled and standing forth in distinct outlines, embracing his Christian life since his conversion up to the present day. There it may have been the sin, or indifference, or insensibility of *years long past* ending in conversion. The pages of his old life are written in faded, half obliterated characters, while the newer part of the volume is fresh and legible. His life is also, in its later stages, a more *positive* experience, spent in the actual presence of Christian motives and truths, just the same which he is called to enforce upon the people of his charge, while in the earlier stages it may have been *negative*, a withdrawal of his mind from the influences of the Gospel, a disregard of the truth, forgetfulness or carelessness. Thus his experience as a Christian is more vivid, and supplies him with better means, perhaps, of judging concerning other Christian hearts.

But perhaps the minister may say that his experience is vivid enough since the beginning of the new life, but that it is of the most discouraging kind. And who of us, my Christian brethren, may not sympathize with him when he describes his life, in strong, perhaps in *unduly* strong terms, as made up of struggles against sin, with frequent defeats and almost barren victories, of oscillations of a soul almost evenly balanced between earth and heaven, of slow advances towards a higher life, with the eye often directed towards the things that are behind. But ought we to sympathize with him if he should turn his experience into an argument, and should say, what hope can I have of building up the Church of God, when my toil upon myself has been so unrewarded? Shall we admit his conclusion, even if his premises, his gloomy views of his own Christian life should be, in the main, true? Ought *he* to admit *his own* conclusion? He certainly might, if religion in the soul were a thing of natural development, but he certainly cannot, if he believes in a principle of grace and a quickening Spirit. Thus much, at least, we can say to him: that his Christian course can help him to enter with all sympathy into the faults and sins, the sluggishness and moral weakness of his brethren. If the Christians of his flock are oppressed with worldliness, and often fail of honoring the Gospel, may not this have been the case with himself? And if they need a kind voice to warn, a kind hand to lead them on toward heaven,—*whose* experience qualifies for this blest office better than his own? He pities himself, must he not also pity like sufferers? And if he could only tell them of his sorrows, would not even that be a kind of encouragement to them, when they think that God has not forsaken him? Then, again, his experience makes the virtue of patience and forbearance so much the easier for him. Ministers sometimes lose their temper, when they see Christian believers full of apathy and worldliness. They feel as Moses did, when he said, "Hear now ye rebels, must I draw water for you out of this rock?" Must I give line upon line, precept upon precept, when it all bounds back from your hearts, as from impenetrable stone? But his experience has taught him a diviner charity. He has more cause to be impatient toward himself, for he can trace his own slothful, fitful progress, but there may be in them a holier life than appears on the surface. So then, in charity and patience, suggested by what he knows of himself, let him work on to build up the Church. In so doing he may, peradventure, build up himself also, and may, ere long, possess and feel a new power.

But a more important thought still remains to be considered. Whatever his religious experience may have been, if he be a true Christian, he cannot help believing both in the reality of spiritual life and in the Gospel's power to make that life grow. That he has not been permitted to fall away—is not that something? That, when he has been cold and dead, a self-reforming power has been put forth in him, that by some spiritual magic his sins themselves have worked their own cure—is this nothing, or can this be accounted for without a principle of grace? That the truth of God, for a while seemingly lifeless, has spoken to him at length with a voice of mighty power, with the charm of resistless music,—can this teach him no lesson? And must he not admit, that, on the whole, he has made some headway since his conversion, and that part of his dissatisfaction with himself has proceeded from the *sharpening* of his spiritual faculty, from the *greater sensibility* of his spiritual eye, which sees sins where it did not before, and has measured the vastness of perfection? If so, his experience ought to encourage him. He ought to build up his Church in hope.

His past history does not make him despair of becoming a better man himself,—to do so would be treason. Why should he despair of bringing others nearer to the standard of perfect manhood in Christ Jesus? He *is* really pressing towards the mark, and *has been*, in spite of his small success. Should not his experience help him in urging others to do the same? In his past life he can see the truth and Spirit of God at work, and sometimes with unusual power. Can his experience fail to convince him that a permanent power for the life of the Church is treasured up in the Gospel, and that the Spirit of Life is ever in the world? Thus, even if his experience is an unsatisfactory one, he can work with hope: how much *more* if he can discern a progress, if his choice of the ministry itself was made in the spirit of consecration, if, as he becomes better acquainted with the Gospel through his experience, he sees in it more and more the resources of an infinite mind for the holiness of Christian believers.

III. In the third place the experience of the Christian minister is fitted to encourage him amid the cavils and objections to the Gospel with which our age abounds. Every age of great mental activity, since Christ came, has tried to pick flaws in His religion; but never was greater learning or more science opposed to it, so far at least as its evidence and its authority are concerned, than now. Hostile criticism is attacking its facts and its inspiration with remorseless minuteness of scrutiny, while a new philosophy denies the possibility of a revelation and of miracles—if there could be any revelation—in its support. Philosophy goes farther than this: it denies the personality of God, puts man under the law of a fatal development, and holds that sin is a necessary stage in a finite being's progress. The Christian minister has to encounter these forces of unbelief: they come up in his studies; they fill the atmosphere through the lighter literature of the day; they have, we will suppose, affected minds in his congregation. As he sees the cloud which first gathered in Germany, passing on its gloomy way over the British channel, and, like some plague of cholera, breaking out on this side of the Atlantic, he may naturally be filled with alarm. The pillars of the Gospel seem tottering. The interests of society, of the Church are at stake.

Now in such a time as this, whose beginnings only we as yet discern on our shores, the Christian experience of the minister is eminently fitted to bring hope and courage back into his soul. For as the Gospel won its way and established its convictions in his soul not by its historical evidence simply, but by its adaptation to the wants of our common nature, by its peace offered to him when he felt his alienation from God, by the satisfaction which it held out to his longings for a higher and holier life, so he knows that it may affect the hearts of his fellow-men. It is a magnet drawing souls to itself by its inward essential power, and its main proof is the experience of its excellence. "He that believeth on the Son of God hath the witness in himself."

Let us select for tests of the power of experience two extreme standing-points of unbelief. The first shall be that doctrine of pantheistic philosophy, according to which the soul is not free, and sin is a necessary stage of development for a finite mind. The substance of such a doctrine, so far as it directly affects character, is that the sense of sin is a delusion, and that it is idle to talk of redemption. If such a philosophy could reign over Christian nations, it would soon eat out Christianity altogether and destroy our modern civilization. But can it reign? Not unless it can alter the nature of man, not unless this undying sense of sin, this self-condemnation which is so vivid a part of our experience, can be destroyed. Sin, in short—the Christian man knows by experience—is one of the great realities of our inner life; no hardening of the conscience can wholly deaden its smart; no carelessness or occupation can wholly turn the mind away from it; no philosophy can wholly destroy essential human convictions. A few minds may perish of such philosophy, but doctrines that strike against human nature must in the end suffer shipwreck.

The other case occurs where historical and critical objections to the New Testament,—both to its truth and its inspiration—are presented in their most plausible forms.

The Christian minister sees them spreading around and bearing bitter fruit. Young minds are perplexed and bewildered by them. Some professed believers are so employed and disturbed in encountering them, and in reaching a satisfying faith, that they almost lose the power of doing good, and the healthy unfolding of their characters seems to be suspended. He may himself admit that these objections have their force, and may be tempted to think that the received views in regard to inspiration need to be reconstructed. But will all this alarm him? Not if he can fall back on a clear and definite experience. These discussions may do great harm, they may land some souls upon uncertainty and unbelief, but they do not after all reach the essence of the gospel; they do not obliterate our deep convictions; they do not supply a solid resting-place; while the system of the gospel is found to bring peace, hope and courage both to those who can and those who cannot examine arguments. The man with an experience looks on the baleful path of the forms of unbelief as he would on a tornado or a flood; they have but a short-lived sweep. The world of souls will surely return to the gospel. Faith, in its citadel, has not been reached, only some outworks have been stormed. Man needs and is drawn to Christ.

IV. In the last place we remark that the Christian minister's experience will supply him with encouragement and hope in regard to the universal spread of the gospel. It seems at first view a desperate undertaking for the church in these last ages, after having stood still for centuries, to rouse itself to the conversion of the world, to be making up, as it were, for the inactivity and sloth of many generations. Especially does it seem to some a fool-hardy thing for the church in our land to take this burden on its shoulders, when the wants within our own borders, the conflict with heathenism and irreligion at home, is becoming a greater task the more rapidly the nation spreads. Such is the feeling of even benevolent unbelief, which likewise exaggerates every difficulty growing out of the inferior culture of heathenism, out of national prejudice, of language, and of whatever else holds nations asunder.

But for every difficulty attendant on this greatest and noblest work of our times the Christian minister's own life and experience provides a counter argument. He was not converted to Christ because he was an Anglo-Saxon, or had Puritan ancestors, or partook of the superior culture of the nineteenth century, or was brought up to weigh evidence, or was familiar with the story of redemption. How many he can point at possessed of all these qualifications, who are more unimpressible than heathen; and does he not find that familiarity with the truth, knowledge of obligation and of danger, tend to paralyze the power of religious motives? But he was led to Christ as a sinner, by his desire of forgiveness and of peace with God, on a path which a child or a heathen can take, where no subtle analysis of processes or clear view of doctrines is necessary. And so he feels that the same Gospel is as well adapted to the mind of the dark idolater as to his own, that it has a universal power, that it can meet men in all stages of culture with an offer of salvation, which can be expanded by one intellect into doctrines of the divine government, and by another is received as a simple promise from God. His experience then has taught him, what no perception of the mind could so well teach, that Christ is for mankind, that all men come to him in the same way of faith, that the same question meets all—"Shall I break away from my sins and take this Saviour for my master?" What turned his heart, can in like manner as easily turn the heart of any other, anywhere, who listens to the story of Christ. Nor does he stop at the conclusion that the Gospel appeals to the common principles of all nations and races; his experience suggests to him the well-grounded probability, that if God, in His providence, spreads such a universal religion through the nations, some everywhere will receive it, and that there cannot fail to be some harvest, sooner or later, gathered over all the world for Christ. The world is prepared to welcome Him, even where it seems least prepared. Thus the Christian minister co-operates with missions in hope, and even in expectation. To him, the same Spirit that taught him the way of life promises, as it were, the conversion of mankind.

Thus has the encouragement supplied to the minister, by his experience, been considered under *four aspects.* He is not disheartened when he beholds the *insensibility of men in their sins,* for he too, was once at the same distance from the Gospel. He is not disheartened when he sees *lifelessness in the Church,* but his experience, as a believer, teaches him patience and sympathy, and, although it may be an unsatisfying one, furnishes him with hope and with the power of wise counsel. He is not disheartened when he sees *philosophy and criticism making earnest and fierce assaults on the word of God,* for his experience tells him, that there are convictions and wants deep down in the soul which infidelity can never reach, and that it is on these that the truth of the Gospel fastens. He is not unhopeful of *the conversion of the world,* for his experience brings him to perceive clearly the nature of the Gospel as a salvation for mankind, because the dark Pagan has a dim sense of sin, which Christ can relieve, and can come without a long process of mind, by the help of intuitive convictions, to the reception of Christ's word.

And now, in closing this discourse, we will suggest two reflections, which can be left in the minds of our hearers without long remark. The first is that experience ought to make the preacher *bold in declaring the truth;* the other is that it ought to make him *a preacher of Divine Truth and not of human systems.*

As for the first, it is only necessary to say that religion, like every moral movement, demands something more than intellectual conviction from those who stand up before the world on its behalf. Such a kind of conviction is not earnest, it is not courageous, it gives no assurance of success. Far different is that experience of the Gospel which is attended with a deep impression of its reality. In this case the soul is committed to the cause. There are no misgivings; the preacher appears before men to testify rather than to argue; he knows what the Gospel can do from what it has done in his own case. He is not ashamed of it, for it is the power of God unto salvation. The most earnest appeals to men in their sins have come from those who have had the deepest sense of sin. Assurance of one's own Christian estate gives great plainness of speech in addressing other Christians. The man of moral courage and Christian heroism is he on whose soul Christianity has impressed the deepest feeling of its reality and its importance.

And is it not plain also that experience is an important aid in making a man a *scriptural rather than a theological* preacher? That which he has felt within will, whether he is conscious of it or not, be a guide in his manifestation of the truth to others. But it is the truth of God's word that has awakened, turned, and edified him. Those views of sin and of Christ which have been used to renew his character he will naturally use to benefit others. The Spirit did not convert him by logic and system, by showing him the consistency of religious doctrine with itself in its several parts, or with other truth belonging to the kingdom of nature or of mind, but by awakening a sense of want and of guilt, and by revealing the sufficiency of Christ. This saving truth is scriptural and Divine. It is true that a man may be narrow if he have a partial or limited experience; but he cannot be narrow if the whole Gospel has had its appropriate sway over his soul, if his character has been developed by it in harmony. Then will he preach a better, truer Gospel than he could if, without this experience, he had all theological learning and all logical power. Then, too, learning will do him good as a help, but not as an original source.

And if this be so, that which is most needed, in an age of intense worldliness, or in one of increasing unbelief, is a Christian life in the ministry, built on a deep and large experience of revealed truth. Other things may be important, but this is *all* important. Men may ask how preaching may change its style in order to be more effective, or how theological training may be improved; or they may strive to reform theological systems, or may devise new ways of reaching men in their sins, or, possibly, may contrive some new organization for the Church of Christ. But let them remember that it is the old Gospel of Christ, proclaimed by men who have felt and experienced it, that must convert the world.

SERMON XXI.

THE BENEFITS TO CHARACTER OF IGNORANCE OF THE FUTURE.

ACTS i. 7. And he said unto them it is not for you to know the times or the seasons, which the Father hath put in his own power.

ONE department of knowledge, as our Lord here teaches us, is kept by God within His own power, or, in other words, is reserved to Himself, and not laid open before the eyes of mortals. The laws of the kingdom of nature He has in part spread before us for our study, and in that field is leading mankind continually further into the deeper, more hidden recesses of His counsels. These laws, when we have once gathered them up from the examination of the past, become our almost certain guides for the future. It is true, indeed, that even in this department, all things are not naked and open to our eyes. The phenomena of the atmosphere cannot be predicted with unerring accuracy, and the earth still contains many secrets which may never be reached. It is, however, yet true, that in the material world, where God acts by laws which partake of His own immutability, He allows us to predict what He will do hereafter, and gives us firm ground to stand upon in our plans which reach into the distant future. "Thou hast established the earth and it abideth." "Forever, O Lord, Thy word is settled in Heaven."

There is, however, another department, where knowledge cannot be reduced to simple laws, where everything is complicated, and the future is hidden from the foresight of man. This is the department in which the agencies of God and man meet, where the plan of the great Ruler and the plans of countless finite beings run across one another, where the creatures of God are influencing and changing and thwarting one another in manifold ways, and God Himself is using them with or against their wills, by spiritual, invisible means, to accomplish His plan for the human race. So many agents, so many interactions create a confusion and complication which none but infinite skill can disentangle, the results of which only God can foresee. Thus the divine government over men, where one would think beforehand, from our knowledge of man himself, that all ought to be clear, is really hid in impenetrable clouds. The coming history of the world, the future life of every individual man lies beyond conjecture. Even the events which are to affect His own kingdom of grace God has kept in His own power. He has disclosed a little, He has made the final winding up sure, but this is a region of knowledge where He reigns alone, and shares the particulars of the boundless plan with no other.

It may be profitable to give one or two illustrations of so plain a subject. And first we find, every one of us, in our own experience, that the times and seasons of human life God has put in His own power. All of us who have passed the boundaries of youth can testify that an unexpected future has been unrolling itself before us through all our years. We make new acquaintances and they affect our condition and prospects. Small circumstances may have proved to be turning points in our lives, when we had no suspicion of their importance. Our plans are ever interrupted by novel events wholly unforeseen. Disease, misfortune, the death of friends, our own mortality, as well as the prosperities and joys of our earthly condition, are as much hid from us as if the lot determined them. No sagacity escapes from this ignorance, which is indeed proverbial.

Another illustration is drawn from the strange mistakes of the most practiced men, as they stand on the threshold of great events. There are vast revolutions in society and government, which alter the whole course of the world, and must have had deep foundations laid for them in the past; yet the statesmen and philosophers of the time are slumbering without anxiety on the sides of the volcano. Nay, if some one, confident in the sway of general law, assured that the divine government will have its way and will claim its rights, ventures to predict in vague terms a coming disaster, the men of his time will laugh at him as a wild guesser. But the storm which he foreboded has come, and has left desolations by wind, and flood, and lightning, which the predicter himself did not anticipate.

Thus at the fall of the Roman republic, how little did the Senatorial party augur, when they required Cæsar to resign his command on a certain day, that they were urging on measures which would destroy the power of the aristocracy forever, would change Rome into an empire, would bring on an immense revolution in society, law and government! How little did Caiaphas or Pilate dream, at the crucifixion of Christ, of the power that would go forth through all the ages from that submissive man who lay under their hand! How little did Leo X. and the leading Italians imagine that Martin Luther would make an era, and start a movement that would never stop! Who thought a little before the French revolution, unless some dreamer regarded as wild, that all the thrones of Europe would be shaken, or that a man of Corsica would hold half the continent under his foot? We call ourselves wise in matters of revolution on this side of the Atlantic, but if any saw the cloud of our present troubles arising, they measured not its vastness or its duration, and some there were among the leaders of the nation who ventured on predictions that the storm would blow over in a little space, only to earn for themselves the rebuke of levity and folly. "O Lord, I know that the way of man is not in himself; it is not in man that walketh to direct his steps."

Nor can I forbear giving one illustration more, which seems to have a close relation to the text of my discourse. The prophets and apostles, whose minds were divinely enlightened concerning the future, were yet kept to a great degree in ignorance of that future, so that the times and seasons—that is to say, the length of the interval between events, and the fit opportunities of divine action, or the crises of the kingdom of God—were not brought within their range of sight. Some persons seem to imagine that when God set apart a prophet to reveal His counsels to His people, the man acquired a telescopic sight which penetrated into all the details of the remote and the future, as though he had become a partaker of the divine mind. But this is far from being true of those comprehensive visions, in which the prophet foresaw the stages of the kingdom of God on earth. We prophesy *in part*, says Paul, that is imperfectly. And if the word *to prophesy* here denotes *utterances concerning the divine will in the present*, and these are declared to be partial or incomplete, much more partial must be the *utterances concerning the divine intentions in the future.* "The prophets of the old time," says Peter, "searched what or what manner of time the Spirit of Christ which was in them did signify, when it testified beforehand the sufferings of Christ and the glory that should follow." All was vague but beautiful before their eyes, enough to keep hope alive, for which object they were set a-prophesying, but not enough to satisfy curiosity. And so the Apostles knew not when their Master would appear again on the earth: without doubt their feelings and hopes antedated an event "the times and seasons of which God had put in his own power," which He has kept hidden until now from His church, and which will come, when it comes, like a thief.

Such being the blindness of men in regard to the future history of mankind, and such being the plan of God in this department of His kingdom, we may profitably ask

w. at are the moral uses, the purposes of discipline for the character of the individual and for the welfare of the Church, which this arrangement of His was intended to serve? Doubtless an instinct, like that of the bird, presaging the storm or providing against winter, could have been given to us; some foreboding or presentiment, such as certain persons seem to have now and then, could have run through our lives without tearing in twain the veil that hides the future from our eyes. But man is left to his traditions, and experiences, and hopes, and moral convictions, with no divine finger to warn or guide him, while the lower animal has in one sense a closer union with its Creator, and feels the cord which ties him to the Supreme Reason. And the cause of the difference is, that to the brute events are every thing, but character nothing, while to the man character is every thing and events nothing, save as they act on character.

Among the reasons why the events which make up human life and history are concealed from the prescience of man, we mention,

I. *First,* that in the province of individual effort uncertainty as to the future, united with probability of success, taxes the energies of man and develops his character in a desirable way.

Our life is directed to a great extent by calculations of the probable, and the possible, derived from the past, and applied to the future. Hope and fear are ever on the watch, looking forward for something to be secured or avoided. We know that what we hope for may fail to be realized if we relax our efforts. It is obvious that this system of things runs through life and gives to it that energy, industry and precaution, without which life would end in calamity. The man who is certain of future good feels no impulse to secure it by exertions of his own, for failure is regarded as impossible. The man who is uncertain has every motive to prevent ill success, and will avail himself of his powers, of the helps afforded by the laws of nature and by human experience; he will understand his own strength by putting it to the trial; he will guard against those faults which can obstruct his way, and will, all the while, be gathering new power as he goes forward. Not only can he accomplish as much as he hoped for, but in many cases a great deal more. He thus grows and advances, while he who is certain of the future, who lets causes beyond himself have their way and floats down the stream, is not disciplined by the work of life and learns from life little or nothing..

In particular the difficulties which we are to meet with in every good object, especially in endeavoring to improve our characters, do not take us by surprise, as long as we are ignorant of the future. We admit the possibility of them, we allow for their coming, and for their coming when we can *least* foresee their approach, we work and rest as in the neighborhood of enemies. Thus we are not stunned by any force which they may bring against us but hold out courageously, and are prepared for new exertions even when baffled and overthrown.

So too, while our uncertainty as to the future enables us to take possible difficulties into view, it enables us also to admit the possibilities of ultimate failure. Success is uncertain. Countless failures in smaller things are teaching us that the grand result may never be reached, that something may interpose to render it impossible. Thus we adjust our minds to the order of things appointed for finite beings, and have the foundation laid in our character for submission to a higher will.

Thus are we, hardened, made wary and careful; thus the virtues of prudence, forethought, diligence, vigilance, courage, and a train of others which move in harmony with these, are cherished in our souls.

We have considered the effect of uncertainty as to the

future thus far upon the character, whatever may be the moral condition of the individual before God. Doubtless a race of fallen beings is by this discipline made much nobler and fitter for good, and contains within itself more possibilities of recovery and progress than if it were endowed with prophetic foresight, and like God saw the end with clear vision. But how does this law of our condition act in respect to our spiritual and eternal interests? How does it act in relation to the interests of God's kingdom on earth.

As for the first point, our eternal interests, it is plain that *entire* inability to estimate the course of our future life would cut off motive, and entire certainty might plunge us into despair if the foreseen end were evil, and into carelessness, if it were good. But now we have the highest motives to exertion,—a probability of success, if our efforts are commensurate to the greatness of the issue, and a certainty of failure, if we let earthly things take the control of our lives. Nothing final is assured to us before the end of our course by the gracious decree of God or by our own exertions. "So run that you may obtain" is the rule for our natures, and while by acting in conformity with this rule we secure all good and escape all evil, we gain upon our way everlasting benefits for our characters. The struggles through which we pass are the means of purifying us from sin, and the result is worth them all.

As for the other point, the interests of the kingdom of God, as long as the law of the kingdom is that nothing is brought to pass but by the co-operation of God and man, and that nothing but promises of ultimate success, no immediate, sudden triumph of the principles of Christ, is held out before the servants of God, it is plain that they are in circumstances most favorable to strenuous exertion. Nothing goes on without them; there are only moral forces working without magic against the mass of evil in the kingdom of heaven and these forces they must wield. They know not the result of each effort, they know not when or how the kingdom will come in all its perfection. But they have every motive for acting, each in his sphere, and as a body, for carrying the work along through successive generations. The failure of others to do their part cannot wholly prevent my efforts from bearing rich fruit, and my failure to do mine can be a hinderance and a delay to the general success. Those same motives act then here, those same virtues of character are strengthened in the church, which are encouraged in any co-operation for a future earthly object.

II. It is well that we cannot foresee the mass of difficulties which may beset and discourage us in our future lives, and that all our trials do not press on us at once. The trials of character which men meet with through ignorance of the future sometimes break down the most stout-hearted, and lead the most determined to give up an enterprise. Nay, it often happens that an *apprehended* difficulty will unnerve and terrify the soul so that it loses all power of action. Suppose now, that this stage of ignorance were exchanged for a state of certainty; that we saw in long array, the trials, hazards, losses, pains, contempts, that were to attend on our plans; that we could take a measure of the bodily toil, the mental anxiety or tension, the spiritual struggles, the perplexities and contests of our entire lives, is it not evident that the mass of them would seem too great for human strength to move, and, even if final success were within our reach, should we not feel unequal to the number and severity of the exertions required to secure it? Ignorance, then, of the sum total of our difficulties is a great blessing for us, and without it, we should not have courage to undertake anything good and great. We *now* encounter our toils and anxieties one by one; we conquer them in detail, and sweet hope lives through all the efforts. But *then* a great cloud would hang around every new enterprise; a great mountain or wide sea would be ever in our way; the present and the future would conspire to terrify and dishearten us. I ask you, if any man is equal to the endurance, beforehand and at once, of all the pains that are allotted to him through all time,—to the full prospect and adequate conception of all that is to try him until he reaches his goal? Only one man through all the ages has had such knowledge,—He who "died every day He lived," the death on the cross for our sins. And He, without a perfect faith and consecration, would have sunk under the burden.

A few illustrations will set this truth in a clear point of view.

An inventor is a man who gropes in the dark, confident that the laws of nature in her different departments may be made to conspire for a certain result, and yet not knowing how. He works on through profitless experiments, now elated with hope, now depressed by disappointment; the world calls him a visionary who is wasting his property and his life on a project; a thousand times he wishes that he had had a different lot and a different nature. By-and-by, after many despairs and an amount of toil and thought beyond calculation, he has gained what he sought and he is happy. But let the end be as bright as it may, if he could have taken one clear, full look of his long, dreary conflict with difficulties, at the time when he laid his plan of life, who believes that he could have held on his way in courage and hope? Would he not have fled from such a career? and thus is not the world indebted for much of its progress, for many improvements in science and art, to man's ignorance of the future?

Another illustration, which we all must feel, is suggested by the present war. If we had foreseen its length, its costliness in money and life, its ill successes interspersed among its victories; if the soldiers, as they thought of enlisting, could have foreseen their hardships, wounds, defeats, is it not more than probable that the strength to persevere would have been taken out of us, that a majority of the people would have shrunk from the contest, although certain of ultimate success? Of how many public and private efforts the same thing can be said. We can resolve nobly, we can grapple with each trial as it comes, but the whole load of the future, which God in His mercy distributes over months and years, it is beyond our powers to carry.

So also, when a man has devoted himself to the work of preaching Christ's gospel, it is best for him to live in ignorance of the future. The Apostles saw trials, bloody ones, before them, and in prophetic foresight foresaw a falling away from the faith. But it was a mercy to them that they did not see the slow rate at which Christian truth has moved over the world, the days of Mohammed, the days of papal darkness, the days of a divided, distracted church. Had all this arisen above their horizon, the sadness and discouragement of the sight would have benumbed even them. Like them a minister goes hopefully into his field. For long years his labors are crowned with small fruit. The church declines. Men do not forsake their sins. Those from whom he had hoped most disappoint him utterly. Like Elijah he is tempted to request God to take away his life. Yet if no one else is saved, he at least is purified by seeming ill-success, and a seed may have been sown which will be reaped when he is at rest. But if he had foreseen all, if he could have cast his eye forward on the gloomy future, more than mortal strength would have been needed by him to enter into his work for Christ.

There is another illustration which must commend itself to all who have been endeavoring to live for God through many years of this earthly life. Who of them is not painfully conscious of fruitless struggles against sins, of a slow and fitful progress, of frequent declensions, of great perplexities on the momentous points of truth and duty, of despondency and uncertainty in regard to the inward life? Now if all this had been foreseen at the beginning, when as yet Christian virtue, unhardened and feeble, was but a tender plant amid the weeds of sin, who could have collected courage enough to endure so much for the attainment of so little? We may safely say that the life of the soul would be quenched at first, if the soul could look forward with a full realization of all the trials of its earthly pilgrimage.

And you, my young friends, whose hearts beat strong with hope, you especially have reason to bless God that He has kept the times and seasons of your lives in His own power. You may feel a natural curiosity sometimes to know what will befall you in the world: Where shall I be when I finish my college and professional life; who will be my intimates; what my condition; how long the duration of my lot? Such questions you may ask, but God be praised that there is no oracle to answer. For if you could look, as through some opened door, upon a series of pictures representing exactly all your burdens, all your disappointments, all your heart-griefs, all the obstacles in your way, your energy and courage would flag, your hopes would spring up no longer, life would lose the health of its tone and its power of growing better. Such would be the effects of a knowledge and a foresight which happily are not imparted to mortals.

> I would not be much concerned,
> Nor vainly long to see
> The volumes of Thy deep decrees,
> What months are writ for me.

III. Finally man's ignorance of the future aids the spirit of piety. And of this large subject I have time to dwell on one or two points only, as that the present limitations of our knowledge concerning the future help us to realize that God has a plan for us and for the world; that they suggest to us our dependence and awaken our faith.

Let no one impute to me here the opinion that ignorance is in such sort a handmaid of piety, that, if we could foresee the operation of all causes, we should eliminate God's providence and activity from the world, but that, as we cannot do this, we label with the name of providence what we cannot explain. Perhaps, if we had insight enough to refer all phenomena, those of the material world and those of human life, to their complicated causes, we should detect the secret invisible string which the Great Ruler holds in His hands for swaying free minds and controlling history: perhaps, however, even then we might doubt, and be able not to see God, if He stood before us. But proof of this sort, I do not value much, and this is not the way, in which God impresses His existence on our souls. A healthy mind assumes Him; He is the *petitio principii.* His manifestations in His works may awaken a sense of God, but do not produce it. The preparation for our faith is laid in our very nature and its natural development. Doubt of Him is the daughter of sin.

Such being the readiness of our nature to receive the presence of God in the world as an ultimate fact, the simple inquiry now is, in what constitution of things are we most freed from the sway of the visible world, and most thrown back upon an invisible God,—when we can see our way clear and distinct before us, or when uncertainty hangs around our future? The answer given by all experience is, that when we feel surest of the success of our plans, when we are strongest and most stable in our own opinion, when we least fear disaster, then God is farthest off from us; and that, when a deeper impression comes home to us of the uncertainties of our condition, when we can make the least calculation of the future, then the reality and sway of God are forced upon our thoughts.

The finite, dependent being is preserved in a sense of his dependence, not by a process of reasoning, but by realizing that he is not his own master, that he cannot foresee or secure his own way, that confidence in himself as the guardian of his own interests is presumptuous. The uncertainties of our lives, our ignorance, our weakness suggest the feeling of our dependence, and the sense of our dependence is a prime essential of piety.

But our ignorance of the future is an aid to *faith* also. We trust, where we do not know. We rely on character because it is a security and because we cannot foresee events. The character of God is a guaranty for that which shall come to pass. But why, one may ask, should a finite mind, ignorant of the future, trust rather than distrust, believe rather than doubt? Without question, our ignorance opens the door both to faith and to the want of it, and just here lies the trial of our characters. But when our dependence on a Supreme power is felt, when the fact is admitted that God has plans running through every life and all history, then faith, and not distrust, is natural, for such plans are good, they cannot fail; he who is in harmony with them shall prosper, and God will protect his interests. Thus much *natural* religion could discover. Doubtless, a spotless soul, without a revelation, would grow up into confidence in God, would feel safe under His care, in danger would look to Him as a present helper, would commit its future into His hands. But how much more is faith excited by the united influence of a revelation which gives us a right to trust in God, and of our state of ignorance concerning the future which impels us to faith because we have neither strength nor sight.

I cannot lay this subject down, without suggesting, as I close, two thoughts that follow the train of our remarks. The *first* of these is, that according to analogy, prophecy will never shed more than a dim, uncertain light upon the future before its fulfillment. The propheci.s relating to

Christ were such, that worldly minds could misinterpret them, and this the Jewish spirit was sure to do. Christ gave no satifaction, as we have seen, to His disciples, when they questioned Him concerning the future destinies of the kingdom of God. So, too, when Peter, in idle curiosity, asked his Master what should befall John, he received but an ambiguous answer,—"If I will that he tarry till I come, what is that to thee? Follow thou Me." And so Paul went to Jerusalem, not knowing the things that should befall him there, save that the Holy Ghost kept assuring him, as he traveled on his way, that bonds and affl ctions were in store for him. And the history of interpretation shows, that thus far the Church has made little progress in applying prophecies to particular events.

Now according to our Saviour's words in our text this ought to be so. It is not for us "to know the times or the seasons which the Father hath put into his own power." And if we have discovered the purpose of God in keeping us ignorant of the future this ought to be so. Prophecy gives us light, that the Church may not lose its hope in the dark hours of its discipline. But the light reveals neither the length of the way, nor the severity of the trials, nor the exact nature or extent of the final triumph, for such full knowledge would prevent those influences with which the present state of things acts on character, and which are better than knowledge.

Finally, he who gains character out of the uncertainties of life is a great gainer. He who struggles on to what is called success may gain nothing. *If this world were our all,* he who after long effort has secured his prize, has only gained that which is less sure than life itself, and has besides passed through the healthy discipline which comes from a life of work and uncertainty. *But if this world is not our all,* what has he gained? What uncertainty of the future life has he provided for? May he not by limiting his plans to this world have lost every thing? May not preparation for the life to come be the very point towards which finite ignorance was meant to conduct him? Must he not perish if he opens his eye to all the uncertainties and risks of this life, while he has no forethought for the great limitless future?

But on the other hand he who gains character out of the uncertainties of life gains everything. He has learned in the dark not only those qualities of character which make him a good actor in these earthly scenes and which generally insure success; but he has learned also how to depend on God, to trust in His providence, to act with Him in His plans, and to secure His co-operation. He is thus fitted for eternal life, for its employment, for its revelations. He has gained from his condition here what God meant he should. Soon this earthly darkness shall pass away. Soon a boundless field of knowledge be open to him; soon perfect certainty be within his reach. He now knows as he is known. Is not this gain? *

* 1864.

SERMON XXII.

THE STABILITY OF GOD'S THRONE.

Psalm xciii.

THE subject of this magnificent Psalm is the stability of God in His natural and moral kingdom. He is represented as a king upon his throne, robed in majesty and girded with strength: to Him the world is indebted for its stability, since He is from everlasting and His throne was established of old. Against Him, thus sitting on His throne, the wild, turbulent floods rise in their fury, as if they would drive Him from His established power, but the Lord, seated on high, is mightier than all the disturbing forces—whether of nature or of nations, which lift themselves against His authority. And of this stability His law and moral government partake: His testimonies or precepts are very sure; they may be relied upon, for they have the permanency of God in them. Holiness becometh His house forever; there are fixed proprieties in the worship of Him and in the relations of the worshiper, which will not pass away.

The irregular forces of the natural world are elsewhere represented under the image of a wild and swelling sea. But some interpreters suppose, that the type includes the moral commotion, also, of agitated, disquieted nations. In the 65th Psalm the two kinds of disorder are spoken of together as subject to the sway of God—"which stilleth the noise of the seas, the noise of their waves, and the fury of the people." I shall give this latitude to the meaning here, so that the doctrine of the Psalm is the stability of

God on His throne amid the natural and moral forces of the world which seem to threaten the order of His government.

In illustration of the truths set forth in this Psalm, I remark,

I. That the stability of God presented to us in the Scriptures consists in His fixed character and purposes, backed by unlimited power. It is not *law,*—regular and uniform sequence, dependent on the necessity of things—to which the Bible refers the order of nature. There is a will above law, and a character of infinite wisdom and goodness behind will, which is the support of the universe. If ever the Scriptures seem to represent God as arbitrary, as willing and decreeing without a reason, the representation, which is made in order to set forth, in a strong way, the unalterableness and irresistibleness of the decree of God, is corrected by other passages where the decrees of God appear as His counsels, the results of His perfect wisdom and moral excellence.

But this wisdom and moral excellence could not sit upon a throne, God could not be a king without power equal to His wisdom. Separate the two, conceive of wisdom without power, or power without wisdom, and there could be no stability in the system of things. Power alone would be ever fashioning and destroying; wisdom would be ever contriving without accomplishing, or else would confine itself to the field of its own limited resources, because it would be unwise to push further. God's majesty and strength as a ruler, is in fact, the union of His perfect attributes.

How unlike is this scriptural representation of God to the conceptions of many heathen religions and heathen philosophers. The god of heathenism is bound by and under the control of the order of nature. A higher something, fate or law, sits above him, limiting his movements and making him its vicegerent and subordinate.

His will is a capricious, unreasonable decree, formed at the time, or after a short foresight and deliberation; he has no plans reaching from the beginning and embracing all things. The order of the world is not his work.

The heathen philosopher, on the other hand, tried to strip the Deity of all limitation and change, of every influence from finite things and every relation to them; and so he reached the notion of bare *entity*. The stability of God in his view was such, the idea of Him was so broad and abstract, that all personal attributes and works must be denied to Him altogether. Thus, for all practical purposes, the world was left to itself, and the Deity was stripped of all that could awaken the feeling of awe and respect in the human soul.

II. The stability of the world results from the stability of God. It is the place where He unfolds His fixed but progressive system.

The world makes the opposite impressions on the observer. First, it is a scene of endless change and alternation. Life and death, growth and decay, the wearing away of the solid structure, and the reconstruction, the sinkings and upheavings of its surface—phenomena like these show a want of stability, a war of opposites. But again, as the observer looks beyond these immediate appearances, he sees steady, unwavering law, which may have had its way through countless ages, and shows no sign of growing weary or coming to an end. "One generation passeth away," he will say, "and another generation cometh, but the earth abideth forever."

The convictions also, of mankind give their testimony to the stability of the system. We believe, we know not why, in the permanence of the order of nature. This primary faith is no mere result of experience, but is a necessary law of thought for the unthinking and ignorant as well as for the philosopher. It does not assume that there was no beginning of material things, or that there can be no end, but only that there is so much assurance of the continuance of the system, that all fear of present change may be dismissed, and all plans of man, even if they embrace ages, may be rationally prosecuted. The God who gives stability to the universe has revealed this stability to mankind, that they may work their work demanding foresight and long preparation without disquiet and anxiety.

But the system of the world unites progress with stability. The ancient thinkers could not reach the knowledge of this great fact, which geology has disclosed to our eyes. The world itself, so fastened on its rocky base, has been moulded over and over again; has risen and sunk; has received new forms of life rising in dignity up to man, the newly settled tenant,—in short, has had a marvellous and steadily advancing history, since it has been a fit abode for animated beings.

These glimpses, which science gives us of the progress of the system, accord with the declarations of Scripture, concerning the unfolding of God's counsels in regard to creation, redemption, and the world's future destiny. But these great movements are no evidences of change—they rather manifest a steady, onward march—an established plan which needs many milleniums for its full accomplishment. "The world is established that it cannot be moved." This stability is an emanation of the wisdom and power of God,—of wisdom which has contrived it as the theatre, where He is carrying forward His great plan, and which must be kept in its place as long as the plan demands, and of power which deals with unyielding matter, as easily as the potter with the clay.

III. The Psalmist proceeds to speak of forces natural, and perhaps moral or human, whose violence seems for the time to obstruct the plan of God and to endanger the stability of the system.

Casting our eyes *first* upon the seemingly irregular

forces of nature, with what awe we behold the great deep agitated by tempests; overwhelming after a brief resistance the well-compacted vessel with all its treasure of human lives; breaking down great cliffs along the coasts which it has undermined with caverns; sweeping over great tracts of level ground planted by the husbandmen; tearing away dykes and dams so as to let in a flood upon lands that have been reclaimed from its dominions. How fearful, also, and wild are rivers in floods, when even the scarcely noticed brook seems clothed with a new power of death; how in a moment devastation is spread over meadow and plain, and streams find out another channel than that which for ages they have followed. Still more irregular is the air in tempests, sweeping over thousands of miles and destroying the works of man in its way; yet more fearful the lightning with the thunder;—the most inevitable, when it strikes, of all foes. But of all earthly forces the earthquake seems most like an insurrection against God, as if the earth itself were no longer under His curb—the earthquake tumbling cities down, cleaving the ground with great chasms, giving the watchword to volcanic fires to pour themselves forth anew, and sending the sea far up in destroying waves upon the populous shore. These are wild, convulsionary forces, but others wear away or alter the earth in silence. In a course of ages what vast effects are produced by moisture, by heat and cold, by the soil descending with the currents of rivers, by melting snow and the decay of vegetable matter. But notwithstanding all these powers, violent or quiet, the world is established that it cannot be moved. The agitated sea and air, the flood and the lightning, do their work, and that on the whole a beneficent work according to God's laws, without endangering the safety of the system. Since man has been placed on the earth its face and frame-work have remained nearly the same. Nay, earth outlasts all attacks upon it, whether occasional and violent, or silent and continual, and will endure until it shall be remodeled again to become a dwelling-place of the saints.

It is worth remarking also that there is a stability and power of resistance in some of God's very minute works, as if He were determined that life in all its species should go on safely through all the disturbances of the elements. The eggs of the smallest animals show a vitality in extremes of heat and cold that is truly surprising. Of the little shell, the fragile tenement of a living being, a poet of our day says that it is

Frail, but of force to withstand
 Year after year the shock
Of cataract seas that snap
 The three deckers' oaken spine,
Athwart the ledges of rock.

But, *again*, in the moral system among men, forces yet more terrific lift themselves up against established order. The commotions of nations are more fearful than floods or swelling seas or tempests in the air, or even than the earthquake. It is no exaggeration when the Hebrew prophets speak of them in figures borrowed from the agitations in nature. "Ho to the multitude of many people, says Isaiah, which make a noise like the noise of the seas, and to the rushing of nations that make a rushing like the rushing of mighty waters." "The earth is utterly broken down, the earth is clean dissolved, the earth is moved exceedingly. The earth shall reel to and fro like a drunkard, and shall be removed like a cottage; and the transgression thereof shall be heavy upon it, and it shall fall and not rise again." "The multitude of the strangers shall be like small dust, and the multitude of the terrible ones shall be as chaff that passeth away; yea it shall be at an instant, suddenly. Thou shalt be visited of the Lord with thunder and with earthquake, and great noise, with storm and tempest and the flame of devouring fire."

The insurrectionary forces here are those of blind desire, furious will, ignorance and hatred. Sometimes, when some of these reach a certain pitch of violence in a single man, they are frightful. But how sublimely awful they become when a whole people, millions of men, are filled with fury together, and are banded in the pride of power and in desperate resolution to do something unjust and unholy before God and men,—when they court ruin rather than consent to retrace their steps.

There is a difference between these violences in the moral system and those in the kingdom of nature. The wild forces in the latter case obey an established law and do a beneficent work—all at least, except the earthquake, into the purpose of which men have not yet been able to penetrate. But violence in the moral world, the fury and wild force of nations, as of individuals, is not only against moral order but also against the original conception of the system. The fact of sin, then, the impetuous rage of sin on the great scale, looks as if finite beings were getting the better of God, as if they were disappointing Him, and marring somewhat the majesty of His throne, when they lift up their waves against Him. But it is far otherwise: the Lord on high is in the end shown to be "mightier than the noise of many waters, yea than the mighty waves of the sea."

For *first* the law of retribution is continually coming into play, when nations commit great crimes. The blind force of finite minds punishes itself, and thus clothes God before the eyes of His creatures with majesty, and establishes His throne. It is a glorious thing when national wickedness is punished; God seems to come nearer then than in the earthquake and the flood; He speaks a word of rebuke and warning to many millions all at once. As He sees them madly given up to falsehoods, He leads them by false hopes or rash counsels or the dissensions of selfish ambition to disaster and disgrace, or He blows upon them with His pestilential breath, crippling their strength as in a moment, and filling them with dismay. A nation sometimes gives up faith in Him. But there is a law of His kingdom, which makes religion necessary to national weal, and so these misguided men, who thought to drive God out of His world, find Him coming back armed with terrors, a consuming fire, a dread avenger. They shall see Him though they bandage their eyes against the flashes of His lightnings; He will bring Himself back to their minds; men shall know there is a God that judgeth in the earth.

And *secondly*, God draws good out of evil. As in storm, and flood, and lightning, so here His final purpose is beneficent, although, through the perversity of man, not always attained. Sometimes He chastises their pride, and a humbled nation, bowing in repentance before Him, will henceforth have in its hand the key of prosperity, will respect the rights of others more, and learn lessons more readily. Sometimes a vast structure of injustice on which they set their hearts, which they upheld by all sophistry in defiance of truth and God, is made the source of their present ruin, but out of the trunk grows up again a vigorous tree, which will flourish for ages. A lesson of justice has been burnt into them which they will not forget. Sometimes they cast God away in voluptuous refinement and heartless skepticism. They are punished by dissolution of civil order, by wild passions in society, by strife of class with class, by political revolution. They are shaken until they acknowledge God again and become able to have an orderly and established government.

Thus, nations lose their stability when they come into conflict with the stability of God, with those principles of eternal truth and justice, which are deeper foundations of His throne than natural law and infinite power. So has it been in our case. A nation enjoying every blessing, has suddenly been thrown into the thickest of a political storm most vast and terrible. And why? Because it lifted itself up in pride and boastfulness, because it sanctioned manifest political injustice, and fell into political corruption. God would not let it perish without an earnest attempt to save it. How signal has been the chastisement! The more guilty part of the land has been led in demoniac madness into a state where they are ground as between the upper and nether millstone. The less guilty has been called to severe sacrifices, to humiliation, to anxiety, to the discovery of its dependence on God, and it knows not what it is destined still to endure. May we not hope, however, that when this war shall end, when the Lord on High shall have shown Himself mightier than the noise of many waters, this nation, stripped of its political injustice, humbled, made more honest, seeing God in its history, will be prepared for a bright and high destiny? May we not hope, that, mended like a watch, and moving in harmony with divine order, it will fulfill its high calling, which it had, in a great measure, abandoned, of spreading a sense of justice, a pure political example, the blessings of freedom and of the Gospel, through the nations?

II. The Psalmist passes on by an easy sequence to teach us that God's testimonies or precepts are sure, that is, are true, permanent, and to be relied upon. If the swelling waters that lift up their voice are symbols of disorder among nations as well as in nature, the transition is yet more smooth; for from the majesty and power of God as displayed against rebellious nations we go directly to His precepts which they have violated and which He upholds by His judgments.

From the stability of nature we could not infer at once the stability of the moral system. But our nature compels us to refer this stability of nature to God, and to attribute to the author of nature a moral character, a plan of government, a kingdom. Nay, if we should separate in thought the natural attributes in God from the moral, they would, standing alone, awaken no respect in us; a king of limited power, but with a soul alive to justice, would stand higher in our veneration.

But if God has a moral nature it must be a fixed one. The great system of righteousness must take a permanent place in a mind of boundless wisdom, which has no bia-ses and needs no experience. And not only this, but the moral in God's sight must have a far higher value than the physical; righteousness is the stability of His throne; it were better for heaven and earth to pass away than that He should favor or sanction one jot of injustice. If so, His precepts are sure, they can never be abrogated, never be made light of. They are the reliance of all who love righteousness, individuals or nations. And thus holiness becomes His house for ever. Having a character of holiness which will never alter, He demands a like disposition from those who worship Him. The forms of His worship may change, but its *essence is the same for ever,* spiritual union with God, consecration to Him as a holy, wise, true, merciful King and Father.

1. In closing this subject I remark first that whatever adds to the strength of the conviction that God and His precepts are immovable, adds also to the power of the righteous in this world. We live in a world of irregularities where good and evil seem to have oftentimes about equal strength; nay, the complaint has arisen in many ages from the servants of God that evil is the strongest. To meet this faintness of heart God appeals to His omnipotence. "Lift up your eyes on high and behold who hath created these things, that bringeth out their host by number, why sayest thou, O Jacob, and speakest, O Israel! my way is hid from the Lord, and my judgment is passed over from my God?" Shall He who spread the heavens as a tent to dwell in, who created the earth, and

settled it on its foundation, shall He have no stability of purposes, no uniformity of views in regard to what takes place among men? No, it cannot be! He must hate fraud, injustice, faithlessness, malice and furious rage more than you can, O Christian. Confide in Him then. Go forth to your work in the world with courage, trusting in the unchangeable righteousness of God. Every thing right that you do as a man, a citizen, a Christian, has His sympathy. He unchangeably loves right and must love you. Is not a man strong, will not a church or a righteous nation be strong, if it can entertain faith like this?

2. Times of natural and moral convulsion are pre-eminently times calculated to bring God before the mind. They bring Him from behind the cloud, He seems to show His face, and to those who humble themselves before Him He speaks words of encouragement and hope. We have already referred to God's dealings with the nations that lift up their wild cries against His sway, as seen in His punishments and corrections. In this way Napoleon was a preacher of righteousness to Europe; as the scourge of God he awakened many from their dreary infidelity and atheism. A German gentleman once told me that amid the disasters of Prussia, about the time of the battle of Jena, he first began to feel that there was a God in the earth, having been a Pantheist before. And not only do the inhabitants of the world learn righteousness at such times, but the servants of God are brought near to Him. Humbled before His majesty for their sins, they are fit to be exalted. Seeing God in His majesty they trust in His strength, in His righteousness. They are enabled to commit the interests which are dear to Him into His hands with the assurance that He will do well. They rejoice in His control, and love Him when He smites them and theirs. In the noble words of Tennyson their love and faith

"Hear at times a sentinel
That moves about from place to place,
And whispers to the vast of space
Among the worlds that all is well.
And all is well, though faith and form
Be sundered in the night of fear;
Well roars the storm to those that hear
A deeper voice across the storm."

3. How glorious the system of God will appear to those who shall see it in its oneness and completion.

Microscopic beauty, displays on a small scale or for a brief space of time, suit our minds now, but immense outlines, long stretching plans are too great for us. With God one day is as a thousand years and a thousand years as one day; but it requires a special training for man to rise to the comprehension of His counsels, so that the brief experiences of our lives are constantly coming into conflict with what He has made known to us concerning Himself. And if we were merely individuals, without the bond of race and the experiences of the race, we could have no conception of a great plan running on through time, and destined to issue in something glorious when time shall end.

Of such a plan He makes us aware in His word, and the stability of His character, His unalterable wisdom, is pledged to carry it through. History, when it arises to the height of some critical epoch in the world's affairs and looks through many ages, confirms the existence of such a plan; although, if revelation did not furnish the key it could not solve the mysteries of Providence, nor be quite sure that there is a Providence.

Faith and hope, which are prophetic powers in a servant of God, go still farther: they argue from His character and His promises, the certainty, the stability of His system. Hence, the visions of faith are sometimes rapturous. But how much more glorious will be the aspect of the system to those who shall be initiated in a future life, into the wondrous counsels of God; who shall see beginning, middle and end; the interruptions, the oppositions, the steps forward, the victory, the closing triumph? God will not seem slow or slack then, but majestic, almighty, all-wise, one and the same through the whole drama. We look upon some vast mountain of solid rock; we call to mind that it has defied the elements for ages; the flood rose and fell leaving it as it was, the rains and snows have scarcely made an impression on its surface; it has outlasted all human works and will stand until the doom. Such, to illustrate great things by small, will the stability of God's system appear, when surveyed and traced out from the heights of Heaven. But even in this world, we may expect that at some future time, there will be a most profound impression pervading mankind, of the stability and oneness of God's counsels; general history will, one day, be more wrought out than now, and will be brought into harmony with revelation. When such a time shall come, the world will appear to be one more than now, and the race one, and the counsels of God one from their germ to their perfect fulfillment. Then the perverted will of man, the schemes of imperial power, the theories sanctifying injustice, the great systems of oppression will seem to have been used by God to spread His glory. As then the enlightened eye shall look back on obstacles, which, at their time, seemed insurmountable, but have now faded away in the distance,—on the wrath of man opposing God or defying Him, on revolutions in opinion and in society, they will seem like the storm of yesterday, which has left no trace on the sky, while the steady laws of God run their constant race. "God has triumphed, He has triumphed;" they will then say: "The floods lifted up their voice, the floods lifted up their waves. The Lord on high is mightier than the noise of many waters, yea, than the mighty waves of the sea." And so we may hope that human experience, running down in the channel of history, will unite with faith and revelation, that a rectified opinion of mankind will ascribe to God His proper majesty and His place in the affairs of men, that a deep conviction of the stability of God's moral system, of the unchangeableness of His holiness, will drive unrighteousness from the world, and help to purify the nations.*

* Written in 1862.

SERMON XXIII.

THE STABILITY OF THE CHRISTIAN CHURCH.

ISAIAH lx. 20, 21 (in part). The Lord shall be thine everlasting light— Thy people shall be all righteous, they shall inherit the land forever.

ISAIAH lxvi. 22. As the new heavens and new earth, which I will make shall remain before me, saith the Lord, so shall your seed and your name remain.

THE Christian Church is not the conqueror of the Jewish polity, but the heir and successor. The new covenant has been developed out of the old. There was no break when Christ came, but a fulfilment and a completion. And so the promises were handed down in the Christian line, among which these from the latter part of Isaiah, relating to the *stability* of the ancient Church, are not the least remarkable. They declare that God is an *everlasting* light to His people, that their permanence is like the permanence of the creation of God.

The permanence of the Christian Church in the world, if it be a fact, is unlike all facts of history. Everything human decays and passes away. All institutions, forms of government, civilizations, have their day and decline. No one doubts that the old religions of India and its castes are doomed to perish. We cannot, therefore, be assured from history, that Christianity may not perish also. Still, when you look at its origin, its power of growth, its vitality, when everything around was dead; its changes of form joined to unchangeableness of principle; its power to correct evils within its pale; its predominance among the influences that act on mankind; its universal character, and its consciousness—so to speak—that the world is its own, you cannot feel it to be otherwise than quite probable that it is to be man's guide to the end of time.

Think how, at the first, before a church, in the external sense of the word, arose, before a compactly organized, body, acting together in all places, with officers guided by a common spirit, sent its power over the world,—how, at its very birth, it was strong to resist and to oppose, and strangled the serpents sent to destroy it in its very cradle. What courage, what feeling of strength there was in those men who went forth alone to preach Christ, calculating beforehand that they should die in the struggle, but sure that they were planting that which should live. Or cast your eyes on that later time, when in all quiet, by simple appeal to men's hearts, it spread itself over the Roman empire, disarmed persecutors, got supreme power into its hands, and rooted out the forms of heathenism. Here it showed itself not only stable but dominant, and this very dominion, by bringing causes of corruption within the Church, put it to the severest test. But its stability stood the test. It showed an inward vitality in the cures which it applied to its own disease. The power of self-reformation in a man, or in bodies political or religious, is surely an indication of an inward life. Or, if you look at what the Church is doing now—bringing back the apostolic age in endeavors to convert the world, grappling with all the hard problems of society, standing its ground against the metaphysics of pantheism and of sensation, and raising the standard of personal godliness,—you find her animated by the same spirit, and at the old problem with renewed courage. Thus, though history is not prophecy, though it cannot with authority predict the universal and final sway of Christ's Gospel and of Christian institutions, it reveals, at the least, a working power, a tenacity of life, a hopefulness, a benevolent energy, which are not inconsistent with stability and with continuance until the end of time.

To what is this stability due? We shall look at several causes to which it is *not* due, but to which, on a superficial view, it might be ascribed; and then, shall endeavor to show how in right reason it may be accounted for.

It is not owing, then, to strength borrowed from governments. A Roman pro-consul in Asia Minor, writing to his emperor, in the year 104, could say that the contagious superstition of the Christians had then spread not only through cities, but through villages and the open country, until the heathen temples had become desolate, the sacred festivals were neglected, and victims for sacrifice were in little demand. To stop this, was the office of persecution. Thus the Church grew without help from the government; it grew also in spite of long efforts of the government to destroy it; whenever it has been protected by the State, it has been injured in proportion to the closeness of the union, and it has flourished most when most left to itself. It submits to all sorts of restraints and grows; it grows under neglect, but the embrace of the powers of the world tends to stifle it. It can no more form an alliance with those who have the power and the glory of the world in their gift, than its Master could bow down and worship the tempter, bringing in his hand the same offerings.

Nor is the stability of the Church due to the stability of its forms of discipline and order. These have passed through a great variety of changes, from the times of the nascent Church, when there was little of established order, down through the ages of hierarchy, to our times, when the Church thrives in a great variety of forms, and with varied theories of government. Some forms indeed injure it, because they interfere with its spirituality and its freedom, but it remains at this time to be proved, that the Gospel cannot accommodate itself to any order of discipline which permits its untrammeled development; and its future form of organization is still a problem: we cannot tell whether it will be outwardly one or outwardly many, and, if one, what will be its shape.

Nor yet is the stability of the church owing to the stability of theological systems. It grew, it almost reigned, before any received dogmatic statements of its sacred truth were current. It has outlived theories and expositions innumerable, and indeed nothing connected with Christianity has been more changing than the scientific arrangements of its truths. We do not deny that a theology incorporating falsehood into its system may be detrimental to the Church and to the soul, but it is refreshing to think that within certain limits of variation in its theology its faith and hope are the same. The same Gospel cheers and vitalizes two opposite churches which denounce one another: Augustine and the Greek Fathers, Luther and Zwingli, Calvin and Arminius, Whitefield and Wesley thought differently, but at the bottom felt and hoped alike. Amid all the varying chimes of theological bells the same old hymn has been sung by the church, "Blessing and glory and honor and power be unto Him who sitteth on the throne and to the Lamb forever."

Nor can the stability of the church be explained by saying that it got the control of opinion and kept thought in leading strings, so that when science was emancipated, new conditions full of danger to the church began. It arose in spite of a reigning heathen opinion and philosophy, which it overthrew and put another in the place. It has in its healthiest state favored all knowledge in the confidence of being itself together with every other true thing from God. That some opinion and some science have been hostile to it and would undermine it, if universally admitted, is beyond question, and could not be otherwise. That on the other hand some received dogmas of the Church may have to be modified or thrown away is quite possible, but nothing as yet shows that there is on the part of physical science, as obtained by a study of nature, or of history, the science of human progress, a hostility or even a want of sympathy with the Church and with the Saviour.

Nor, lastly, can the stability of the Church be attributed to the condescending patronage of large-minded men, who saw in its justice and humanity a help for the world to be found no where else, but yet did not believe in it themselves. There have been such men without doubt, who have held Christianity to be an excellent religion for the masses, who would uphold it even by law and by establishments, but did not call themselves Christians. But in truth they have had very little hand in sustaining the Church. Perhaps their not entirely honest relation to the Gospel may have done more harm than their support did good. It is not unlikely that if they had persecuted the Church, they would have done it still more good. And it seems quite certain that such aid on earthly grounds to religion will do little good and little harm to those who seek the heavenly, to those who will have a religion from God if they can find it in the universe, to those whose justice and humanity and pains-taking for mankind flow out of Christ the fountain, and out of irrepressible convictions in their own hearts.

To what, then, is the stability of the Church due, if all these reasons are to be set aside? And to this question it is no sufficient answer that the Holy Spirit is ever in and with the Church. For the Spirit's office is to act on men according to the laws of character by Divine realities. The question, then, still recurs, to what causes in the hands of the Divine Agent is the permanence of the Christian Church to be ascribed?

I. It is due, I mention in the first place, to this: that the Gospel, on which the Church is built, works out some of the great problems which lie on the heart of man, in a way to give lasting peace and satisfaction to the soul. I refer to practical rather than to intellectual problems, although even the restless questionings of the mind either meet with an answer from the divine oracles, or are carried up into a higher realm of truth. The power inherent in Christianity itself, as a way of reconciling God and man, and of raising man above sin by great truths and great hopes, is a real and a permanent power. It is suited to all natures and capacities, to all races and times. Of course, if a soul or an age rejects the Gospel, it can have no effect on life as long as the unbelief lasts; but unbelief is a forlorn state for every earnest mind. As unbelief consists of mere denials and doubts, it only increases the natural unrest which is the fruit of sin. The proofs of the truth of the Gospel are not demonstrations, so that it does not rise above the possibility of being doubted and rejected. But it puts its trust not on its cogent arguments, addressed to the understanding, but chiefly on those appeals to the soul which carry with them their own evidence and gain the consent of the whole nature. True, doubts will arise in the intellectual region after the reception of Christianity, as clouds in the atmosphere: there is no known, there is no possible explanation to the full of the relations between the finite and the infinite. These, however, are of small account, if the experience of the soul assures it, that there is a light above the clouds, a real Sun in which there is no darkness at all.

We assume in what we say, that mankind need and will have some religion. It is as necessary for the race to be bound to God by this cord, as to be bound together in societies by institutions and governments. For this reason, when Christianity is first thrown among pagans, it may naturally be looked on as an enemy. It strips souls of their hopes, and they know not what it has to offer to fill up the gap. Hence opposition, persecution, the death or exile of those who bring the tidings from heaven to unenlightened coasts. But it conquers, because man is, or at least some men are, prepared for it. It tells them what they half knew before, it offers an unspeakably great gift, it comes with an honest countenance that silences suspicion and distrust. Frivolous souls turn from it, but they do not make opinion, they pass for nothing in the general weight of affairs; while earnest souls, even in paganism, have a longing for something higher than they can reach, and if satisfied, will die for their convictions. "This was the God I called upon to save my child," said an Indian woman to Mayhew, when he, for the first time, preached the Gospel to the Nantucket Indians, and she received the message which spoke of divine pity. Her heart was ready for a resurrection, and the voice of Christ raised her from the dead.

And so the Gospel, as it travels along the ages, finds many who will not open their hearts to it, but finds many others who count it their chief treasure. They feel it to be solid ground. It does not quake under their feet. Its hopes and motives last for a life-time, and they expect to live with its steady light shining upon them until their eyes close in death.

If, on the other hand, Christ had furnished man only with a relief from the earthly woes of a corrupt religion, a vicious society, a grinding despotism, His Gospel might have been embraced and diffused, but, as soon as conquest and a new race had overturned the old order of things, such a secular Gospel would have fulfilled its work, and, like all the births of time, have been swallowed up by time. Or if there had been a flaw in it, if it had not worn well, as tested by experience, if it had offered what it could not give, had promised rest to souls whose unrest no physician of souls could remove, the weakness of its pretensions would have been found out. The second or third century would have witnessed its decline. On the other hand, the stability of the conviction presupposed and confirmed by Christianity, the lasting satisfaction attendant on its method of salvation, the unchangeable grandeur of its aims, and of the motives by which it acts on mankind, its peace and joy which are found to be abiding—these, tested by experience, insure the stability of the Church, composed of minds the same in their wants, and in their capacity of receiving spiritual realities.

II. The stability of the Church is due, in the second place, to those permanent features of the Gospel, which bind men together in a brotherhood pervaded by the spirit of love and fellowship. It would be a great thing if each soul lived by itself in its own separate sphere, amid incommunicable joys and hopes. And there is, indeed, in every Christian breast a closed and locked chamber of most inward feelings, where God and Christ alone are the guests. But how poor and unsuited for such natures as ours would a religion be, which lived thus beyond the eyes and ears of friends and fellow-men, which was no bond or cement of society, no companion in social life! Is it not one of the highest glories of Christianity, if there is that in it which fits it to enter into the common interests of men, which ties believing souls together, makes them one body, unites them in common worship, causes them to express their feeling of brotherhood in Christian institutions, and gives them that spirit of mutual help, which renders the whole community strong? That there are such principles of union, which not only bring different minds into harmony, but almost of necessity give birth to institutions, there can be no doubt. The existence of the Church of Christ was involved in the Gospel itself, and it would have grown up without any positive rules, from the necessities of Christian intercourse, or of Christian instruction, from the impulse of common feelings, from a common faith and common hopes. Man has been called a political animal, as led by the cravings of his nature to enter not only into society, but into society which is organized under law and government, and has thus a permanent life. But much more will a Church grow out of the spirit of the Gospel, because here not only *society*, but *brotherhood*, a fellowship of similar minds, is provided for by the very spirit with which Christ is received into the heart. This brotherhood, furthermore, must be *stable and permanent*, because Christ and the relations of believers to Him are permanent; because the Scriptures are in a fixed form, and because the needs and the aims of a spiritual life, and the hopes of immortal life, are permanent.

But here an objection is made; it will be said that the church has changed and must change; that within a particular church there are diversities of intelligence, of character, of Christian progress, of degree of faith which cannot fully be united, and that in the general body of believers there is no external, and little internal union. In the Catholic church, as soon as intelligence overcame the stagnation and paralysis of the middle ages, sects of philosophy began to dispute, monks of different orders quarrelled, the papal and the episcopal principles, or monarchy and aristocracy, contended together. In the Protestant world the right of private judgment carries division much farther still, and dogmatic differences are here of far higher importance than in Catholic Christendom, where a generally received authority puts a check on the excesses of private judgment.

We accept of this summary of facts as a fair one, with whatever spirit it may be made. We do not believe either that the right of controlling the opinions of the major part of society by a select few has any validity, nor do we believe multiplicity of sects to be a blessing. We do not see that there is any pledge in the Gospel against corruptions, against abuse of Christian liberty, against infusing human ingredients of weakness into the divinely constituted church. The problem here, as in society, is to harmonize liberty and order. The problem is not to avoid all change, to bind men with fetters, so that they shall think and act exactly as Christians did in the age of Augustin, or even in the age of the apostles. It is the great desideratum to have a church flexible and yet fixed, obedient to the necessities of the times, yet adhering to the unchanging principles of Christianity. Just as in the English constitution, with all its great alterations since the sixteenth century, there have been certain fixed principles of justice, certain fixed, or nearly fixed, rights of the people, certain political landmarks; so and much more is it with the Church, or if I must so say, the churches of Christ. There is an evil in divisions into sects, as there is in strata of society. But the *real church* under all its shapes subsists through all the evils. With heart-burnings and jealousies and unfounded suspicions there is a general unity. They sing each other's hymns, they pray together, in affliction they comfort one another by the same grand truths treasured up in the divine word. God's forgiving love, Christ's sacrifice of Himself for all, the Holy Spirit leading Christian hearts into purity and peace, the foundations of morality in love and obedience, immortal hopes—*these precious things fixed as the solid mountains* are dear to all in spite of differences in dogma or in discipline. The time may come, and seems approaching, when there shall be no mystical Quakers, no logical Calvinists, no emotional Methodists, no Baptists or Ritualists shut up within the close pale of a rite or of a church, but even now the true church runs through and into them all, as true to the general principles as if there had been no separation. Nay more, I cannot help believing that the time is not a great way off when godly Roman Catholics, as they hold to the same conversion from sin with Protestants, to the same sacrifice of Christ, to the same love from God and to God, will find their hearts too large for their narrow church, will hold to a brotherhood of saints in which all partake, and will say, as was said in apostolic times, "We believe that through the grace of the Lord Jesus Christ we shall be saved even as they."

III. And this leads us *thirdly* to remark that the Church

owes its permanence in part also to its self-reforming capacity. We hinted at this in the beginning of our discourse, but it is too great a thing for a brief and passing mention.

The human and the divine have ever mingled and will ever mingle in the historical progress of Christianity, as they mingle in the development of a Christian life. No thinker, who rightly weighs past facts or the nature of the case, can expect that a supernatural religion will keep out all corruption from its own province. Men and ages may fall away from the high standard of Christian life, which the gospel holds up, and so they will pervert the truth, for surely the idea is preposterous that a fallen man or a fallen age will cling to the truth with the same fidelity and interest which were showed in days of unworldliness and purity. "It must needs be that offences come." "In the latter times some shall depart from the faith." "Many shall follow their pernicious ways, by reason of whom the way of truth shall be evil spoken of." Such sayings of Christ and His Apostles are our guide. Full of good sense, they show that Christianity was neither founded nor spread by idealists who thought that a world of sin would offer no trials or sources of corruption to their followers. They encountered bitter opposition, they expected to die for the truth, and they did not rate the corrupting influences of the world upon a successful and triumphant Church at all too low.

There are then unavoidable sources of corruption in the revolutions of society, in the growth of wealth, in the love of self-gratification, in the increase of worldly comforts. There are other sources in the ignorance of untrained Christians, in the ambition of the clergy, and their love of dominion, in the rewards offered within the Church to the aspiring in formalism, in a dead orthodoxy. With the conversion of Constantine came, as an ancient Christian writer says, an unspeakable amount of hypocrisy into the

Church. The conquest of Europe by the Germanic race, necessary as it was for the ultimate good of the Church and of mankind, spread over that continent brutal half-heathen men, ignorant of every thing, and this revolution in society could not but retard the progress of Christian light, as well as bring bad men into the Church itself. But *the worst of all corruptions* are those silent ones which arise from a decaying or a material or a hollow civilization, which creep over men's souls to destroy the energy of Christian life and neutralize the power of Christian truth.

Now how are these corruptions to be removed? The answer is that at the lowest ebb of Christian life and knowledge there remain within the reach of the Church the sources of a better spiritual state, so that it can reform itself as it has done more than once. *First*, as long as the *Bible* is acknowledged as an authority, there is an appeal to it from all other authorities, from popes, and councils, and philosophers, and the current opinion of the time. *Next*, there are at the times of greatest declension men who are somehow led, as we believe, by the Divine Spirit concurring with the word, into a deeper experience; they rise above their times, they reach convictions which are irrepressible, they must proclaim to the world at any cost what they found out as the resting-places of their souls; they become the starting points of a reform which sweeps over all Christian nations. Let, for instance, the grand truth of free remission of sins, without our works and deservings through the mediation of Christ, be obscured in the Church or half-forgotten, some man will appear who has learned it anew from the Bible, and from the experience through which his own soul has past. From him that reform, that rectification of opinion and life, which he has undergone, will spread all around; nor can any tyranny over human thought, any dread of public avowals of faith, any fear of the consequences of separation wholly destroy the movement. Thus the Church is ever coming back to the old principles and feelings, *because the Bible is the same Book,* old yet new, the treasure-house of spiritual power, and *because* when it is believed *the same old effects* follow that showed themselves when Christ was first preached.

IV *Lastly* the stability of the Church is ensured *by the stability of Christ.* "Jesus Christ, the same yesterday, today and forever." Here we will dwell not on the objective truth which clusters around Christ, and emanates from Him as the centre of the system and its essence, so much as on Christ fitted by His nature and work to be the attraction of the Christian soul. If the truth which lies at the foundation of Christianity could lose its hold on the minds of men, of course the Church and all positive religion, together with the meaning of life and the best qualities of modern civilization, would perish. But the hold which Christianity has depends on *Christ,* and the hold which *Christ* has is chiefly dependent on those personal affections and reverential regard which souls that receive Christ entertain towards Him. Every thing then in the stability and durability of the Church turns on these two points; whether *He* is fitted to attract the soul towards Himself, and whether any change of feeling towards Him can be detected in Christian minds through new tendencies of thought or of civilization, or through any other cause.

As it regards the first point no one can doubt, taking Christ's personal life and work together, that He is fitted to *draw all* men unto Himself. If Christians or any great number of them really love Him with a love surpassing that which they feel towards the nearest earthly friend, if He has held His place for centuries so that Christian poetry and painting, Christian song in its union of voice and music, *all* love to draw their subjects from His life and death, this is pretty good proof of what has been the cord that binds the soul to Christ. So it was yesterday.

Is it so to-day, and will it be so forever? We may be certain of this, that there never will be a new edition of Christianity with Christ left out of it. If He is given up all positive religion, all authority which speaks to us men from beyond our own nature will perish with *Him.* He is the principal part; the drama would be stale and empty without Him. But are there no signs of a rejection of Christ, and *can He stand the mass of attacks,* critical, historical, metaphysical which are made against Him? There are signs of a conflict from which some return with deeper confidence to the Saviour, simplifying their faith by pointing it more exclusively towards Him; while others go away and deny Him, yet generally not without deep reverence for His character. And thus we see that in the struggles of doubt His character rises above all question. It remains amid all the difficulties with which the understanding concerns itself, *a point of attraction* for the soul, *an assurance of His sincerity, a proof that His clear consciousness of what He was did not deceive Him.* Christ then is a *fixed* Saviour for the present and for the future. *Doubt is of to-day, but He is of all time.* Once let a soul feel its sins and have a longing for a better life, and turn in simplicity to Christ, and discover how He can satisfy its longings, and how in all boldness and in all love He reveals Himself as its Saviour, *that is all;*—He is received and loved. He is a *permanent possession for the soul.* He does not wear out in a life-time. He is *the permanent possession of the Church* in all its ages and changes. He does not wear out while there are men to long for redemption. He is, in the words of the Apocalypse, "The true and faithful witness, the first-begotten from the dead;" and so the Church cries out, in the words which follow these, "Unto Him that loved us and washed us from our sins in His own blood, and hath made us kings and priests unto God and His Father, to Him be glory and dominion forever."

The stability of the Church, we add in closing, is fitted to inspire us with courage. It may have its ups and downs, its bright days and dark days: men's hearts, when they see doubt, denial, the follies and the faults of Christians, may fail them for fear, but it is an unreasonable fear. Doubt about your own endurance, if you will, although that is the part of little faith ; but do not doubt that principles of salvation, which have stood their ground against sin in so many minds in all the varying forms of society, can work out and will work out the same results and more glorious ones in the future. If the Gospel has ever corrected your mistakes and follies, believe, as you may fairly, that it may do the same for the Church. If it has held its own and perhaps made advances in your heart, believe that it can do the same in the world. If you have had times of trial or of darkness, and the Gospel was your stay, believe that it may be the general stay of all believers. Let your experience put new life into the promises of God, and the promises will put new life into you. To this we must come at last, that whatever Christ can do for us He can do for all ; that if we can testify to an abiding hold of His Gospel on our souls *it has in itself stability, and the Church built on it has stability also.*

SERMON XXIV.

LONGINGS FOR THE HEAVENLY CITY.

HEBREWS XI. 14–16. 14. For they that say such things declare plainly that they seek a country: 15. And truly, if they had been mindful of that country from whence they came out, they might have had opportunity to have returned. 16. But now they desire a better country, that is a heavenly, wherefore God is not ashamed to be called their God; for he hath prepared for them a city.

THE language which comes from the lives of godly men is that they are pilgrims and strangers on earth. Such was the declaration made by the patriarch Jacob to the king of Egypt when he inquired of him his age. "The days of the years of my pilgrimage," he replied, "are an hundred and thirty years; few and evil have the days of the years of my life been, and have not attained unto the days of the years of the life of my fathers in the days of their pilgrimage." This confession of being a pilgrim was not drawn from the patriarch by his feeling of the shortness of life, for he considered his fathers who had reached a much greater age as pilgrims also. Neither was it drawn from him by the feeling that his life had been passed among strangers away from his kindred and the graves of his ancestors. For as the sacred writer says, if such had been the feeling of the patriarchs, if they had sought an earthly fatherland, they had constant opportunities to return; they needed only to cross the Euphrates at the same old ford in order to find their kindred again and be among the traditions of their fathers. But this was not what they meant, when they felt as pilgrims and longed for a home. The longing was a spiritual one; and even should we suppose that they knew little of a future life, their feeling was an aspiration for more of God and of blessedness in God than they could have here. They had a kind of sacred discontent with the best that earth could give, and a sense that without more maturity in godliness and more knowledge of God the end of their existence was unfulfilled. This was the deep source from which their pilgrim feeling proceeded; and hence the feeling continued, as long as they were away from God. They thus recognized God as their portion, and in turn He was not ashamed to be called *their God,* that is, *not their object of worship but their protector* and guardian. Well He might thus be called, for He had prepared for them a city. He would not suffer these longings of theirs, which were founded on faith and love to Him, to be unsatisfied. He had built a city on purpose for their reception. They were to have, instead of tabernacles, in which they removed from one pasturage to another, *a settled home;* instead of a dwelling among strangers a *dwelling among the truest friends,* instead of a lonely tent *a thronged city,* instead of a residence without rights or security, *a share in* that safe commonwealth, *that heavenly polity* over which God reigns.

The text, as thus expounded, supplies us with several subjects for reflection, among which I name first *the longing* which the godly have for something better than this world can give. Here we may notice *first* of all *the difference in kind* between this longing and sinful *discontent on the one hand,* and the difference between it and *the noble aspirations* of worldly minds *on the other.*

II. Discontent is the spirit of self-will, displeased with the ordinances of God, or denying a providence and complaining of its destiny. This temper *is insubordinate,* for it would remove the disposal of things out of God's hands: it *is proud and selfish,* for so far from being willing to take an humble place in the universe it would take the highest, and bend everything to its own arrangements: *it is worldly,* for the excessive desire of earthly good, which by the nature of the case must be ungratified, gives it birth: *it is not only miserable in itself, but the source of new misery,* for it leads the soul to look on the dark side of its earthly lot, and to make the most of whatever counteracts the desires.

Compare with this discontent the temper of the godly man, as he looks with dissatisfaction upon this world. He may be in a depressed condition of life and surrounded by the wrecks of hopes, but his tendency is not to complain or to chafe against the dispensations of God. He is not dissatisfied with trials as such, for he views them as intended to bring him into a state of holiness which will more than make up for them. He is not dissatisfied with God's providence, for he sees in it infinite reason and love. He is not even dissatisfied with the world, for the reason that his renewed nature has lowered his expectations and anxieties in regard to worldly good, and changed his estimate of the nature of blessedness. There is then in his feelings nothing of disappointment, or of that bitterness towards human life, which we call misanthropy, and which is as truly hatred of God, as it is hatred of man. He is not disappointed and cannot be, because he has expected nothing inordinately great from his outward condition. He has entrusted his fund of hope to one who cannot be false to him: he has laid up his treasure in heaven.

The dissatisfaction of the godly man with this earthly life is a feeling which can exist in the highest prosperity, when the wishes are all gratified, when not a cloud is on the sky. It has no reference whatever to external fortunes; no height of prosperity can extinguish it, and the depths of sorrow only increase it. It has a divine source, and is aroused by a sense of absence from communion more precious than any on earth, by a sense of imperfection which no progress in godliness has repressed, by a sense of want of spiritual enjoyment for which no earthly enjoyment can compensate. With such a dissatisfaction the highest contentment is compatible. The man may be willing, yes, he may rejoice to stay amid his trials and in a world of sin, in the hope of working for God and of fitting himself for everlasting life. He is not like the chained beast which howls with rage and bites his chain, nor even like the caged bird, that sings as he flies about the walls of his little prison but seizes the first chance to escape: he is rather like the soldier in the garrison, with whom he has often been compared, weary it may be with the constant vigilance and the toilsome defence, but stationary until his commander allows him to depart, and giving himself up meanwhile, with energy of will, perhaps with heroic joy, to the defence of the fortress.

2. The feeling of the godly man towards this world, so unlike the spirit of discontent, resembles much more the higher aspirations of mere human nature. There are men who seem to have by nature a high standard of character and attainment, who, if they lived alone and were uneducated, would have a certain dignity about them which is not allotted to all. These men are not made to be worldlings; the toils of covetousness, the intrigues of ambition they despise. If they engage in the pursuits of life, their ideal follows them along their whole course. In art, if they are artists, it places before them an excellence they never reach. In poetry or eloquence, though they may give high pleasure to others, they always keep a sense of imperfection within themselves. They are philosophers not of a sensual school, but of an ideal or spiritual; they live not by the rules of a prudential morality but with lofty, perhaps with misty, aims. They set themselves to the improvement of their own character or to the reformation of mankind. They are severe, exacting, unsatisfied with the present, pushing forwards, it may be to an unattainable point in the future.

Now these men have *this resemblance* to the godly who are our *true* pilgrims, that they are at a wide remove from earthly-mindedness in its worst sense, that they never reach the goal of their choice, and that thus they gather a dissatisfaction, often a very great dissatisfaction, with themselves and the world. But they *differ* from them in this: that they have not surrendered their native self-will, and that their standard, however lofty, is not spiritual. As they fail to take their proper place in God's kingdom, there is nothing to prevent them from running into the wildest complaints in respect to their condition. Such men, who most need reliance and submission to God, oftenest show the most improper temper, when they are disappointed. How much of the biography of genius consists of unfulfilled visions, of discontent with one's self, and yet of complaints of the world's injustice, of weariness of life. How many have taken the work of ending this scene of dissatisfaction into their own suicidal hands; unlike the heroic martyr at the stake, who longs for the palms of Heaven, but will not shorten the hour of agony one jot, since he is witnessing for God. How many have lived like Rousseau, jealous, wretched inhabitants of this world, neither pleased with themselves nor pleased with the attentions of others, unlike the meekly suffering Christian, whose cheerfulness is a bright lamp for the feet of others, revealing to them the goodness of a divine Father.

And again, these idealists, even the noblest of them all, have *nothing truly spiritual* or godly in their aspirations. We must admire them when we find them grasping at something beyond the attainment of man; we must sympathize with them in their struggles and their despondency, but we ought not to mistake the quality of their endeavors. It is not communion with God, or likeness to Him after which they long; they do not, under the sway of the divine promises escape the corruption that is in the world through lust, and so become partakers of the divine nature. They may retain their aspirations after what is true and great, after perfection in art or science, or even in character, without lifting their eyes above the level of this life, and taking God into view. They are thus essentially distinct from the religious men after the scriptural standard, who, though they may be rude and unlettered, though they may have no appreciation of art and no high ideal, yet have taken into their souls a longing for God and for communion with God. "Their souls thirst for God, for the living God; when shall I come," they cry, "and appear before God?" Now, though these aspirations may be covered up and half-crushed by sinful worldly anxieties, they *exist;* and *they* alone fit the soul for a higher life, in which more glorious manifestations of God will satisfy those who awake in God's likeness. But the aspirations of taste, science and self-discipline have no such preparatory influence; they rather take the place of that more godlike sort of longing, and cheat the souls where they lodge into the persuasion that they need no transformation and no purer source of blessedness.

II. The text leads us to remark in the second place that the godly have an opportunity to return to their former state and make this world again their portion. By not doing this they show that they seek a heavenly country. The confessions which proceed from their lips and lives prove that the world has not yet satisfied them. But if their earthly desires are not subdued and controlled by heavenly principles, they have abundant facilities for making new experiments upon the world. They can immerse themselves in it again, as they did in their days of thoughtlessness. They can assume that their ill success in securing for themselves earthly happiness was not owing to the nature of man and of the objects offered to him in the world, but to want of prudence or some wrong direction of their efforts, or some sinister conjunction of circumstances against them. They have the power to throw themselves into the pursuit of this kind of good with as much eagerness as the merest worldling. There are, moreover, temptations lying in their way, inviting them to return to a worldly life, or to remain awhile amid earthly enjoyments without thinking of their pilgrimage. The world is ready to welcome them back, for it does not relish the silent reproofs which a non-conformist to its rules utters, as he withdraws from it. There are ways of life for which something plausible can be said, which excuse inordinate, engrossing love of the world, and dignify the exclusive minding of earthly things with the name of virtue. Add to this that they find within themselves something which conspires with these outward tempters. They meet with difficulties which perplex them; sloth calls them to present repose; fear suggests future dangers; the world to come often seems unreal and a great way off; the good they expect shrinks, and present good swells in its dimensions. Thus they have not only opportunity to return *at times*, but their whole course is filled with such opportunities. Some who seemed to be like them have gone back, and made it plain that the world was their home, and that they had mistaken their way, when they professed to begin the *pilgrim-life*. These have never returned to the path on which they set out, and by their careless, quiet satisfaction with this world condemn those who look beyond it. Others are always halting, doubting which way they shall go, going forward with averted eyes, and leaving their sins with regret. You cannot tell what they are seeking most. Certain it is they seem to make no progress on their pilgrimage.

Amid these defections and haltings, these temptations and opportunities to return, the man of a heavenly mind utters his pilgrim's confession by his life, sings his pilgrim-song and goes forward. If his longings had been for mere happiness he would have served the world like the others. He would have refused to set out for heaven, or have returned, for it is destined for those who have only happiness in view to make continual mistakes, to look for it where it is not, and fail to see it where it is. Such have no eye of faith to pierce the reality of things. But he with opened eye is seeking for a *better country, that is a heavenly.* It is not the extent of his dissatisfaction with the world, or the strength of his resolution, or the force of circumstances, or a peculiar nature which leads him on in his chosen course, but the conviction that *there is a better* country to which he can attain. And *it is better* not simply because it promises a greater amount of good, or more lasting good such as the earth gives for a few years, but because it lays before his hopes *another kind of good,* as different from earthly as possible. This difference between spiritual and temporal good was always a reality of infinite importance, but he could not perceive it until his eye was opened and his affections transferred. Since that great revolution in his character, weak and tempted and often vacillating as he has been, he has resisted the invitations of the world to return to his old plan of life, because his desires are fastened on a new object, on the heavenly inheritance, which comprises all that is holy and truly blessed.

III. Owing to these heavenly desires, to this spiritual mind of the Christian, God is not ashamed to be called his God. As his God and protector, God takes care of his interests by preparing for him a city.

The aspirations of the heavenly mind point towards God, and do homage to God not only as a lawgiver and controller, but as a hope and portion. Now will God be ashamed of such a heart, that breathes towards Him the new language of love and confidence? Will He reject from His service one who desires to be with Him and to work for Him? Will He make no difference between the condition of those who have clung to this world in spite of all divine influence, all warnings, all demonstrations of the emptiness of their hope, and those who have forsaken the world to find Him? If He had made these *no* promise, could He forbear to show them His complacency in their choice; and if he has made them *promises great* and *precious,* will He fail in the performance? They throw themselves, by an act of faith, on Him, take Him as their God, resolve to cleave to Him, prize heaven because He is there, and turn away from the earth because they cannot see enough of Him here: will He not value *such faith,* such longing after Him, such surrendry of their happiness into His hands? Assuredly He will. He is far from being ashamed of such service, far from disappointing such hopes, far from showing to the universe, that such consecration is of no account before Him, when, moreover, His own Spirit inspired it. Therefore He enters into covenant with them: since they make Him, by an act of faith, *their God, that is their object of supreme veneration, their hope, their guide, He becomes their God, that is, their protector*—in which protection is included all necessary guidance by His Spirit and Providence here, together with the hopes of immortal life. *They* are not *ashamed* before the world to *make Him their God; He is not ashamed to be called their God.*

Acting as their God—the sacred writer proceeds to say —*He hath prepared for them a city.* His preparations are as large as their hopes. His foresight has, from the foundation of the world, arranged all things, so that whatever changes overturn this world, there is an unchangeable share in immortal life prepared for them. Others cannot step in and take their inheritance. It is theirs by preparation, by the predetermination of God.

It is not without emphasis, that this portion prepared for them is called a *city.* We have already, in brief, summed up the notions that can lie in this word. Let us now again give to it a moment's meditation.

It is a *city* which is prepared for them in contrast with a *tent;* it is *something abiding and stationary,* in contrast with this *temporary and uncertain* state of existence. The dwellers in tents, as they drove their flocks from place to place, beheld at a distance, perched on a hill-top, the cities which the industrious Canaanites had built. While *they* were fastened to no one spot, the *city dwellers* lived within their walls year after year; one generation of nomads passed away after another, and still the city was there, shining at a distance in the sun, with houses built to defy time, whose walls were never taken down to be transported to some other spot. The city became to the owners of flocks an emblem of what was lasting: the tent became to the citizens an emblem of what was short-lived and transient.

The man of God dwells in a tent or tabernacle in this world, and not only *wants* no *city* here, but feels that he can *find* none. Still his nature longs for something abiding. Death, decay, change, uncertainty are alien from his nature, they run counter to the longing for immortality which is within him. Such an abiding-place God, his God, hath provided for him. It is a city which *hath foundations,* whose builder is the everlasting one, and which the skill of such a builder has made indestructible. It is a permanent home. No more does he who is admitted into its gates need to be moved about in quest of a new settlement. He is no more an emigrant or a pilgrim; he is no more left to uncertain conjectures in regard to his future condition. This city henceforth is to be his continual home, and his rest.

Again it is *a city* which is prepared for the godly man, in distinction from *a lonely tent among strangers.* So that his feeling of being by himself away from his best friends will have an end. As the traveler in the East passes from the bazaars and thronged streets of some capital, to the border of the wilderness, where the Bedouin is encamped for a season, he finds a new sort of people, who have no turn for city life, who are retired from the haunts of men, and when nearest to cities feel wholly estranged from them. Something so do godly men feel amid all the ties and joys of this world. Its spirit is unlike theirs; they have no home-feeling in its neighborhood; they have, while they live closest to it, an unsatisfied sense of absence from something most akin to them, a sense of emptiness for which hope alone furnishes a relief. The city which God, their God, hath prepared for them fills up this want. There they are to be among friends, in whom they can fully confide,—with God, Christ and the redeemed,—there they will no more have that sense of loneliness, which saddened them in their night-wanderings through this world. The city is the great gathering place of God's chosen ones, where nothing that hates or destroys can enter.

Again the place which God, their God, hath prepared for them, is called a *city*, as being the *heavenly polity* where God reigns. If the Bedouin or Tartar be carried from his wild usages, to the rules and institutions of a well-ordered commonwealth, he finds at once the entire contrast with his old way of life. He cannot adapt himself to the healthy control and method of a society so wholly unlike his own spirit of license.

It is quite otherwise with the Christian. In this world, as he wanders through it, he sees disorder, lawlessness, unbridled will: God reigns by natural law, but not over human hearts or society. And thus whatever institutions arise on earth, they tend to acquire a godless character and to decay. But this city, which God, his God, hath prepared for him, is a commonwealth of well-ordered, sanctified minds, of citizens whose highest idea of freedom is to serve and love with the entire devotion of the heart. It is a place where the rights of God as a sovereign are acknowledged with joy. It is a city, where no citizen violates the rights of another, where there can be no conflict of interests, no faction, no revolution, nor any fear, penalty or restraint. It is a place of perfect harmony, a perfect commonwealth.

The reflections to which I have called your attention in this discourse enable us to discover that heavenly longings and the feeling of the pilgrim can be ascribed to no earthly origin.

There are those who think that what is divine in man, as they call it, if unimpeded by counteracting causes and refined by education, would blossom out into an unworldly, heavenly character. There is something in man which discerns dimly or feels its celestial origin, and can be made by the proper encouragement to trample the world under its feet. The aspirations after ideal perfection, which we considered in the early part of this discourse, can be made without any help from God or revelation to fasten specifically upon heavenly things, and either to put on the nature of what is called faith in the Bible, or to take its place.

This view of the capabilities of human nature is false, but akin to truth. A great poet has said that "Heaven lies about us in our infancy," while "shades of the prison-house begin to close upon the growing boy."

"The youth,"

he continues,

"Who daily farther from the east
Must travel, still is nature's priest,
And by the vision splendid
Is on his way attended;
At length the man perceives it die away,
And fade into the light of common day."

Now I believe and most cheerfully admit that if human nature had retained its incorrupt state of child-like faith, if the stream of gratitude and veneration had not almost dried up in the bosom of man, if he had lived in sympathy with whatever is pure,—I admit that in this case, as the faculties expanded, the recognition of a pure and infinite [illegible] have been received into the mind even [illegible] distinct proof, that with a feeling of his true destiny man would have embraced a faith in immortal life, and that heaven would have lain about us in childhood and in manhood, like a sky into whose blue depths our eye could penetrate. But from the wreck of this happy innocence what has survived save longings that either gnaw the soul or content themselves with an earthly object? What is there in the heaven or future life of any heathen mythology that indicates this child-like purity of the race, or that acts as a strong motive upon the man environed with earthly things? Homer knew what men are, when he made Achilles among the shades say that he would rather be a field laborer in the service of a poor man, than be king over the dead. No! my friends, there is *enough* of relationship to heaven left, since our fall from innocence, to make us without excuse when from love to this world we turn our backs on celestial hopes, but *not enough* to exalt us above that world-worship in which we are sunk, and which is the very kernel of our sin. If we had affinities to a heaven where God manifests His presence, we should on the first news of it receive it as a message of life, but worldliness is as intense, there is as little love for a spiritual and heavenly inheritance among the money-loving and earth-loving inhabitants of Christian lands, as among the most besotted idolaters. There is need then of a new revelation, that the dark mind may have a light brought into it in spite of itself, and of a new creation, that a love for spiritual things may be awakened. Thus only can the soul be led to lift its aspirations towards a heaven of unspotted holiness, bright with God's presence; thus only will it believe and trust in the sure promise of God, and overcome earthly allurements. It is not enough that there be a revival of a child's mind in the midst of manhood,—although even that amid the world's resisting forces were impossible—but there must also be a deadening of the old worldly by the power of a new heavenly principle. Not without this can we receive the promises as motive powers into our hearts, nor be persuaded by them, nor embrace them, nor confess that we are strangers and pilgrims on earth. *Without this* remoulding of his nature, the most aspiring, the most ideal will form for himself an earthly paradise; *with this* the Christian of the coarsest mould will put on by degrees heavenly properties, and become transfigured into an inhabitant of the *city* of God.

SERMON XXV.

THE RELIGION OF THE FUTURE.*

MATTHEW xxiv. 4. And this gospel of the kingdom shall be preached in all the world for a witness to all nations, and then shall the end come.

IT is the doctrine of the New Testament that the dispensation which was introduced by Christ is to continue until the end of the world. The whole strain of the New Testament shows this; and such passages especially as "Of His kingdom there shall be no end;" "He must reign until He hath put all His enemies under His feet;" "This gospel of the kingdom shall be preached in all the world for a witness unto all nations, and then shall the end come," are proofs, with many others like them, that the Founder of Christianity and His disciples regarded it as the final act of God's moral system for the human race. The very nature of Christ's religion would be enough of itself to demonstrate that it must be, if true, not a stage in a progress, but the ultimate form of religious truth and thought, the last of God's economies, the fruit which, when fully ripe, is followed by the plant's death and the end of the year. As the completion of whatever was imperfect in Judaism, as intended for all mankind, and claiming for itself to satisfy the religious wants of all, it cannot be superseded by any new form of truth, or supplemented by a later and improved revelation. All the progress of mankind until the end of time, and all the hopes of mankind are treasured up in it, if

* This was originally preached in the College Chapel with omissions, and was afterwards enlarged and published in the *New Englander* for July, 1869.

its claims are just. When it shall have done its work, the present condition of man on earth shall come to an end, and a state of things wholly new, a state of retribution, shall succeed.

There are many persons in the present age who refuse to admit these pretensions of Christianity. It is not to be the universal, nor the ultimate religion of the world. In some respects it may have been a very great improvement on whatever of religious doctrine preceded it, and it has carried the nations of Christendom to a higher state of culture than was ever before reached; but it is like all other religions in having no historical basis and no divine authority. The progress of the world, hereafter, will consist in setting aside the exclusive claims of Christ, in retaining all that in His moral precepts which will endure the storms of time, and in giving the guidance of the future to science and human insight. The religion of the future will be a religion with all that is peculiar to Christianity cast away, while something of its spirit will be retained; and, with the help of this spirit, without a revelation, the coming ages will reach the point of perfection that is attainable by man.

The enemies of Christianity are divided among themselves. As Atheists, Pantheists, and Theists—the latter of various classes—they even oppose and sometimes denounce one another. Of this irreconcilable difference of opinion, however, we intend to make no use. We will suppose that the Theists are at length to triumph;—that they who receive the doctrine of an infinite God, and a divine plan in governing the world, and who hold to a system of morals something like that of Christ, are to gain the day over all other thinkers;—that the destinies of the world are to be put into their hands;—that the religion of the future is to be as they shall shape it. Their way of thinking, we will suppose, has had its perfect work. The reign of Christianity is over. That religion which soothed sorrows and inspired hope, which took up man amid the despair of decaying antiquity, was his only protector through the middle ages, and led on modern civilization; which has encouraged philosophy to reproduce the thoughts of God; which has given security to states by its lofty morals, and exalts the poorest of men by awakening the feeling of human brotherhood and the sense of human rights; which has controlled and modified art and letters,—that religion, we say, is fallen, its stronghold of facts is demolished, its miracles, whether to be explained historically or not, are discarded as inconsistent with the laws of the universe; its Christ is only a man, its God has retired behind the curtain, never to reveal Himself in human affairs. He spoke not to the fathers by the prophets. He speaks not to us by His Son. He will never speak to mankind. Men must do the best they can without Christ and without a Gospel.

Let us make the most favorable supposition the case admits of—that these foes of Christ's religion are sincere, earnest, philanthropic men, haters of all injustice and of all falsehood; that they begin their work of destruction with the purpose of introducing something better, and really believe that the progress of men can only be reached through their systems of thinking. Let us suppose too, that unbelief creeps over the Christian world not all at once, like a stroke of paralysis, but by a slow undermining of the foundations, by an abandonment of one point after another. The Christian faith ceases not at once to be respected or admired, but becomes by degrees conscious of its weakness, loses hope, retreats from the more educated to the less, lingers longest with the poor, the widow, the afflicted who have no weight in the world, and at length dies out and is forgotten, to be counted among the many religions, which she herself, drove away from among mankind.

Now, we ask, What the world will do without a positive,

historical, revealed religion. Let the religion of the future, as we will call the rival of Christianity, start on its career with all veneration for the spirit of the Gospel; can that veneration last? What doctrines will be left to rear their heads above the deluge of unbelief? What motives in favor of religion will survive the decay, the extinction of Christianity?

We propose to attempt to answer some of these questions in a spirit of candor, to look at some of the disadvantages, which, will of necessity, attend on such a religion, and to consider what prospects it can have of spreading over and of bettering mankind.

And here let it be permitted to us to say once for all, that we compare the resources and powers of the Gospel with systems of Theism, but that, if what we are about to urge, has any weight, it will be still more weighty in the comparison between Christianity and Pantheistic religions. The point again toward which we turn our remarks, is not directly the truth of the religions placed side by side, nor directly their services to mankind, but rather to find out whether any religion, which lays no claim to be a revelation, even although holding fast to a personal God, can fulfill the offices of a religion for the world, and whether, if it cannot, progress or civilization can take its place.

I. Our first position is that the absence from a religion of historical facts is a very great weakness, or, in other words, that the supposed religion of the future, being unable, as it must be, to take the form of facts and of history, must be without a very great source of power.

Christianity is historical in its very nature, and cannot, as we maintain, be torn apart from history, without both ruining the religion and belittling the whole story of the world; for the system of redemption through Christ is a progressive work going on in the world of men, and culminating in the manifestation here below of the Son of

God. The religion being a story, and a story concerning God, its evidences, it is quite natural to suppose, must not merely make an appeal to the moral judgments and sentiments, but, like all other story, must depend on the veracity of witnesses, on the truth of facts in the outer world. Moreover, as religion is a practical thing, as its highest aim ever must be to be taken up into the lives of men, and hence to interweave itself with all actions and all history, it must exhibit life, or truth conviction and principle in action, before our eyes—that is, it must be historical.

All this, the great founder of Christianity and His first followers were aware of, more so, perhaps, than any of their successors in the following ages until the present time. He sent them forth as witnesses; they took this attitude before the world and felt that this was their leading vocation. Their view of the strength of the Gospel was justified by their success. It spread by the simple telling of a story, even among the most prejudiced, among the Jews to whom a suffering Christ was a stumbling-block, and among the Greeks, to whom a new religion, bursting in upon the events of the present world, was a thing not so much as dreamed of. It is true that it contained a system of doctrines, a philosophy suited to man's wants, to his convictions, to his deepest nature, but it is equally true, that the philosophy could not have existed separate from the facts and that by the facts it was recommended, impressed, and established.

To this force of the historical element in religion the systems of heathenism bear testimony.

On whatever principle we account for the religions of nature, it is evident that their mythologies and their worship indicate a desire to bring the Deity out of the region of abstract thought, to represent Him to the human senses and in contiguity with man, to call Him within the limits of space and time. The great interest, the great charm of heathenism consists in its mythology, as India, Greece, Scandinavia, and even the new world bear witness: if its views of the Divine Being had not taken the form of a narrative, if the gods had not been represented as living and moving and acting among men, it would have lacked the power to fascinate and in a measure to satisfy the human soul. The Romans, who had at first a sober religion without image worship and with a scanty mythology, to a good degree deserted their earlier and vaguer system for the more beautiful, more copious, more imaginative fables of the Greeks. Upon mythology worship in a considerable degree depends; the sacredness of particular spots, the reasons for particular rites, the character of the rites themselves, are all to be referred to ancient and venerated traditions. Poetry too and art are shaped by mythology; they draw their materials from its fables, they act originally as its handmaids. And, when heathenism decays, as decay it must, the overthrow grows out of philosophical views and historical criticism rejecting the narratives handed down from ancient times. All these and many like considerations show that religion would appear dead and barren to mankind if it assumed an abstract, philosophical form, that it would not come home to the soul, or have a sway over the life.

Even the decay of heathenism in the Roman empire, that strange time when the old religion tried to brace itself up against the spread of doubt and of Christianity, indicates a longing for the appearance again of the Deity amid human events: the magic rites, the mysteries, the theurgic processes by which men sought to come into communication with the spiritual world, were, as it seems to us, so many testimonies of human nature that the Gospel, by means of its narrative form, that the economy of our religion from the first by its history, is most wisely accommodated to human nature and human wants; so that they who expect much from a religion of mere abstractions must be most signally disappointed.

And this experience of mankind under heathenism and Christianity makes it probable that the nature of man itself, rather than anything so variable as the style of culture and of knowledge, pronounces an historical form to be necessary for the sway of religious ideas among mankind. This is made more than probable by several considerations. Our nature, except when under strict philosophical training, of which few are capable and from which many turn away in disgust, revolts from abstractions and delights in concrete realities. We are made to take pleasure in personal existences and in their actions. Our sentiments need some object on which they can fasten. *Reverence* is not content with existing as a vague feeling, but seeks for some reality which may be the object of worship. *The feeling of dependence* needs to have that on which we are dimly conscious of depending body itself forth in some apprehensible form. *Thankfulness* implies the purpose of a known personal object to confer a benefit, and so all our feelings go forth only towards distinctly apprehended personalities. But personalities evidence and manifest themselves through actions which have to do with life and the world. So also the imagination is distressed—so to speak—if it cannot give form to the invisible and the ideal. The Christian religion could not hold its ground in the world but through a personal attachment to Christ. How then can a religion, with no attraction derived from history and personal power, expect to be met by human sympathy and to spread through mankind?

But, again, a religion which has no history must be destitute of the power of life and example.

Life, considered in relation to religion, is the embodiment and test of doctrine or principle. Example is an illustration or acting out of principle in a particular case, and implies an influence on the imitative nature of man.

Nothing gives so much power or weakness to a man as his life. Nothing tests a religion so much as the way in which it moulds the life of men. The life of Christ is the central power in Christianity. The treasury of the Church is the good lives of all faithful Christians, not because they can do more than they ought, as the Romanists supposed, but because they act just as they should. The blood of the martyrs is the seed of the Church, not so much because they dared to die for what they prized, as because there lay behind the martyr's faith a life that rose above the ordinary level. If Christianity had not put on a living form, if it could not have passed at once from high and loving precepts into the shape of pure men and women, we should not be defending it now. Forgiveness might have sounded sweet in precept, but if Christ and His dying disciple, Stephen, had not forgiven, where would the humanity of the world have been at this time?

It seems certain, then, that the strength of Christianity, as of Judaism before it, lay in its history, in the lives which it formed, and especially in that one life which it set up as a perfect model. But for facts in the life of Jesus, the cloud of witnesses would not have surrounded us, the host of shining ones would not have arisen in our sky. Mere precept, although invested with celestial authority, can effect little; an abstract standard of character, not realized in the life, will be almost destitute of power for the great mass of mankind.

But the man whose religion, as he thinks, is to control the future, may ask whether it cannot become the "heir of all the ages;" whether all that has been good and pure in the lives of men, under the Gospel and under heathenism, cannot be collected and used for the good of mankind? Why may not Christ, with His saints, stand on the calendar of that religion, even as the heathen emperor, Alexander Severus, built a temple to Christ, and counted Him among his gods? Meanwhile, he will say, the religion itself will be forming its own examples of a higher than Christian virtue, and setting them up for the veneration of all future time.

What success this proposed religion may have in the way of making godly and finished lives we do not propose now to consider. But this is certain, that a great part of the glory of Christian lives must then be effaced and lost. For Christ will have become a self-deceiver, and the view of His own character under which He acted was false. You cannot separate His consciousness of a peculiar relation to God from His life itself, and you cannot separate the life of His followers from a faith in Him as divine, and from the power of those truths which He taught, and which, on the supposition, have turned out to be false, or to be without divine authority. Either, then, veneration and respect for the character of Christ and of the best Christians will, in a good degree, cease, or it will be accounted a thing of small importance, whether that be true or false which controls the life, since falsehood has attended the development of the noblest characters known to the world.

II. The supposed new religion of the future must be a religion without authority, a religion constructed by human reason alone. The Christian religion claims a twofold divine authority; it is from God and by God,—it is a revelation contained in inspired writings. Even if you gave up the latter source of authority, you would not cut all its connection with heaven, unless the claim to inspiration be part and parcel of the revelation itself. Nor is the Christian religion solitary in advancing such claims, but all over the world, wherever religions have sprung up, they have declared themselves to be disclosures of the Divine will. Nor is it important for our argument to decide whether these religions have been the product of imposture, or of the myth-making power, or of a self-deluding enthusiasm. If impostures, they confess a need of some authority beyond their inventors. If the offspring of a myth-making age, they clothe themselves in the garb of a revelation from an instinctive sense that religion ought to wear such a dress. If they grow up in an individual mind of large imaginative power, the same craving for a connection with God and for an inspiration from Him is manifest.

It is further evident that the reception of religion in the world has much depended upon faith in its divine origin. That Christ was a teacher come from God was an essential element of His power, without which many would have refused to listen to His words, and few, if any, would have followed Him. The churches founded by the apostles were founded on faith in a divine interruption of the natural order of things. And so the written word is indebted for no small part of its power, for the attention originally given to it in spite of its defects of composition, for the hold it has had on the best minds of the world, to a belief that it is in some way authorized to give the news of a plan of God, which man's own faculties could not discover, that it contains facts and truths above nature and above the reach of reason. And hence, if at any time the evidences for the Christian Scriptures lose their hold on the faith of any age, the religion itself is abandoned. We are now thrown back upon reason; we must decide between different schools of philosophy, or follow our inward light, or be tossed on the uncertain waters of skepticism. And the need of divine authority for the guidance of our faith and conduct is felt by many of the strongest minds to be so great, that it is only with extreme reluctance, and by a kind of necessity which is harrowing to the soul, that they blow out the light that was their guide and commit themselves to the direction of reason. They feel when they reject the Gospel that some authorized guide, some standard of truth, some charter, speaking pardon and spiritual hope, would be divinely precious.

The contrast between Christianity, as authorized to make God known to men—not indeed shedding full light on every side, but satisfying and stimulating without suppressing reason,—and a religion of man's devising, is one that reaches to the very foundation of the soul's life. Religion in the soul would shrink into pitiably small dimensions without the guidance and authority of a supernatural revelation. What is to become of faith in spiritual realities, in what God thinks of conduct, in what He is and how He will treat men, if the Scriptures are of "private interpretation," if Christ spoke without authority, if no one hath come down from heaven to tell the world of heavenly things? What will trust find to lean upon, if the "great and precious promises" are of human origin? Where will repentance go for refuge if there is no assurance of pardon? How will the soul be made strong enough to resist sin, if there is no certainty of divine assistance? How can such a hope of heaven as reason can establish fortify the erring against earthly trials, and help them to die in peace? In short, since every religious feeling, every virtue, all morality, all practical benevolence are now maintained, as Christian experience demonstrates, by the voice of God in His word, will there not be an end of all these things, and must not religion become so uncertain, so weak, when Christ shall be given up, as to have next to no power over human life and society? Without divine authority, evidence and motive power are taken away from religion, and without these what can it do for the good of man? Nay, without assurance concerning those great questions that perplex unaided reason, will not the main energy of human thought be turned towards the problems of philosophy and away from practical virtue? Can a religion drawn up out of man's own soul satisfy his reason? Will there not be eternal questionings, as there were among the old philosophers? Will not the main strength of the greatest minds be spent in finding out truth, instead of reducing it to practice and using it for human improvement? At present to a very great extent Christianity satisfies the cravings of the soul by its truth and by its evidence. What can any other religion which claims no such authority bring into the world save doubt, restlessness, self-dissatisfaction, and wandering, unsuccessful efforts after rest?

To make the immense importance of divine authority more apparent, let us briefly sketch the progress of subjective religion, as we find it arising and increasing under the Gospel. In the first instance there is a recognition, founded on positive precepts, of a divine law reaching to the thoughts and intents of the heart. This the moral sense approves and adopts as its rule, but what would become of the standard of action, if the outward authority were to be disregarded and denied? Is it not certain that the divine requirement, as things are, originates and sustains all the convictions of the necessity of a religious life, and awakens a sense of want and a sense of sin by which the soul is led to God? Then again in the pathway of our return to God, we are met by positive assurances of danger on the one hand, and positive offers of forgiveness on the other, without which it is certain that religion on the Christian plan could not begin to exist. And the terms of forgiveness, contained in these revelations which the Gospel makes, are the outward resting-place on which the peace of the soul through a long life reposes. What assurance can it find within itself, or in the plan of the world large enough to fill the place of this authority? Then the whole of internal religion is obviously maintained by declarations of Scripture, some of which, singly, have afforded more comfort than all the reasonings and self-encouragements of unaided minds since the world began. A life of inward morality and of holiness is built on the Scriptural exhibition of God and His holiness. A life of benevolence is a following of the precepts, and of the lives which are precepts, that the Scriptures afford us. A life of hope needs distinct statements, and these must embrace both worlds. A life of unworldliness and self-renunciation needs promises to support it in its weakness, lest it should have given up everything to gain nothing. And so whatever aspect religion presents to us in the soul, whether it consists in escaping from sin, or in reconciliation of heart to God, or in acts of morality or of philanthropy or of piety, or in the development of certain feelings, or in the formation of a certain character, it needs throughout and actually uses the support of the Scriptures, as the guide of faith, the directory of life, the strength of every feeling of the heart. What then must happen when this revealed word shall have been abandoned, when its former influence shall have ceased, when its light shall have faded away from the world's atmosphere, but that religion must lose its hold on the world, must dwindle down into a feeble, sickly, timorous thing, looking every way for help, if it do not quite expire?

But it will be said by a portion of those who hope to see a new universal religion rise up on the ruins of Christianity, that *their* faith is in a certain sense from God and is attended with authority from Him. Every good man, every man who walks according to the inward light is in a sense an inspired man. Christ had with Him more truth than any other human being, because He was better than any. Thus there is a kind of natural inspiration of the human race, which is slowly perfecting truth, eliminating errors, bringing man from the outward and historical, from the claims to divine authority—proved now to be unreliable and yet for a long time serving as stepping-stones in human progress—to the pure ultimately recognized inner light of the soul.

There is much of beauty and attractiveness in such a theory as this, but it cannot stand the test of truth and sound philosophy. It takes no account of the weakness of human reason, as demonstrated by the history of opinions,—of the vain efforts, for instance, made by the Greek philosophers to attain to theological truth, and of their hopeless diversity of views ending in skepticism. It takes no account of the subsequent history of philosophical thought, which has failed down to the present time, notwithstanding all the efforts of highly gifted minds in the idealistic and pantheistic schools, to reach any assurance in regard to any doctrine of religion. It takes no account of the diversities of opinion, into which men of insight have been or may be led, either from confounding their insight and the conclusions of their understandings, or because insight itself, at least in the present condition of human nature, is an unsafe guide. It demands that a man should be good in order to have a true insight, but how is he to be good except by truth which insight discovers, and how is he to be followed by those who have no such clear insight as his? Would Christ have been a lawgiver and an example for mankind if He had spoken out His own private feelings without any claim to divine authority? The theory then will at length discover that it is decking itself in the robes of Christianity, that its illumination and insight are really borrowed from the Gospel, that whenever it shall succeed so far as to destroy faith in a historic revelation, at once darkness and distrust will begin to creep again over the minds of men whom Christianity had somewhat enlighted.

This theory, moreover, discloses its own inconsistency and falsehood by the position which it takes in regard to Christ. The wisest, best, humblest, and most unselfish of men, as is conceded, He made the most stupendous mistake in regard to Himself, and brought it about that this mistake became engrafted on His religion, nay—that it gave to His religion its distinctive character and its power in the world. So much light with so much darkness, such lofty purity united to such false claims of exaltation above the measure of a human being—this was the wisdom and excellence, this the insight of Jesus Christ. If He had insight and nothing more, is not His insight wholly unreliable, since He failed to see into Himself?

III. The supposed religion of the future will of necessity have a very limited range of doctrines.

Religious doctrine is the measure and sum total of the motives which a religion can bring to bear upon character. If the doctrines are false or immoral, they will form perverted or defective characters; if scanty, they will have little effect on character; if merely metaphysical and not ethical, they will have no effect on character whatever. It has been claimed by the friends of Christianity that it is intensely practical, that its grand truths or doctrines, especially those which are connected with its grand facts or history, have a direct and most healthy bearing on human life, that it contains enough of truth to finish human character on all its sides, and that, when believed, it actually forms characters of the highest excellence. The question then is how much of loss of power over human nature will arise from a rejection of the most important and distinctive doctrines of Christianity; by the side of which question stand others already answered, How much power will be lost by losing the vital force of a historical religion, and how much will be lost by losing the authority of revelation, and throwing men back upon the results of human speculation?

It is impossible at this time to predict what shape the doctrines of the new religion of the future will ultimately take. But thus much we can say, that if it should start with a certain apparatus of doctrines, part of them will at length be broken or not used at all, and that owing to the influence of Christian education, which its advocates cannot now escape, its motive power and seeming excellence will be greatest at first, and will be growing less and less afterward.

But let us try to form a candid estimate, as far as probabilities will allow, of the amount of truth and motive that will be within the reach of this religion of the future, and that can be used in endeavoring to give finish to moral and religious character.

First, whatever is especially Christian, as distinguished from natural religion and from the conclusions of human reason, must be given up. The doctrine that the Word became flesh, that God sent His Son to redeem men from sin, will be looked upon as a fable, as an unaccountable claim on the part of Jesus or an unauthorized addition to His teachings. Thus, His relations to God and to man being put on a wholly different basis, He ceases to be a great personage governing the world's history, and sinks into a teacher who mistook His own nature most fearfully, and from whose most authentic doctrines very much must be lopped off. That this alone would make a revolution in the world, greater than any since the birth of Christ Himself, cannot be questioned. Oh! what other throne, what dynasty of high-born kings reaching through ages and famed through the world, could fall, which man might not forget in a century! But this kingdom over hearts, this invisible sway of Christ beginning in the self-consecration of the soul and ending in the entire renovation of society and of government,—when can it cease to be regretted? Oh! what lapse of time, what changes in outer things will prevent the world from bleeding at every pore through a feeling that it has lost its guide and the pledge of its stability!

Secondly, the doctrine concerning God and His providence must be reduced to its lowest dimensions. Whether the reigning form of this new religion will cling firmly to the personality of God, as a cardinal point, and drive Pantheists as a heretical sect beyond its pale, cannot be distinctly anticipated. But suppose its standard doctrine to be that human nature within itself, apart from proof, contains a recognition of a Deity, when we come to the doctrine of providence and of spiritual influence, the ground is more uncertain. To a Providence, in any such sense that any interruptions of the common course of physical law can be admitted, it cannot subscribe, for it rejects all the miracles of the past. And thus it can scarcely teach, with any show of consistency, that prayer can in any way affect the order of things, or be an argument with God for bestowing blessings on the worshipers.

Moreover, without a positive revelation, that speaks of a God near at hand and around His creatures, it is increasingly hard to put faith in that high doctrine, for every advance of science thrusts Him to a remoter distance. He has left the reins on the neck of time, and inhabits His eternity as a vital energy, without concern or pity for man. What check can the religion of the future apply to this tendency to shut God out of the visible and actual present? Must it not succumb to the relentless blows of science, and lose its faith in a hand guiding the world, since positive and natural religion together find it so hard to furnish strong enough antidotes against skepticism?

The doctrine of spiritual influence, for aught that we can see, it may with consistency admit. But who can tell whether such influences can be hoped for, since they proceed from the free will of a sovereign, who has made no promises either in an external revelation or to the soul? May they be prayed for? What encouragement is there even to begin to pray, much more to persevere in it, when everything is so uncertain? May it not be the appointed lot of man to struggle alone against internal evils, as he must by the law of his nature against outward? In this state of uncertainty there will not be much prayer, and without Divine help the hope of improving the character will decline. Does not this single consideration show that a great part of practical religion will be cut up by the roots?

Thirdly, the doctrine concerning man which Christianity has taught us will need great modification. If the Gospel's view of sin could be retained without its remedial provisions, if a sense of guilt, with no assurance of forgiveness, could settle upon souls under the new religion as now, mankind would cry out against it in desperation, they would flee away from leaden clouds of death which let no rays of hope through, or would wander, if not desperate, into all kinds of heathenish ways of propitiating God. Will it be said, that the glimpses which we catch without revelation of the Divine clemency and forbearance would be enough of an assurance for sinning men? We answer, that they might satisfy a weak sense of sin, but could not comfort a deep one. The sense of sin, then, as of a malady at the root of our nature for which each one of us is responsible, might very much fade away. God never having, by any revelation from heaven, disclosed His wrath against all ungodliness and unrighteousness of men, what sufficient evidence would there be that sin is a very great evil, how would it be seen to alienate the soul from Him, what reason would there be to dread His frown? Nor is it unlikely that sin would be regarded as a transitional state in the necessary progress of human nature. And it seems likely, that the efforts against it would be confined principally to the rectification of society, to the removal of ignorance, to the relief of the lower classes, on the ground that human nature is not bad, that evil emanates from society and can be effectually obstructed and dried up by outward reformations. However this may be, it is certain that by some anæsthetic process, what we call a sense of sin, would be benumbed. But is it not evident, that the cost of this would be immense? Must there not ensue a weakening of the very foundations of morality? Could the family, could society endure this? Will the religion of the future be able to endure it? Will not faith in God, and faith in unalterable morality, in holiness and justice, stand or fall together with faith in sin? Must there not then be a further plunge of a demoralized world into Atheism?

Fourthly, the doctrine concerning the last things will very probably be an open, unsettled question. Only a glance at the history of opinion down to the most recent times is enough to show that man has in vain sought to solve the problem of the immortality and future destiny of the soul. But let the religion of the future pronounce a decisive word on these high doctrines; how little will it gain since it has no new proofs to bring forward, and has nothing but human insight to rest upon. And then, a future state being admitted, are there to be rewards and punishments? May sin, here, affect our state in that future life? If it may, we need some help from God, which the religion does not make sure. If it may not, of what value is the future life in relation to conduct? What is the future life in that case but a barren fact standing a great way off? Thus, whether we consider the uncertainty in which the religion must remain concerning a future life, or the slender use it makes of this doctrine in the way of a motive and of elevating man above worldly things, it will be found quite indifferent whether the doctrine be retained or discarded; at the best, it will be an appendage of no importance.

The whole of what we have said thus far, and especially the consideration of the slender stock of truth at the disposal of the religion of the future, makes it clear that the motive power of such a religion, its influence on life and character, must be exceedingly small. Some room will be left for reverence, and for the sense of dependence; thankfulness also may be awakened to a degree, although crippled by doubts concerning Providence. But how narrow will be the range of trust, how feeble the vigor of hope, having no promises to feed upon; how poor a part will be played by faith in things unseen! And if the doctrine of immortal life gives an immense amplitude to human action, enlarges our sense of our own importance in the universe, and adds untold force to the reason for improving our character, how lame will all efforts at moral excellence be, how small the motive, how trifling the issues of conduct, when this great truth shall be feebly held or quite discarded!

But in lieu of all other considerations touching this point we urge that the new religion will have no fuel for love towards God, that the harmony of the human and divine soul will be nearly impossible. The justice of this remark will stand in a clear light if we consider what excites the emotion of love,—of love, we mean, as involving complacency, confidence, and general harmony of spirit,—and how it differs from some other feelings that play a part in religion. The feeling of reverence will be aroused according to the laws of our nature, although we may have a very dim perception of the power that we revere. So the sense of dependence implies indeed an object on which we depend, but gives no light in regard to the qualities of that object. But love needs for its existence some sort of disclosure or revelation of the feelings and character of the object towards which it goes forth. Between man and man love cannot arise, unless one party has a manifestation of the character and feelings of the other. We cannot love an unknown person, nor love on conjecture, nor love an intellect. It is the same in the case of the Divine Being. There must go before all love to Him some conviction of His moral excellence, and as love is reciprocal, some assurance that He can love in return. And hence, again, there must be some persuasion that He can regard sinners with favor in spite of their sins. The history of heathenism, the convictions of our own sinful natures will show us that a sense of guilt without an assurance of pardon must drive men from the face of God; they will show us the justice of those words, "We love Him because He first loved us."

Now then if the Gospel which pretends to be a revelation of God's character and of His mercy is to be abandoned as untrue, what room is left for man's love to Him? He has become an unknown God; how can we love Him of whose character we know little, and of His feelings towards us next to nothing? Will it be said that something within us leads us irresistibly to conceive of Him as absolute moral perfection? Were we to grant this, which the diversities of human religions do not justify, yet love requires more, it demands some knowledge of the relations between Him and ourselves; and how do we gain any information on this point from our insights and instinctive judgments? If our nature assures us that He loves the good, must it not equally reveal to us His alienation from the morally evil? How then with our conscience of sin can we love Him whom we have offended, love Him of whose pardon we have no assurance, love Him in whose sight our nature is unholy? Love, then, in its highest and noblest forms must be a stranger to the religion of the future. If love to God is the crown of our character, if to call such a sentiment into life constitutes one of the chief glories of Christ's religion, as well as one of the great sources of its strength, must not a religion that knows little of God, and nothing of forgiveness, be incapable of forming beautiful lives? Must it not perish and become despised from its very weakness?

In short, the religion will be of this earth, getting next to no influence from the unseen life beyond this world, or from the unseen life above this world. It lacks, therefore, the power of faith and the possibility of a life of faith. Can the age when it shall be established fail of being intensely worldly, and epicurean? Think of the art and literature of such an age: think of the spirit they must breathe; think of the loss of motives for morality and a religious life at which we hinted just now. Can such a prospect fail to excite deep alarm?

IV. We remark very briefly that the new religion of which we speak will be without the strength derived from a church and its institutions.

The Christian Church of the present, with all its faults and weaknesses, is the salt and the light of the world. As holding, preserving, and spreading the faith of Christ, as built on the feeling of brotherhood, and on trust in a common Saviour, as bound together by social worship, sacraments, a ministry and a discipline, and as containing in itself a self-reforming power, it is one of the bonds which bind mankind together, and on it the hopes of mankind in a great measure rest. Its influence extends far beyond its own pale, and beyond the religious interests of man; it originates or aids every effort to make him wiser, happier, and more manly.

What now can take the place of the church, or compensate man for its fall, as fall it must, if the old historical religion is abandoned? What common hopes, what common object of reverence or love will the new religion have to offer to its professors, nay, what common faith can it supply them with, except a few meagre shreds not large enough to cover the nakedness of reason? It must have worship, but what kind of worship? That in which sentimentality and taste take the lead, with the fewest, the weakest appeals to religious feeling. Will it introduce prayer into its public services, when the question of an answer to prayer is unsettled, or denied; or thanksgiving, when a Providence is doubted, and blind law accounts for all things? Can it have institutions? Institutions of a historical origin are out of the question, because the religion has no history from which to draw them. Institutions made for the sake of having them it can invent, but how weak the hold on the mind of man of such institutions, how small their venerableness! What can it have or find to replace the sacred supper? Compare the fellowship pertaining to such a dead skeleton of a religion with membership in Christ. Compare its preaching on a narrow round of dogmas with the inexhaustible themes of the Christian pulpit. Must not, in fact, morality take the place of religion in the pulpit, and religious doctrine be no more looked to as suggesting the great motives of action? Compare the probable zeal for its propagation with that resulting from the nature of the Gospel, and from the command of Christ, "Go ye into all the world." Can there be much zeal for its diffusion, especially as long as its friends maintain that the systems of heathenism involve all the essential truths of religion? Wherever we turn, then, we discover its weaknesses, we cannot find one element of power. It will make no place for itself in the affections of human souls.

V. If these things are so, human progress must cease, and civilization, whenever the world shall throw away its faith in revealed religion, must decline.

We seem to ourselves to have shown, that, whether the form, the evidence, the substance, the motive power, or the social influences of the new rival of Christianity be taken into view, it is wholly weak and unreliable. Can the destinies of mankind be safely entrusted to a religion without facts, without authority, with a minimum of doctrines, and with no institutions at all? Must not the advancement of society in all that is good cease, if Christianity is to lose its hold upon the faith and love of men? If a large factor be thrown out of the account, must not the product be greatly lessened?

There is but one answer to this question: such a decline

must take place, unless in the future other influences are to make up for the diminished power of religion. Just this, we suppose, is what many thinkers anticipate, who have rejected the claims of Christianity. We apprehend, that, as a class, those who have looked upon bare Theism as the heir and successor of the Gospel, do not put very much of dependence upon this predicted religion of the future; we conceive that it is expected to take its place as a handmaid and not as a mistress, while civilization, or progress, is looked upon as the coming Queen of the world. The bitter taunt of the Greek poet is to be fulfilled, who makes his sophist say, that Vortex or Whirl has expelled Jupiter from his throne; God is to cease to reign and Progress will take his place.* This doctrine of progress may adopt the form of a fatal development, or that of a free advance in accordance with a divine plan. The first form, or that which it must assume in a pantheistic theory of the world, does not now concern us. The other form, or that which a Theist, who rejects the Scriptures, can embrace, will be something like this: that, in the course of time there will be such an accumulation of knowledge, such a lifting up of man above nature, such improvements in government and legislation, such refinement diffused through society, that even in the lowest classes, the propension will be towards sobriety, honesty, chastity, and kindness. And so a very little influence from religion, very little knowledge of God, or concern about Him will give all needed aid to the advancement of mankind.

A theory of human progress like this deserves, on account of its importance, an extended examination; we must content ourselves, however, with two or three remarks that bear on our subject more immediately: we observe, then,

First, that the facts do not justify the hope of such a

*Aristoph. Nubes, 381, Δῖνος reigns *vice* Διός.

progress; we mean, that the improvements which have been made in society must be ascribed chiefly to Christianity; that advances in physical science have no great weight in bringing about moral ones; and that ameliorations of governments and of society can scarcely begin, cannot be made permanent, without the aid of religion.

It is apparent that a benevolent feeling aroused by the Gospel has, in fact, had very much to do with modern reforms; with reforms, for example, in prison discipline, in the houses, habits, and privileges of the poor, in promoting temperance, in putting an end to the slave trade and to slavery, in sending light to the ignorant, in endeavoring to spread the spirit of peace. Christ's religion has in fact taken the lead in schemes for the benefit of society, and it will be scarcely maintained that, while thus at the head of this blessed movement, it has crippled or suppressed other benevolent forces, which can take its place when it shall become extinct. For where are they? Were they in action when the Gospel overcame heathenism, and were they put in the background by it as by some jealous monarch? On the other hand, without the Gospel the field and the energy of benevolence will be vastly lessened. The field will be earthly relations almost exclusively. The energy will be paralyzed, when the conception of God's kingdom on earth, when faith in divine influences, shall be discarded, when the doctrine of a future life shall be disbelieved or just clung to amid the waves of uncertainty.

Again, the advance of science does not, in fact, secure the advance of society, notwithstanding all the efforts of Christians and other benevolent persons. As far as the past can teach us, science may add indefinitely to its stores, while society continues corrupt or degenerate. There are armies of thieves and of reprobates, worse than heathen, within sound of the voice of the great lecturers of Paris. Officers of preventive and of correctional police have plenty of work to do in all large cities, both in Europe and this free land. In some respects the dangerous classes in large towns are worse than they were. They know more, and are more excitable. Their knowledge, having nothing to do with rules of conduct and the meaning of life, being in fact such as a class of men without religion would gather, makes them craftier, more able to combine, more able to evade justice.

Nor is there any necessary connection between the advance of science and the improvement of political institutions. Even the theory of politics may be conformed to true science in a nation, while yet the body politic may have no power to govern itself or to shake off abuses. The moral energy, the spirit of self-sacrifice, the courage to attempt reform in the right way, the hope of success, the healthful tone of opinion in society concerning justice, all these and other sources of national health are far less dependent on the state of science than on religious and moral influences. Nations, in order to grow great, or become free, or remain free, must, like single men, have strength of character, and this is mainly from moral and religious culture, or from a certain simplicity of life which is lost in high cultivation.

2. But in the second place, theories of human progress, like that at which we are looking, misconceive of and underrate the power appropriate to religion in the civilization of the world, and also give an exceedingly earthly view of life.

They misconceive of the civilizing power of the Gospel. At least they seem to conceive of Christians as thinking that religion of itself, without the aid of any other agencies, is the sole source of human improvement and civilization. But the true and received statement is that religion controls the forces which mould and refine the soul and society. It is the main-spring or the governing wheel which gives motion, and it also regulates and harmonizes all movement. It is in harmony with all truth and in sympathy with all improvement, but it acts not only through its own direct invisible power, but through the laws of nature, of the soul, and of society. It looks on the science of nature with favor, because this is an exposition of the thoughts of God, and thus science has a strong, healthy growth under its fostering influence. It sends the individual's thoughts within, and thus aids the science of the soul. It makes him aware of his rights and his duties, and thus helps to build up a true philosophy of man in the state, as well as a just society. It elevates his feelings and purifies his taste, and thus gives wing to true art. It is the foe of vice, and thus of all ignorance and of all oppression. But its glory lies in making "all things new," not *without* other agencies, but *through* its control over them, and *through* its sway over the individual soul.

Again, in such theories of civilization, the power of the Christian religion seems to be greatly underrated. In the first place, a due value is not set upon that which is distinctively Christian, as compared with that which belongs to Judaism and to natural religion. The history of Christian art, the examination of religious experience, if we look to no other sources of proof, will show us that the great sway over life and society proceeds from that which is new in Christianity, from Christ in His person, life, and work, from forgiveness of sins and redemption, from the doctrine of the Holy Spirit, from the judgment and the future state. Take all this away, and you take away, if we are not deceived, nearly all that constitutes the superiority and the glory of Christian civilization.

But again, such theories contemplate the civilizing forces of Christianity as standing side by side, with those of literature, art, science, law, and government. Tariffs, roads, and printing presses, are held to be as original and as efficient benefactors of society, as Bibles and sermons.

But this seems to be a very serious mistake, which grows out of another, still more fundamental, concerning the nature of man,—an assumption that he is unfallen, that he has all power within himself without the aid of new truth from Heaven, to elevate his condition. Is it not evident that the system of practical forces, which makes up the Gospel, must, if believed and loved, govern the will, heart, and life of the individual, and that through the amelioration of the individual, all civilizing influences will be either perfected or originated? What the Gospel has done or can do in the way of benefiting society, the institutions it founds, the science it warms into life, ought not surely to be alleged as reasons why we can get along at some future day without the Gospel. The Gospel is not the schoolmaster who leaves the grown-up pupil to be guided by his own reason; it is the leaven hid in the meal *until the whole* mass *is leavened.*

The conservation of society can be entrusted only to moral and religious forces. If religion has no moving, preserving, checking, or balancing power, or if, as is true of heathenism, it is itself immoral, then art, literature, whatever promotes the advance of society, is paralyzed or corrupted; and there comes on a decline of society, as in Greece after Alexander and in Rome under the emperors, without hope of recovery from any internal power. On the other hand, if, as is true in the case of Christianity, the religion is ethical in the highest sense, in the sense not only of teaching morals but of enlarging the conception of what is right, and supplying the highest motives for the ennoblement of character, then there is a foundation laid, on which society, with all its interests, can rest, and there is opportunity for all that progress which is possible in consistency with the condition of man.

We are now prepared to say, that if the influences from the Gospel should be withdrawn, a most earthly civilization, one having its own doom written on its forehead, would take the place of that which Christianity has been the leading agent in forming. Suppose, for instance, that all thinkers should lose faith in the immortality of the soul. Is it not evident, that with the abandonment of this one truth, the concerns of the present world would begin to assume a new relative importance, that all motives drawn from a life to come would be feeble, that self-gratification must rise in value, and self-denial fall, that all the aspirations of man must droop and wither? Is it not evident, that something of that mingled frivolity and despair which Atheism engenders, and of which heathen society, especially in its decay, when its faith is lost, gives us examples, would brood over the world? For how could civilization fail to decline, when frivolity blighted the taste and depraved the moral judgments, and when despair, the sense of the emptiness of life, took away the stimulus from all noble endeavor?

3. Finally, in one very important respect the very progress of society demands the assurances and supports of positive Christian truth. As knowledge and refinement increase, the standard of character tends to rise, and along with it will deepen the feeling of responsibility and the pain of falling below the standard. A sense of imperfection—of sinfulness, if we may call it so, as keen as any other sense and more indestructible, will then be in vigorous exercise. How is this sense to be satisfied without a Gospel? Heathenism has had its method of satisfying the consciousness of sin, its reconciliation of man and God, in which lay no small part of its strength. Christianity has its method, and herein lies much of the service which it has rendered to mankind. But naked Deism, the religion of human insight and natural reason, says nothing of pardon and redemption, nothing of a helping, life-giving Spirit. In this respect it occupies a much weaker position than that which is taken by the systems of necessary development. They legitimately deny the reality of moral

evil. It has for them no existence, because the will is not free, or because sin, being a necessary stage for finite minds, is not objectively evil. But a system, in which a personal God is a central principle, cannot extinguish the sense of sin or deny its reality. Nay, the farther the true refinement of society is carried, the higher the standard of character is raised, and the vaster the creation is shown to be by science; so much the more grandeur and glory are spread around the throne of God. Sin, then, tends to enlarge in its dimensions before the eye of a refined age which has not thrown aside its faith in the moral attributes of God. But Deism has nothing to satisfy this sense of sin but baseless hopes and analogies drawn from the unexplained dealings of God. If God ought to forgive because the best conceptions of human virtue include forgiveness, He ought to have indignation against sin, because that too enters as an element into our ideal of perfect character. And how terrible that indignation! What distance so vast as that between the Infinite One, inhabiting His dwelling-place of holiness, and a soul conscious of selfishness and of impurity! The course of things, if Deism should be the ultimate form of religion, can easily be foretold. As long as the recollections and influences of Christianity survived its fall, earnest souls would hope on, they would stay their soul-hunger on the milk drawn from the breasts of their dead mother. But a new age would toss about in uncertainty, if not in despair; or else, throwing aside their Deism which brings before their wearied minds the unsolved problem of the relations of sinning man to a holy God, they would hunt after peace in the fields of Atheistic or Pantheistic philosophy. Civilization with God, but without Christ, leads to a terrible dilemma. If the sense of sin remain, the life of all noble souls will be an anxious, gloomy tragedy. Or if that burden, so crushing, is thrown off, as in a life struggle, then the standard of character will fall and the sense of sin grow faint to such a degree that the pardon from God craved in heathenism will not be needed, and the utmost frivolity will be reached of life and manners. In either case, the progress of civilization will be stopped; the world of the future will be doomed; and the "religion of the future" will turn out to be a miserable raft, unfit, after the shipwreck of Christianity, to carry the hopes and the welfare of mankind down the ages.

STANDARD WORKS

AT

GREATLY REDUCED PRICES.

	REDUCED FROM	TO
FROUDE'S HISTORY OF ENGLAND. Popular edition. In twelve volumes 12mo. Per vol.	$3 00	$1 25
—— The set in a neat case	36 00	15 00
FROUDE'S SHORT STUDIES ON GREAT SUBJECTS. One volume 12mo	3 00	1 50
MOMMSEN'S HISTORY OF ROME. In four volumes crown 8vo. Per vol.	2 50	2 00
—— The set in a neat case	10 00	8 00
DEAN STANLEY'S JEWISH CHURCH. PART I. Maps and Plans. One volume crown 8vo	4 00	2 50
—— PART II. One volume crown 8vo	5 00	2 50
DEAN STANLEY'S EASTERN CHURCH. One vol. crown 8vo.	4 00	2 50
ARCHBISHOP TRENCH'S STUDIES IN THE GOSPELS. One volume large 12mo, cloth	3 00	2 50
LORD DERBY'S TRANSLATION OF HOMER'S ILIAD. Containing all the author's latest revisions and corrections. Two volumes in one	5 00	2 50
FORSYTH'S LIFE OF CICERO. Two volumes in one	5 00	2 50
CONYBEARE & HOWSON'S LIFE AND EPISTLES OF ST. PAUL. Complete and unabridged edition. The two volumes of the London edition in one, with the Text and Notes entire, and the Maps and Illustrations	7 50	3 00
DR. J. ADDISON ALEXANDER'S SERMONS. Two volumes in one, crown 8vo	4 00	2 50
DR. J. W. ALEXANDER'S FAMILIAR LETTERS. Two volumes in one, crown 8vo	4 00	2 50
DR. SCHAFF'S CHRISTIAN CHURCH. Three volumes in two	11 25	7 50
DR. SHEDD'S HISTORY OF CHRISTIAN DOCTRINE. Two volumes 8vo	7 50	5 00
DR. SHEDD'S HOMILETICS. One volume 8vo	3 50	2 50
MAINE'S ANCIENT LAW. One volume crown 8vo	3 00	2 50
BRACE'S RACES OF THE OLD WORLD. One vol. cr. 8vo	2 50	2 00
DR. JNO. LORD'S ANCIENT HISTORY. One volume 12mo	3 00	1 50

These works to be had of all Booksellers, or sent, post-paid, upon receipt of the price, by the publishers,

CHARLES SCRIBNER & CO.,

654 Broadway, New York.

POPULAR AND STANDARD LIST OF BOOKS

PUBLISHED BY

Charles Scribner & Co.

IN 1869 AND '70.

ALEXANDER, H. C. Life of J. A. Alexander. Two vols. crown 8vo.......$5.00
ALEXANDER, J. W. Forty Years' Correspondence with a Friend. *New Edition.* One vol. 12mo........ 2.50
ALEXANDER, J. A. Sermons. *New Edition,* One vol. 12mo........ 2.50
ANDERSON. Foreign Missions. One vol. 12mo........ 1.50
BOWEN, Prof. FRANCIS. Am. Political Economy. One vol. crown 8vo.. 2.50
BROWNING, Mrs. E. B. Lady Geraldine's Courtship. Illustrated. One vol. small 4to........ 5.00
BUSHNELL, HORACE. Women's Suffrage. One vol. 12mo........ 1.50
CONYBEARE & HOWSON. St. Paul. *Complete Edition.* One vol. 8vo. 3.00
COOLEY, Prof. Le ROY C. A Text Book on Natural Philosophy. One vol. 12mo........ 1.50
——— A Text-Book of Chemistry. One vol. 12mo. 1.25
DAY, Prof. HENRY N. The Young Composer. One vol. 12mo........ 1.00
——— The American Speller. One vol. 12mo........ .25
FISHER, Rev. GEO. P. Supernatural Origin of Christianity *New Edition.* One vol. 8vo........ 3.00
FROUDE, J. A. History of England. Vols. XI. and XII., cr. 8vo., per vol.. 3.00
——— Vols I. to XII. inclusive. 12mo., per vol 1.25
HAMILTON. Reminiscences of J. A. Hamilton. One vol. 8vo........ 5.00
HARPER, MARY J. Practical Composition. One vol. 12mo........ .90
HEADLEY, J. T. The Adirondacks. *New Edition.* One vol. 12mo........ 1.75
HURST, JOHN F. D.D., History of the Church in the Eighteenth and Nineteenth Centuries. Two vols. 8vo........ 6.00
ILLUSTRATED LIBRARY OF WONDERS. Fourteen vols. Illustrated, per vol........ 1.50
JERNINGHAM'S (Mrs.) Journal. One vol. 16mo........ .75
LANGE'S (Prof. J. P., D.D.) COMMENTARY. Romans. One vol. 8vo. 5.00
——— Proverbs. One vol. 8vo. 5.00
LIFTING THE VEIL. One vol. 12mo........ 1.25
LORD, Dr. JOHN. Ancient States and Empires. One vol. crown 8vo.... 3.00
MAINE, H. S. Ancient Law. *New Edition.* One vol. crown 8vo........ 2.50
Mc ILVAINE, Prof. J. H. Elocution. One vol. 12mo........ 1.75
MOMMSEN, Dr. THEODOR. The History of Rome. Three vols. cr. 8vo., per vol........ 2.00
MULLER, MAX. Chips from a German Workshop. Two vols. cr. 8vo... 5.00
PORTER, Prof. N. The Human Intellect. One vol. 8vo........ 5.00
POUCHET, F. A. The Universe. One vol. royal 8vo........ 12.00
SEAMAN, E. C. The Am. System of Government. One vol. 12mo........ 1.50
SHEDD, WILLIAM G. T., D.D. A History of Christian Doctrine. *New Edition.* Two vols. 8vo........ 5.00
——— A Treatise on Homiletics and Pastoral Theology, *New Edition.* One vol. 8vo........ 2.50
SONGS OF LIFE. Illustrated. One vol. small 4to........ 5.00
STANLEY, ARTHUR PENRHYN, D.D. Lectures on the History of the Jewish Church. *New Edition.* Two vols. crown 8vo........ 5.00
——— Lectures on the History of the Eastern Church. *New Edition.* One vol. cr. 8vo........ 2.50
——— Sinai and Palestine. *New Edition.* One vol. cr. 8vo........ 2.50
TRENCH, R. C. Studies in the Gospels. *New Edition.* One vol. 12mo.. 2.50
WOOD, Rev. J. G. Bible Animals. One vol. 8vo........ 5.00
WOOLSEY, T. D., D.D. Essay on Divorce. One vol. 12mo........ 1.75

www.ingramcontent.com/pod-product-compliance
Lightning Source LLC
LaVergne TN
LVHW020107110826
845151LV00001B/88

* 9 7 8 1 4 2 5 5 4 4 4 8 5 *